Turkish Immigrants in Western Europe and North America

I0127450

Public and even scholarly debates usually focus on the integration problems of Muslim immigrants at the cost of overlooking the role of the growing number of migrant organizations in establishing a crucial link among immigrants themselves, as well as between them and their countries of origin and residence. This book aims to fill a gap in the vast literature on migration from Turkey by contributing the neglected aspect of civic and political participation of Turkish immigrants. It brings together a number of scholars who carried out extensive research on the associational culture of Turkish immigrants living in different countries in Europe and North America. In order to understand the diversity and dynamics within Turkish migrant communities living in these parts of the world yet maintaining transnational ties, this book offers a comparative and interdisciplinary approach to migrant organizations in general and civic participation and political mobilization of Turkish immigrants in particular.

This book was published as a special issue in *Turkish Studies*.

Şebnem Köşer Akçapar, PhD, is a Social Anthropologist. She is the Director of Georgetown University's McGhee Center for Eastern Mediterranean Studies. Previously, she worked at the Institute for the Study of International Migration (ISIM) and at the Center for German and European Studies (CGES) at Georgetown University lecturing inter alia on Muslim communities in Europe and North America, and Islam and Gender.

Turkish Immigrants in Western Europe and North America
Immigration and Political Mobilization

Edited by
Şebnem Köşer Akçapar

Routledge
Taylor & Francis Group

LONDON AND NEW YORK

First published 2012
by Routledge
2 Park Square, Milton Park, Abingdon, Oxon, OX14 4RN

Simultaneously published in the USA and Canada
by Routledge
711 Third Avenue, New York, NY 10017

First issued in paperback 2017

Routledge is an imprint of the Taylor & Francis Group, an informa business

This book is a reproduction of *Turkish Studies*, vol. 10, issue 2. The Publisher requests to those authors who may be citing this book to state, also, the bibliographical details of the special issue on which the book was based.

British Library Cataloguing in Publication Data
A catalogue record for this book is available from the British Library

ISBN 13: 978-1-138-11730-3 (pbk)
ISBN 13: 978-0-415-69391-2 (hbk)

Typeset in Times New Roman
by Taylor & Francis Books

Publisher's Note
The publisher would like to make readers aware that the chapters in this book may be referred to as articles as they are identical to the articles published in the special issue. The publisher accepts responsibility for any inconsistencies that may have arisen in the course of preparing this volume for print.

Contents

CONTENTS

Notes on Contributors

Şebnem Köşer Akçapar, PhD is a Social Anthropologist. She is the Director of Georgetown University's McGhee Center for Eastern Mediterranean Studies. Previously, she worked at the Institute for the Study of International Migration (ISIM) and at the Center for German and European Studies (CGES) at Georgetown University lecturing inter alia on Muslim communities in Europe and North America, and Islam and Gender.

Thomas Faist is Professor of Transnational Relations and Sociology of Development at the Department of Sociology, Bielefeld University (www.comcad-bielefeld.de). Formerly, he directed International Studies in Political Management (ISPM) at the University of Applied Sciences Bremen. His research focuses on migration, ethnic relations, citizenship, social policy, and transnationalization. Faist was Willy-Brandt-Guest Professor at the University of Malmö, and DAAD Visiting Professor at the University of Toronto. He is a deputy editor of *The Sociological Quarterly* and a member of the editorial boards of *Ethnic & Racial Studies* and *Migration Letters*. His recent book publications include *The Volume and Dynamics of International Migration and Transnational Social Spaces* (Oxford University Press, 2004); *Dual Citizenship in Europe: From Nationhood to Societal Integration* (Ashgate, 2007); *Citizenship: Discourse, Theory and Transnational Prospects*, with Peter Kivisto (Blackwell, 2007), and *Dual Citizenship in a Globalizing World: From Unitary to Multiple Citizenship* (Palgrave Macmillan, 2007).

Ahmet İçduygu (PhD Australian National University, Australia, 1991) is Professor in the Department of International Relations, College of Administrative Sciences and Economics, Koç University in Istanbul, Turkey. He is also the Director of the Migration Research Program at Koç University. He serves as the national correspondent of Turkey to the SOPEMI-Organisation for Economic Cooperation and Development, Paris, and as a member of the International Advisory Board of Mediterranean Migratory Observatory, Athens. He has conducted research for international organizations such as IOM: the International Organization for Migration,

UNHCR: the United Nations High Commissioner for Refugees, and ILO: the International Organization of Labor. He teaches on the theories and practices of citizenship, international organizations, civil society, nationalism and ethnicity, migration, and research methods. He has published several articles in academic journals such as *International Migration, International Social Science Journal, Global Governance, Middle Eastern Studies, Ethnic and Racial Studies, Population and Environment, Human Rights Quarterly, Citizenship Studies, Journal of Scientific Studies of Religion, Mediterranean Quarterly,* and *Journal of Southeast European and Black Sea Studies.* He has also co-edited a book titled *Citizenship in a Global World* (Routledge, 2005).

Jonathan Lacey is a PhD candidate in the Department of Sociology in Trinity College, Dublin, where he completed an MPhil in Ethnic and Racial Studies. He has published in *Translocations: The Irish Migration, Race and Social Transformation Review.* He is also a part-time research assistant to a Senior Ethnographic Researcher at Intel, focusing on independent living for elder people.

Laure Michon holds an MA of Political Science (University of Amsterdam) and a Research Master from the European University Institute. Currently, she is a PhD student at the Institute for Migration and Ethnic Studies (IMES) at the University of Amsterdam. Her research focuses on how ethnic minority politicians get access to the local political arena and how their political careers evolve. Her article on the Amsterdam case: "Carrières politiques locales d'immigrés à Amsterdam, 1997-2000," was published in *Migrations Société.*

Pontus Odmalm is Lecturer in Politics at the University of Edinburgh. His research focuses on national citizenship, political integration, and civil society in a comparative, European perspective. He is currently working on political parties' attitudes towards immigration and the EU. Some of his recent publications include "One Size Fits All? European Citizenship, National Citizenship Policies and Integration Requirements" (*Representation,* 2007, Vol. 43, No. 1); "Getting Ethnic Questions on the Agenda: Party Formation as a Strategy for Social Movements" with Charles Lees (*Social Movements Studies: Journal of Social, Cultural and Political Protest,* 2006, Vol. 5, No. 1); and *Migration Policies and Political Participation: Inclusion or Intrusion in Western Europe?* (Palgrave, 2005).

Saime Ozcurumez is Visiting Assistant Professor in the Department of Political Science at Bilkent University. She teaches and publishes on comparative politics, politics of international migration, political parties, European Union politics, and governance. Her current research interests include questions around gender and immigration, irregular migration in the Mediterranean, border management, EU politics, immigrant associations, diversity, and health care systems.

NOTES ON CONTRIBUTORS

Esra Özyürek is Associate Professor of Anthropology at the University of California, San Diego. Her work focuses on the relationship among politics, religion, and social memory in Turkey and Germany. Her publications include *Nostalgia for the Modern: State Secularism and Everyday Politics in Turkey* (Duke University Press, 2007); *Politics of Public Memory in Turkey* (Syracuse University Press, 2007); and "Convert Alert: German Muslims and Turkish Christians as Threats to Security in the New Europe," *Comparative Studies in Society and History*, (Vol. 50, No. 1 January, 2009).

Jon Rogstad is a Senior Researcher at the Institute for Social Research, Oslo, Norway. He gained his PhD from the Department of Sociology at the University of Oslo in 2000. Rogstad is the president of the Norwegian Sociological Association. He is also Co-editor of the Norwegian journal *Spotlight on the Labor Market*. He has written several books and articles on different aspects of the multicultural society.

Floris Vermeulen is Researcher at the Institute for Migration and Ethnic Studies (IMES), Political Science Department, University of Amsterdam. His main research interests are: immigrant organizations, development of integration policies in Germany and the Netherlands, and the influence of welfare state regimes and integration processes. He published exclusively on the immigrant organizing process and immigrant organizations in the Netherlands.

Ahmet Yükleyen received his PhD in Cultural Anthropology from Boston University in 2006. His research is on Turkish and Moroccan Islamic organizations in Germany and the Netherlands. He is Croft Assistant Professor of Anthropology in the Sociology and Anthropology Department and in the Croft Institute for International Studies at the University of Mississippi. He co-authored a book published by TESEV (Turkish Economic and Social Studies Foundation) in 2006, titled *Islam, Secularism, and Democracy in Europe*. He has forthcoming articles titled "State Policies and Islam in Europe: Milli Görüş in Germany and the Netherlands" and "Localizing Islam in Europe: Religious Activism among Turkish Islamic Organizations in the Netherlands" in the *Journal of Ethnic and Migration Studies* and in the *Journal of Muslim Minority Affairs*, respectively.

Gökçe Yurdakul is Georg Simmel Professor of Sociology at Humboldt University, Berlin, Graduate School of Social Sciences. She received her doctorate from the University of Toronto. She has published books and articles on immigrant integration, citizenship, Islam in Europe, and issues of Muslim women in Western Europe and North America. She is researching the relations between Jews and Turks in Germany. Her most recent publication is "From Guest Workers into Muslims: The Transformation of Turkish Immigrant Associations in Germany" (Cambridge Scholars, 2009).

Foreword: Turkish Migrant Participation in Civic and Political Life

AHMET İÇDUYGU
Department of International Relations, Koç University, Istanbul, Turkey

The principle of democratic legitimacy requires equal participation by all groups of society in the political process. Given the fact that in recent decades there has been an established and growing presence of immigrants and foreign residents in many countries around the world, the contribution of these immigrants and foreigners to a country's economic, social, political, and cultural spheres further justifies their right to influence the political decisions in the concerned country. Indeed, the issue of the political participation of immigrants in the receiving countries is being debated by the public, politicians, and scholars.

Some recent research has carefully elaborated on immigrant participation in civic and political life in many old and new countries of immigration, mostly as part of the question of how to integrate immigrant communities and strengthen social cohesion. Many receiving countries clearly make distinctions between political and civic rights granted to different types of migrants. Some migrants are granted civic and political rights at the local and regional levels but not at the national level. Citizenship often emerges as a key element to gaining certain basic civic and political rights at the national level. For some countries, immigrants' civic and political rights are subject to different kinds of restrictions. These restrictions vary based on the entry and residence status of individual migrants (temporary migrants, permanent settlers, asylum seekers, and refugees) and sometimes even on their country of origin.

The nature of the civic and political participation of Turkish migrants in various receiving countries provides an interesting case study, firstly because of the presence of sizable Turkish migrant communities in many different countries; secondly because emigration of Turkish citizens has a well-known history dating to the early 1960s; and thirdly because these Turkish expatriates consist of different types of migrants from labor migrants to asylum seekers, from temporary migrants to permanent settlers.

It has been nearly 50 years since the start of large-scale emigration from Turkey to other parts of the world. Although the country has experienced a series of mass outflows of people since the late nineteenth century, those earlier flows were mostly limited to persons with a non-Turkish or non-Muslim background. Therefore, Turkish emigration, in its ethnic or national form, is a relatively new phenomenon.

Unlike the British, Germans, Italians, Greeks, Chinese, or Indians, for example, the Turks had no particular history of large-scale emigration in modern times up until the signing of the bilateral Turkish-West German agreement on October 31, 1961, which initially permitted Turkish individuals to enter West Germany on temporary one- or two-year work contracts and was later expanded to permit the entry of families. In the period of nearly half a century since then, Turkish men and women have emigrated by hundreds of thousands. The great majority of these emigrants went to Western Europe while some others also went to Australia; later, there were large numbers of immigrants to the Arab countries of North Africa and the Persian Gulf and more recently to the new countries of the Commonwealth of Independent States (CIS).

The evolution of this movement was impressive. Starting with the outflow of a few Turkish migrants in late 1961, there were, by the early 2000s, when the population of Turkey itself was some 70 million, more than three million Turkish citizens in Europe; some 100,000 Turkish workers in the Arab countries; some 60,000 settlers in Australia; and over 75,000 workers in the CIS countries. There were also more than a quarter of a million Turkish migrants in Canada and the United States. Thus, at any one time during these years, some six percent of the Turkish population was abroad. As Şebnem Köser Akçapar and Gökçe Yurdakul note in their introduction to this special issue, it is estimated that the number of Turkish migrants as of the beginning of 2009 is about five million.

There is no doubt that the potential impact of the presence of immigrants from Turkey on the communities is more than a function of numbers; it is also a function of exchanges between these migrants and their families and natives of the receiving societies. From the beginning, Turkish immigrants have appeared to engage in various civic and political activities in the destination countries. Many of them have established civil society organizations, some have become members of political parties and associations, some have participated in political demonstrations, some have signed petitions, and some have acquired citizenship in their new homelands. One could expect this combination of massive presence of Turkish immigrant communities and the maintenance of a certain level of civic and political participation to be an important factor of immigrants' incorporation into the receiving societies. Obviously, naturalization is highly central to this process. What is known in the case of Turkish immigrants is that more than a quarter of them have already been naturalized in the countries where they live.

It should be kept in mind that in the beginning of the 1960s no scholar, politician, or migration specialist could either estimate that almost one million immigrants of Turkish origin who live in the European countries would be naturalized there or could imagine that these communities of immigrants would yield members of the parliament and ministers in their adopted countries. Today, Cem Özdemir, for instance, who has been elected co-chairman of the Green Party in Germany, is the first ethnic Turkish politician to lead a major party in Europe. In addition to members of the European Parliament who have Turkish roots, there are many such representatives in the Federal Parliament of Germany. In Denmark, Hüseyin Araç is the only member of Turkish origin in parliament, while Co şkun Gürbüz, Nebahat Albayrak, Fatma Ko şer Kaya, and Saadet Karabulut are members of the Dutch parliament with Turkish origin. Yılmaz Kerimo, İbrahim Baylan, and Mehmet Kaplan were successful in the general elections on September 17, 2006, and became members of the Swedish parliament, while Emine Kır, Fatma Pehlivan, Cemal Çavdarlı, and Emin Özkara still serve as members of the Belgian parliament.

There exists a great deal of research on the various aspects of Turkish migrants living abroad but relatively little is known about their civic and political participation in the receiving societies in which they live. The findings of the articles presented in this special issue are diverse, highlighting similarities and differences among different types of immigrants and also within civic and political spheres in different destination countries. Some of these differences are brought about by different models of migrant incorporation: the "assimilationist" model versus the "ethnic-resilience" model. In the former, the individual characteristics of the immigrants are seen as the crucial aspects that determine their incorporation into the receiving society; in the latter, "structural conditions" are emphasized as the main factors that promote or discourage civic and political participation. Therefore, in order to have a comprehensive assessment of the civic and political participation in the receiving communities, more must be known about the larger context of immigrants' incorporation into their new homeland that is specifically transnational in character. Furthermore, the dynamics and mechanisms of exchanges between the immigrants, their communities of destination, and communities of origin must be studied. This special issue, edited by Şebnem Köşer Akçapar and Gökçe Yurdakul, provides a broad overview of the dynamics and mechanisms of Turkish immigrants' civic and political participation in various countries around the world and is an important contribution to the Turkish migration literature.

Introduction: Turkish Identity Formation and Political Mobilization in Western Europe and North America

ŞEBNEM KÖŞER AKÇAPAR & GÖKÇE YURDAKUL

The overall social, economic, legal, and demographic situation of Turkish immigrants in Europe has changed a lot since the early 1960s, when the first wave of Turkish guest workers started to arrive in major Western European countries. After more than 40 years of migration to Europe and different generations of immigrants, there is now a perception that Turkish immigrants are in Europe to stay as permanent residents.[1] The destination countries and the skill level of Turkish immigrants have diversified too. Today, there are almost five million Turkish people living abroad—almost four million in the EU countries (including naturalized Turkish citizens); 300,000 in North America; 150,000 in Australia; 200,000 in the Middle East; and more than 82,000 in the Russian Federation, who went there between 2001 and 2006 due to contract-dependent labor migration through the Turkish Employment Office.[2] Moreover, Turkish immigrants have started to have more economic power. Contrary to media stereotypes, not all Turks are guest workers, and not all Turks own a *döner kebap* store and live in an urban ghetto. [3] Even Turkish immigrant populations living in the same host country show significant differences in terms of their history of migration, socioeconomic status, and educational background. As the race for skilled migrants has intensified globally, many EU countries compete with traditional destination countries, such as the United States and Canada, for skilled migrants from Turkey. However, the issues today still echo the subjects raised by the research of the migration scholars of the 1970s.[4] Chief among these are unemployment, problems in education, and social and cultural integration. However, although these themes have been discussed for more than 30 years, there is one significant departure: the political integration of Turkish immigrants has now entered the critical agenda, strengthening the discussion and providing a new research direction.[5] Emergence of this new research topic is linked to changes in

4

regulations for immigrant and refugee rights that attempt to set common policies for different European Union countries.[6]

Over the years, Turkish immigrants have formed a large number and diverse types of organizations in various host countries. Creation of these migrant organizations and their subsequent development were not only influenced and shaped by the changing political opportunity structures and attitudes towards foreigners in host countries but ties retained or severed with the home country were also as effective. Often, Turkish immigrant organizations have restructured political, religious, sociocultural, and ethnic identities outside the homeland, and migrant identities have become even more fragmented.[7]

Despite the fact that such diversity in Turkish migrant organizational life calls into question whether there is any representative power of majority, some political parties in the EU countries have discovered the voting power of Turkish immigrants, especially where they are heavily concentrated. [8] For example, local elections in Belgium and the Netherlands in 2006 resulted in the political participation of many Turkish immigrants as both: candidates and voters.[9] Some European countries, like the Netherlands and Sweden, have given foreign legal residents voting rights in the local elections so as to "integrate" non-nationals living in the country, while others, like Belgium and France, have been discussing the issue for some time without any concrete results. After analyzing the integration debate for so long, migration scholars have come to acknowledge that migrant identity and belonging are very much affected by different legal and political integration policies adopted by host countries—for instance access to citizenship and voting rights. [10] However, easier access to citizenship and other legal rights offered by the host country do not always translate into greater political mobilization. By taking the examples of Turkish immigrants in the United States and in Canada, Şebnem Köşer Akçapar and Saime Özçürümez in this special issue argue, that there are other criteria for an effective migrant organizational behavior and a greater democratic participation.

Nevertheless, as transnational relations between immigrant- receiving and sending countries are strengthening[11] and the status of Turkish immigrants in Europe and North America is being transformed, Turkish immigrants have become more politically active. In the United States, despite attempts to participate at the local and state level, there have been no congressmen or senators of Turkish origin to date. In Europe, though, the situation is somewhat more positive. [12] In the European Parliament, for example, there are six Members of the European Parliament with Turkish background—Cem Özdemir (Greens), Feleknas Uca (the Left Party), and Vural Öger (Social Democratic Party of Germany [Socialdemokratische Partei Deutschlands]) from Germany; Emine Bozkurt from the Netherlands; and since 2007, Metin Kazak and Filiz Hüsmenova from Bulgaria. In Germany, many immigrants of Turkish origin are represented at the federal, state, and local levels.[13]

As studies on political integration of immigrants have come to focus on the two themes of voting behavior and democratic participation, and political mobilization and identity formation, this special issue aims to bring together selected articles on Turkish identity formation and political mobilization in Western Europe and North

America as well as voting behavior and democratic participation. This special issue has two main strengths. First, its transatlantic comparison of the political mobilization of an ethno-national group. Making transatlantic comparisons is somewhat slippery ground in migration studies, because nation-states, such as Germany, France, and the Netherlands, have significantly different politics of citizenship and belonging than do settler countries, such as Canada and the United States.[14] Moreover, settler countries may receive more highly skilled immigrants because of their immigration regulations, making it more difficult to make valid comparisons. However, it is important to explore both sides of the Atlantic for the heterogeneity of the Turkish immigrant population to be shown.

Another strength of this issue, aside from the groundbreaking nature of its transatlantic study, is that all articles derive their findings from primary data. The data collected by interviews, participant observation, and questionnaires show each researcher's personal commitment to the issues of immigrants and a keen analysis of the findings. The use of primary data is essential to understanding the immigrant context and to drawing informed conclusions.

Some difficulties arose while choosing articles: first, the literature revealed a heavy critical concentration on Muslim immigrant organizations and the impediments they face to political representation. Further, unlike previous research on "guest workers," the current literature turns Turks into the "Muslims" of Europe.[5] While searching for articles to include in this issue, a proliferation of articles on Muslim Turks was discovered. Substantially fewer articles represent the heterogeneity of Turkish immigrant groups, such as religious minorities, like Assyrians and Turkish and Kurdish refugees from Turkey. Another dimension that needs to be explored is related to the skilled migration from Turkey to Western Europe. As the recent migration trends targeting North America consist of mainly skilled migrants and most of the Turkish immigrant organizations are run by educated and professional elites in the United States and Canada, it would also be interesting to compare the contribution of Turkish skilled migrants in Western Europe in migrant organizations.

Second, the research on Turkish immigrant political integration was concentrated in certain countries. Although there is a significant amount of research on Germany and the Netherlands, [16] original and up-to-date research on France, Sweden, and Austria was unobtainable. Research has been done on Turkish immigrants in Belgium,[17] Austria,[18] and in the United Kingdom,[19] but articles on political integration including primary data were difficult to find, even though a call for papers was placed on different scholarly Internet list servers. Further research is needed in these countries because of their significant numbers of Turkish immigrants. Comparisons to the French case would make an especially interesting contribution to the field because of previous comparative studies between France and Germany.[20]

Third, it was not possible to find gender-specific research on the political integration of Turkish women and Turkish immigrant women's associations in migrant-receiving countries on either side of the Atlantic. More research should be done on Turkish immigrant women's participation in social, cultural, and political contexts to determine gender-specific political integration. This is particularly significant

because of the estimated low civic participation of Turkish immigrant women, especially in Western Europe. It is also important to do comparative research on the
topic of political mobilization of immigrants, not only with "Muslims" but with
other immigrant groups in order to be able to draw meaningful conclusions.

Finally, large-scale, comparative studies that would allow researchers to discuss
the immigrant situation from different perspectives are suggested. Perhaps quantita-
tive data would be useful to support the already existing small-scale qualitative studies. This data would enhance the understanding of demographic changes, labor
market fluctuations, and education trends. Without this data, it is difficult to see the
overall context and interpret the dispersed qualitative findings.

There are eight articles in this special volume. Additionally, Ahmet İçduygu and
Thomas Faist, who are specialists in Turkish migration issues, wrote a foreword and
an afterword, respectively, about the subject matter of this issue. In his article titled
"Turkish Organizations in Europe: How National Contexts Provide Different
Avenues for Participation," Pontus Odmalm starts by comparing different citizenship
policies and understandings of citizenship in France, Germany, and the Netherlands.
Taking the case study of Turkish immigrants in these three Western European countries with distinctive citizenship and integration policies, Odmalm questions how
different policies in different nation-states affect migrant political participation and
claims-making. He argues that the political opportunity approach helps to understand
why migrant political mobilization takes different forms.

In "Turkish Associations in the United States: Towards Building a Transnational
Identity," Şebnem Köşer Akçapar explores the role of Turkish associations in the
United States in creating a transnational identity. She first gives a brief historical
background of Turkish migration to the United States and then she provides information on the organizational attitudes of Turkish-Americans and how these organizational structures differ from those established in Western Europe. She examines
how they have changed over time to serve the needs of a more diversified and
growing Turkish-American community. She argues that organizational dynamics of
Turkish immigrants in the United States are greatly affected by a number of factors
at three different levels. At the macro level, these organizational dynamics are
affected by the general attitude towards immigrants in the host country and the
homeland policies regarding Turkish-Americans as an emerging diaspora. At the
meso (relational) level, they are affected by migrants' relationship with Americans
in general and more hostile ethno-religious groups, like the Armenian and Greek
diaspora, in particular. At the micro level, they are affected by the status of migrants
(permanent or temporary, belonging to a particular social, religious, and professional group). She also comments on some increasing interest and involvement of
Turkish immigrants in American politics, especially during the November 2008
elections thanks to the political action committees.

Saime Özçürümez in "Immigrant Associations in Canada: Included, Accommodated, or Excluded?" agrees with Pontus Odmalm that host society institutions such
as political opportunity structures and citizenship regimes affect migrant participation
and political mobilization. By taking the example of Turkish immigrant associations

in Toronto and Montreal, Canada, and by comparing them with those established in Germany and France, she argues, however, that there are other variables that hinder or encourage migrant collective participation and organizational activities. These variables are size and proportion of immigrant groups, already available integration mechanisms in the host country, emphasis on multiculturalism in host country politics, diversity of immigrant groups, and the perception of discrimination towards immigrants. Similar to the US case, most of the organizational activity is run by elite groups, and diverse groups within the Turkish community in Canada only unite and act collectively when there is a need to promote Turkish culture, when there is a natural disaster in homeland, or when the community feels that they are under a threat of adversarial politics, as with the Cyprus and Armenian issues. Unlike the case of Turkish immigrants in Europe, religion does not provide strong cohesion and higher levels of solidarity within the larger Turkish immigrant group in Canada. Although Canada offers a more inclusive citizenship regime and more open political opportunity structures, Özçürümez concludes that these are not enough to facilitate political mobilization of Turks living in Canada. Gökçe Yurdakul and Ahmet Yükleyen in "Islam, Conflict, and Integration: Turkish Religious Associations in Germany" compare the two largest Turkish Islamic organizations in Germany, Diyanet İşleri Türk İslam Birliği and Islamische Gemeinschaft Milli Görüş. By exploring the historical development and policies of these two associations the authors show how Turkish Muslim associations have defined and enacted diverse integration patterns and policies, specifically in the aftermath of September 11. Although these two religious organizations share the common goal of serving the Turkish immigrant community's religious needs they have different political perspectives and different level of acceptance by the host country: Diyanet is regarded as a supporter of official Islam, as it represents the Turkish state religion in Germany, whereas Milli Görüş' leaders have attracted suspicion both by German and Turkish authorities and have been regarded as a threat to the German and Turkish state. In recent years, however, Milli Görü ş' leaders changed their strict conservative discourse in Germany, and Diyanet started to sympathize with some of their claims on certain issues. Yurdakul and Yükleyen note that it is not yet certain which organization will be considered as a legal representative of Islam in Germany if and when Islam is given a "public law corporation" status in Germany.

Esra Özyürek in "'The Light of the Alevi Fire was Lit in Germany and Then Spread to Turkey': A Transnational Debate on the Boundaries of Islam" focuses on the transnational character of Alevi community in Berlin, Vienna, and Istanbul. She first questions the concept of integration and recognition of Muslim communities in Europe and argues against the view that Muslims have difficulty in integrating into Europe because of their different set of beliefs and traditions. Özyürek further suggests that due to the transnational dialogue among Alevi organizations, religious identities as well as conceptions of belonging and otherness have become more fluid and are largely shaped by the divergent social, political, and legal contexts in Europe. Not only did Alevis find a better space to establish their organizations in Europe but also they discovered that some of the characteristics of their faith that have been frowned upon by the Sunni majority in Turkey were easily accepted in Europe as progressive and tolerant Islam. Moreover, some European Alevi organizations started to define themselves as different from Sunni Muslims because of Germany's efforts to recognize religious minorities as independent units. In return, Alevi identity is first transformed in Europe and then in Turkey, and Alevi identity politics have witnessed heated discussions regarding the nature of religion as well as the group's minority status. Although Özyürek examines a marginal Muslim community like the Alevis, she concludes that her findings display parallels with other mainstream Muslims living in Europe and discusses that a transnational European Muslim identity owes much to the opportunities and restrictions offered by the European Union structures.

The focus of Laure Michon's and Floris Vermeulen's article entitled "Organizing for Access? The Political Mobilization of Turks in Amsterdam" is the link between local politics in the Netherlands and the Turkish organizational field. The Dutch case is especially relevant when it comes to local politics and political participation of foreign residents, as the right to elect and be elected at the local level has been granted to legal aliens since 1985, if they have resided in the Netherlands for at least five years. In this article, the authors assess the role of Turkish organizations in political participation at the local level and question whether migrant organizations serve as an instrument to help Turks gain access to Amsterdam's local political system. After a brief overview of literature on political recruitment and how immigrant politicians were recruited by several Dutch parties, Michon and Vermeulen provide statistics on the political participation of Turks in Amsterdam between 1990 and 2007. Their data also includes interviews with local Turkish politicians about their ties with migrant organizations. One of their findings is that the majority of Turks who were elected to serve at the local level in Amsterdam had some experience in Turkish migrant organizations, and some political parties have recruited politicians via Turkish associations. The authors conclude that migrant organizations do play an important role—though not the most important one—as a pool of recruitment by some political parties and serve as places where people can gain relevant experience in terms of social and political capital. However, they also note that elected Turks for the Amsterdam city council and city district councils seem to distance themselves from Turkish organizations and the Turkish community over time.

The last two articles of this special issue focus on two countries in Europe, namely Norway and Ireland, where research about Turkish immigrants and their organizational life is scarce. Jon Rogstad in "Towards a Success Story? Turkish Immigrant Organizations in Norway" first discusses the differences in organizational behavior of ethnic Turks and Kurds in the country. He points out that although Turkish Kurds make up only 20 percent of the overall Turkish migrant community in Norway, they have twice as many organizations and are mainly supported by Norwegian government funding. According to Rogstad, although this has something to do with the lack of interest on the part of Turkish immigrants in organizational behavior, it is also due to the highly differential treatment of migrant groups in Norway where refugees (mostly Kurds) are allocated more resources than economic migrants (mostly Turks). He further notes that members of these Kurdish organizations define themselves as more Kurdish than Turkish, and albeit in limited numbers, Kurds coming from countries other than Turkey join some of these organizations as well in a possible attempt to establish an "imagined homeland in diaspora." As 34 percent of all immigrants in Norway are second-generation, the author finally notes the importance of generational differences when it comes to political mobilization and democratic participation of immigrants and takes the example of the Turkish Youth Association for a more effective civic involvement among younger Turkish immigrant population.

The island of Ireland provides another interesting case because unlike France, Britain, Germany, and the Netherlands, it has received immigration recently, and Muslim and especially Turkish migration is a new phenomenon for the Irish. Jonathan Lacey in "The Gülen Movement in Ireland: Civil Society Engagements of a Turkish Religio-cultural Movement" explores the transnational character of this movement and the role of their organizations located in Dublin and Belfast. Although the number of Turks living in Dublin and Belfast is very small, this cultural organization of the Gülen followers, act like an interfaith group, being involved directly in integration debates and representing an idealized "moderate" Turkish Islam. As it is the case elsewhere in Europe and North America, Lacey further comments that Gülen followers and their organizations have used "opportunity spaces" made available by governments and willingness of civil society actors to engage with "moderate" Islamic groups.

Şebnem Köşer Akçapar & Gökçe Yurdakul
Georgetown University & Humboldt University

Notes

1. Thomas Faist (ed.), *Dual Citizenship in Europe: From Nationhood to Societal Integration* (Avebury, UK: Ashgate, 2007); Irene Bloemraad, Anna Korteweg and Gökçe Yurdakul, "Citizenship and Immigration: Assimilation, Multiculturalism and the Challenges to the Nation State," *Annual Review of Sociology*, Vol. 34 (2008), pp. 153–79.
2. Statistics obtained from Turkish Foreign Ministry and Turkish Employment Office.
3. Ayşe Çağlar, "Constraining Metaphors and the Transnationalization of Spaces in Berlin," *Journal of Ethnic and Migration Studies*, Vol. 27, No. 4 (2001), pp. 601–13.
4. See Nermin Abadan-Unat, (ed.), *Turkish Workers in Europe 1960–1975: A Socio-economic Reappraisal* (Leiden: EJ Brill, 1976).
5. For previous research on political participation of immigrants, see John Rex, Daniele Joly and Czarina Wilpert, *Immigrant Associations in Europe* (Aldershot: Gower Publishing Company, 1987); Yasemin Nuhoğlu Soysal, *Limits of Citizenship: Migrants and Postnational Membership in Europe* (Chicago: University of Chicago Press, 1994); Gerdien Jonker and Valerie Amiraux*Politics of Visibility: Young Muslims in European Public Spaces* (Bielefeld: Transcript Verlag, 2006).
6. Joanna Apap, "Shaping Europe's Migration Policy," *ERA-Forum*, Vol. 3, No. 3 (2002), pp.151–57.
7. Riva Kastoryano, "Between Europe and Nation-states: The Turkish Transnational Community," in Rosemarie Sackman and Bernhard Peters (eds.), *Identity and Integration: Migrants in Western Europe* (Burlington, VT, Ashgate, 2003), pp. 189–203; see also Samim Akgönül, "Din, Çok Bağımlılık ve Kimlik Korkusu Ekseninde Fransa Türkleri," [Turks in France in the Axis of

Religion, Extreme Dependency and Fear of Losing Identity] in Didem Danı ş and Verda İrtiş (eds.), *Entegrasyonun Ötesinde Türkiye'den Fransa'ya Göç ve Göçmenlik Halleri* [Emigration from Turkey to France and Situation of Migrants Beyond Integration] (Istanbul: Bilgi Üniversitesi Yayınları, 2008), pp. 91–119.

 8. Dirk Jacobs, Marco Martiniello and Andrea Rea, "Changing Patterns of Political Participation of Citizens of Immigrant Origin in the Brussels Capital Region: The October 2000 Elections," *Journal of International Migration and Integration*, Vol. 3, No. 2 (2002), pp. 201–21.

 9. Ayhan Kaya, "Euro-Turks: Dwelling in a Space of their Own," *Private View* (The Quarterly International Review of the Turkish Industrialists' and Businessmen's Association), No. 12 (Autumn 2007), p. 74.

10. For a discussion on cultural identity of second-generation Turkish immigrants in Germany and the United States, see Zeynep Kılıç, "Second-generation Turkish Immigrants in the United States and Germany: Dilemmas of Cultural Identity," in Holger Henke (ed.),*Crossing Over: Comparing Recent Migration in the United States and Europe* (Lanham: Lexington, 2005), pp. 163–81.

11. Thomas Faist, *The Volume and Dynamics of International Migration and Transnational Social Spaces* (Oxford: Oxford University Press, 2000); Nedim Ögelman, "Documenting and Explaining the Persistence of Homeland Politics among Germany's Turks," *International Migration Review*, Vol. 37, No. 1 (2003), pp. 163–93.

12. See Barbara Donovan, "'Minority' Representation in Germany," *German Politics*, Vol. 16, No. 4, (2007), pp. 455–80; for a project on immigrant participation in politics also see Mannheimer Zentrum für Europäische Sozialforschung, "Migranten als politische akteure" [Migrants as Political Actors], www.migractors.de.

13. In early 2009, there were five members of parliament in Germany at the federal level: Dr. Lale Akgün (SPD), Prof. Hakkı Keskin, Hüseyin Kenan Akın, and Sevim Da ğdelen (PDS), and Ekin Deligöz (Greens). There is significant number of MPs at the state (Laender) level, such as from Berlin, Emine Demirbüken-Wegner (Christian Democratic Union), Dilek Kolat, Ülker Radziwill, Canan Bayram (SPD), Özcan Mutlu and Bilkay Öney (Greens), Evrim Helin Baba and Giyasettin Sayan (PDS); from Lower Saxony, Filiz Polat (Greens); from Hamburg, Aygül Özkan and David Erkalp (CDU), Bülent Çiftlik and Metin Hakverdi (SPD), Mehmet Yıldız (PDS), and Nebahat Güçlü (Greens); from Bremen, Mustafa Güngör and Şükrü Şenkal (SPD), Mustafa Öztürk (Greens), Şirvan Çakıcı (PDS), and from Hessen, Turgut Yüksel (SPD) and Mürvet Öztürk (Greens). A number of them are of Kurdish background.

14. Zeynep Aycan and John W. Berry, "Impact of Employment-related Experiences on Immigrants' Psychological Well-being and Adaptation to Canada," *Canadian Journal of Behavioral Sciences*, Vol. 28, No. 3 (1996), pp. 240–51; Ilhan Kaya, "Religion as a Site of Boundary Construction: Islam and the Integration of Turkish Americans in the United States," *Alternatives: Turkish Journal of International Relations*, Vol. 6, Nos. 1–2 (2007), pp. 139–55; Irene Bloemraad and S. Karthick Ramakrishnan, *Civic Hopes and Political Realities: Immigrant Community Organizations and Political Engagement* (London: Russell Sage Foundation, 2008).

15. Ruth Mandel, *Cosmopolitan Anxieties: Turkish Challenges to Citizenship and Belonging in Germany* (Durham: Duke University Press, 2008); Gökçe Yurdakul, *From Guest Workers into Muslims: The Transformation of Turkish Immigrant Associations in Germany* (Newcastle, UK: Cambridge Scholars Press, 2009).

16. Gamze Avcı, "Comparing Integration Policies and Outcomes: Turks in the Netherlands and Germany," *Turkish Studies*, Vol. 7, No. 1 (2006), pp. 67–84; Peter Doerschler, "Push-pull Factors and Immigrant Political Integration in Germany," *Social Science Quarterly*, Vol. 87 (2006), pp. 1100–16; Anja Heelsum, "Political Participation and Civic Community of Ethnic Minorities in Four Cities in the Netherlands," *Politics*, Vol. 25, No. 10 (2005), pp. 19–30; Nedim Ögelman, Jeannette Money and Philip L. Martin, "Immigrant Cohesion and Political Access in Influencing Foreign Policy," *SAIS Review*, Vol. 22, No. 2 (2002), pp. 145–65; Zeynep Sezgin, "Turkish Migrants' Organization: Promoting Tolerance Toward the Diversity of Turkish Migrants in Germany,"*International Journal of Sociology*, Vol. 38, No. 2 (2008), pp. 78–95; Marieke van Londen, Karen Phalet and Louk Hagendoorn,

"Civic Engagement and Voter Participation among Turkish and Moroccan Minorities in Rotterdam," *Journal Ethnic and Migration Studies,* Vol. 33, No. 8 (2007), pp. 1201–26.

17. Dirk Jacobs, Karen Phalet and Marc Swyngedouw, "Political Participation and Associational Life of Turkish Residents in the Capital of Europe," *Turkish Studies,* Vol. 7, No. 1 (2006), pp. 145–61; Therese De Raedt, "Muslims in Belgium: A Case Study of Emerging Identities," *Muslim Minority Affairs,* Vol. 24, No. 1 (2004), pp. 9–30; Christiane Timmerman, "Gender Dynamics in the Context of Turkish Marriage Migration," *Turkish Studies,* Vol. 7, No. 1 (2006), pp. 125–43; Johan Wets, "The Turkish Community in Austria and Belgium: The Challenge of Integration," *Turkish Studies,* Vol. 7, No. 1 (2006), pp. 85–100; Ural Manço and Meryem Kanmaz, "From Conflict to Co-operation between Muslims and Local Authorities in a Brussels Borough: Schaerbeek," *Journal of Ethnic and Migration Studies,* Vol. 31, No. 6 (2005), pp. 1105–23.

18. Sabine Kroissenbrunner, "Islam and Muslim Immigrants in Austria: Socio-political Networks and Muslim Leadership of Turkish Immigrants," *Immigrants and Minorities,* Vol. 22, Nos. 2–3 (2003), pp. 188–207.

19. Talip Küçükcan, "The Making of Turkish Muslim Diaspora in Britain: Religious Collective Identity in a Multicultural Public Sphere," *Journal of Muslim Minority Affairs*, Vol. 24, No. 2 (2004), pp. 243–58.

20. Riva Kastaoryano, *Negotiating Identities: States and Immigrants in France and Germany* (Princeton: Princeton University Press, 2002); Rogers Brubaker, *Citizenship and Nationhood in France and Germany* (Cambridge, MA: Harvard University Press, 1992).

Turkish Organizations in Europe: How National Contexts Provide Different Avenues for Participation

PONTUS ODMALM

Politics and International Relations, University of Edinburgh, UK

ABSTRACT *The purpose of this article is threefold: to identify opportunities and constraints for migrants in participating in their host society; to further explore variance in formal political participation; and to assess how different citizenship policies give rise to different types of participation and different targets for claims-making. The article first discusses how different understandings of citizenship and implementations of citizenship policy give rise to a different set of opportunities for migrants to participate in the political sphere. This is exemplified with reference to Turkish organizations in Germany, France, and the Netherlands. The paths these states have chosen in terms of integration and citizenship policies have resulted in a different set of opportunities for Turks' formal participation.*

Introduction

Migration in Western Europe has steadily become more and more diverse in terms of origin and reasons for migrating. Migration that was often supposed to be temporary, such as the post-war labor migration, has in many cases led to semi-permanent settlement. Continued chain-migration of family members has contributed to the presence of second- and third-generation migrants that has prompted states, voluntarily or involuntarily, to find ways to incorporate migrants into the polity.

Although differences in terms of citizenship acquisition are still prominent, a number of civil, social, and political rights have gradually been made available to resident third-country nationals. This partial dissociation of nationality and citizenship, on the one hand, and identities and rights, on the other, poses particular challenges to nation-states.[1] However, it also provides migrants with a number of different avenues to participate politically in the host society.

It will therefore be important to take into consideration how different types of host society institutions give rise to different types of political opportunities and ways of participating. The most obvious marker is whether formal political participation, for example voting, is dependent on being a national. If this is the case, then non-nationals will be prevented from having an influence on who governs and will be excluded from a key arena of political engagement. Conversely, if an exclusive citizenship regime becomes liberalized, this would alter the electoral landscape in terms of party competition for the migrant vote.[2]

In practice, the citizen/non-citizen distinction is not always clear-cut and nation-states often provide some type of formal political rights to non-nationals. In Britain, for example, non-nationals from Ireland and Commonwealth migrants enjoy national voting rights, whereas in Sweden and the Netherlands resident third-country nationals are allowed to vote in local elections after three (Sweden) and five years (the Netherlands) of residence. Most commonly, however, national level voting rights are the privilege of nationals, and local voting rights for third-country nationals are the exception rather than the rule.

Although the importance of citizenship has been viewed to be declining in the post-national era[3] there is also evidence showing citizenship to be on the offensive.[4] This is most notable in the way that states are beginning to emphasize citizenship as a reward rather than as a tool of integration. This shift indicates that non-nationals are under increasing pressure to show that they are potential citizens through the introduction of formal and informal integration requirements. These requirements are indicative of how citizenship once again is becoming a focal interest for nation-states.

This new situation of tightening access to the polity by making naturalization more demanding provides an interesting paradox among liberal democracies. On the one hand, the formal exclusion of groups due to their non-national status is identified as a problem, and on the other, citizenship is becoming more exclusive and may disproportionably affect the very groups that are considered to be at risk of exclusion.

The aim of this article is therefore threefold. First, it will focus on different citizenship policies and understandings of citizenship in France, Germany, and the Netherlands. Second, the outcomes of these different policies will be discussed in relation to how they provide sets of opportunities for migrants to participate (in conventional or non-conventional forms) as well as how they determine the level where these claims are aimed (host state, supra-state, or homeland). Finally, the study will utilize a key migrant group in Europe –the Turks– as an illustrative example of how different citizenship policies give rise to different types of participation and different directions of claims-making. The article will initially discuss the backdrop for Turkish migration to Europe and then will go onto how different states have responded to this group in terms of citizenship policies and access to rights and, finally, to what opportunities for participation these settings give rise.

Turkish Migration to Europe

Turks constitute one of the largest migrant groups in Europe. An estimated four million[6] of Turkish descent reside across Sweden, Germany, the Netherlands,

Belgium, France, and Austria. Turks are also one of the longest-settled migrant groups in the post-war period, on a par with migrants from the Caribbean and the Indian subcontinent in Britain.

There is, however, variance in terms of the number of Turks as a proportion of the total foreign population. The Netherlands and Germany have a much higher number of resident Turks and their offspring—12 and 25 percent respectively, compared to the five percent that Turks amount to in France.[7]

The German case provides a textbook example of recruiting migrants as "guest-workers," and the Turkish community is very much rooted in this particular migration history. When the recession hit following the oil crisis in the early 1970s and the recruitment ban was initiated, Turks amounted to just over four million and the German government was faced with a difficult task of how to reduce any further inflow of dependents from Turkey. Several restrictive measures were put in place, such as differential child benefit payments and restrictions on employment by family members, which was in line with Germany's resistance to view itself as a country of immigration.[8] Paradoxically, the policies that were supposed to encourage Turks to return to their country instead sparked further migration, in terms of family reunifi-cation, which, while not actively encouraged, was still allowed.[9]

The Netherlands and France were comparatively late in recruiting foreign labor migrants, having initially relied on colonial migration for these purposes. The consequences of this strategy meant fewer foreign-born migrants in the Dutch labor force with an overrepresentation of Turks. In France, Turkish migration has been a post-1973 phenomena and one dominated by political refugees. In a similar vein to Germany, labor migrants in the Netherlands were initially meant to be short-term, but the measures to regulate and control migration were less stringent than in Germany, resulting in migration becoming semi-permanent relatively early on.[10] As in Germany, Turkish migration increased after the official labor halt in 1973 due to family reunification, making Turks the third-largest migrant community in the Netherlands.[11]

Citizenship Policies and Institutional Arrangements for Participation

Citizenship is a key marker in the relationship between the state and the individual. The citizen status sets out the rights and obligations that are appointed to the indi-viduals identified as members of that particular society. Being a citizen also allows these individuals to take full advantage of the political rights associated with this status. A common approach in the literature has been to classify states' policies and understandings of citizenship according to three ideal types. These typologies are said to "define a particular institutional and discursive setting for political conten-tion over migration and ethnic relations" and to distinguish between ethno-cultural and civic-cultural understandings of citizenship.[12]

The first of these, labeled the "exclusive" or "ethnic" model, provides an institu-tional setup which either denies or makes it very difficult for migrants to gain access to the political community through the adoption of a   *jus sanguinis* principle of citizenship.[13] Germany pre-2000 is often used as an illustration of this approach. France exemplifies that second typology, the so-called "assimilationist" or "republican" model, which provides easy access to naturalization through a *jus soli* principle and semi-automatic citizenship for children of immigrant parents. The flip side is that citizenship comes with strong pressures on migrants to assimilate culturally and with little recognition of difference in the public sphere. [14] Finally, there is the "multicultural" model, which provides relatively easy access to naturalization and some rights for cultural difference in the public sphere. The Netherlands conformed, in some respects, to this model but has made some dramatic policy changes over the last decade, thus becoming more similar to France by limiting the public recognition of ethnic identities.

The models give some indication of how receiving states perceive their new population. Furthermore, the typologies also provide an understanding of the opportunities available for political participation, the type of participatory acts that migrants engage in, and to where this participation is directed. However, these models inhabit certain limitations that make them problematic to use analytically. First, since states are classified in a dichotomous fashion, the typologies ignore or oversimplify the complex realities of how nation-states perceive nationhood and belonging and how they construct citizenship policies. Second, states may also change their policies over time—becoming either more liberal or more restrictive—which is not properly accounted for in these models. Finally, the models do not fully engage with intrastate dynamics in terms of how different political actors compete for change in policies and understandings of citizenship. [15] These limitations are highlighted if the formal arrangement of citizenship acquisition is considered. The three countries considered in this article display a number of similarities in this area even though the models would suggest that they should not. For example, access to nationality in all three countries is provided through the *jus sanguinis* principle, through recognition or legitimization (for example, through marriage), as well as through naturalization. There are also further similarities in terms of the additional so-called "integration requirements" that are becoming more common in state policy.[16] These similarities are part of a pan—European trend to upgrade citizenship, which has gained momentum following post—2001 concerns about failing integration.[17]

To understand these similarities, Koopmans and Statham have suggested a two-dimensional conceptualization of citizenship that to a greater extent captures these dynamic relationships.[18] This conceptual space is defined by formal and cultural dimensions of citizenship. The vertical axis runs from an understanding of citizenship that favors ethno-cultural bonds as the basis for the political community, to one that emphasizes a civic political culture based on residence. The horizontal axis runs from citizenship understood as conforming to a single cultural model embraced by all citizens to a culturally pluralist conception that retains or encourages cultural diversity. This conceptualization gives rise to a scale ranging from, on the one hand, civic republicanism—ethnic assimilation—and, on the other, civic pluralism—ethnic segregation.

Viewing citizenship regimes in this way allows for the classification of states as corresponding more or less to these ideal types. It also highlights some of the commonalities shared by countries that would otherwise be considered as polar opposites. For example, both Germany and the Netherlands offered migrant children the possibility of education in their own language. However, in the German case this was intended as a way to facilitate reintegration upon return whereas in the Netherlands the same policy was intended to support and preserve a minority language. Similarly, the typology can be used to position different countries in terms of where the emphasis is placed and allows us to understand changes in policy, for example the introduction of additional requirements such as language proficiency, loyalty to the constitution, etc. At the same time, the Koopmans-Statham typology helps in understanding the different nature of migrant mobilization and the various positions adopted by these actors.

However, citizenship is not only a means by which rights and duties are allocated. It also marks the type of relationship that the state has with its newcomers. It is thus important to also consider the symbolic labeling that is placed on migrants. This enables the understanding of the nature of claims-making (for example, to improve migrants' status in the host society or to gain further recognition for cultural rights) and where the claims may be directed to (host state, supra-state, or homeland).

France defines newcomers as "immigrants," and Germany refers to immigrants as "foreigners," while the Netherlands has adopted the term "ethnic minority." Despite using the same term, the interpretation and definition of, for example, "immigrant" differs between countries. Comparing the French understanding of an immigrant to its Swedish counterpart is particularly illuminating. In Sweden, the statistical definition refers to persons born abroad and to Swedish-born persons whose parents were both born abroad. An immigrant in France, on the other hand, refers to persons born abroad but is also used to indicate a status prior to becoming French or, more informally, to persons who are perceived as being unable to assimilate. Similarly, "ethnic minority" as used in the Dutch context differs remarkably from, for example, the British. In the former, the term is based on objective criteria (place of birth of self and parents) and is used for socioeconomic monitoring of these groups by the Dutch authorities. In the latter, the term is used to signify geographical or ethnic origin (for example Asian, black, and white) through self-identification in census surveys.

These different national understandings of citizenship and ways of officially defining migrants give rise to very different possibilities for participation and may also have a structuring effect on the type of issues around which migrants choose to mobilize. Giugni and Passy point to how the institutional environment is crucial in understanding how migrants participate.[19] In France, they suggest, the assimilationist emphasis and inclusive nature of membership gives rise to, on the one hand, claims that relate to recognition for ethnic and cultural difference, and on the other, a more radical form of mobilization due to the closed institutional opportunities. In Germany, where citizenship policy for a long time made it more or less impossible for migrants to naturalize and thus become part of the political community, the lack of formal political opportunities have led migrants to develop alternative and more civil society-orientated means of participation. This indirect type of engagement, coupled with a "foreigner" status, meant that claims were made in order to improve the status of migrants vis-à-vis the German state or through bypassing the state by aiming for the EU level. [20] In contrast, the Dutch multicultural model of relatively easy access to naturalization and emphasis on migrants being able to retain their cultural uniqueness was complemented by a number of consultative bodies for the recognized minorities to be able to assert influence on policies.[21]

The view adopted by Giugni and Massy is in many ways symptomatic of what has been written on migration and political integration in recent years. This approach has been adapted from the literature on political opportunity structures, which focuses on political institutions and social movements. [22] Accordingly, the state provides a number of institutional settings that make up the political environment and determines the rules and boundaries to which political actors are obliged to adhere. In this environment there are certain conditions that can either facilitate or constrain the political opportunities that these actors face when they pursue their strategic goals. However, these opportunities are not only determined by the presence of the state. Other factors include specific configurations of resources and historical precedents that determine how and what type of groups mobilize. Studying and identifying these opportunities and constraints for participation sheds light on the differences of migrant mobilization and how the contextual structures influence political behavior.

In terms of the political institutions that provide the space available for contestation, a first distinction to make relates to the extent to which France, Germany, and the Netherlands display corporatist or pluralist characteristics. The key distinction is whether a liberal polity is dominated by a monopolized and centralized system of interest organization in which the state formally designates and recognizes only a limited number of encompassing interests (corporatist model) or multiple, overlapping, spontaneously formed, easily abandoned, and politically autonomous associations (pluralist model). [23] The configuration of the polity in this way provides particular types of settings that shape the form of migrant mobilization.

While the Netherlands can be said to conform mainly to a corporatist model with a few state-recognized bodies that represent particular social categories of society, Germany falls in between while France displays few to none corporatist traits.

A second distinction relates to the nature of political conflict. German political life has been dominated by the dividing lines of class and religion, which has, until the entry of the Greens, created a two-tier system, with parties representing the broad categories of capital-labor and religious-secular groups. However, explicit political competition and conflict has by and large been absent in Germany due to what Conradt describes as a striving for absolute solutions in order to eliminate the causes of conflict.[24] This aversion to conflict has thus led to both the elite as well as the general public being unable to accept the need for strong opposition parties or extensive bargaining within and between parties in parliament, opting for a more expert-orientated and legalistic conception of politics.

Consequently, this has generated a strong state presence in the political order that has generated a public sphere that is both highly centralized and bureaucratic, despite its federal political system. Furthermore, the corporatist elements present in the German system provide opportunities for class and religious interests such as trade unions, welfare organizations, churches, business organizations, and so on, to participate in public policy-making. [25] At the same time, migrants and minorities are excluded from decision-making and influence by the exclusive nature of German citizenship as well as by the limitations that the dominating cleavages represent to incorporate the ethnic as well as the primarily Islamic dimension. [26]

The institutional arrangement in Germany, with limited corporatist influence, is also reflected in its way of organizing resident migrants. Migrant organizations are not given a special role or status in the integration policy formulation, and formal links with organizations, similar to those found in the Netherlands, are less well established. Instead, labor unions and churches play a more prominent role than migrant organizations. In addition, few provisions exist on a federal level for the collective participation of migrants, although due to the institutional nature of the German polity one finds significant variance on a municipal level depending on whether the local government is positively orientated towards these organizations or not. There is also a high degree of variance in terms of funding for migrant organizations, which is often left to the discretion of the local government. [27]

Therefore, Germany displays a relatively large number of migrant organizations but of a very fragmented nature. [28] However, regional differences are vast, and the more liberal and multiculturally-orientated cities, such as Berlin and Hamburg, have created favorable settings for the funding of organizations and have also established links between migrant organizations, governmental bodies, and political actors. These differences in host society settings and attitudes open up a variety of roles and levels of engagement for organizations. Yurdakul points to this in her study of Turkish associations in Berlin, where the more open attitude of Berlin's political elite has resulted in close working relationships with certain Turkish associations, primarily in the area of integration. [29] However, in line with the dominating class cleavage in Germany, the Turkish organizations on the left, and especially the Social Democratic ones, have established close links with the Social Democratic Party and also managed to secure more state funding compared to the more conservative and transnationally-oriented organizations.

The Netherlands has traditionally displayed a much higher number of corporatist features compared to France and Germany, both with regard to general policy-making as well as in the area of integration. This process has involved the assertion of individual influence through party channels as well as that of group influence via organizations. These settings constitute a particular institutional framework driven by a top-down perspective where the government recognizes and identifies the needs and rights of immigrants and thus provides the context in which immigrants and their interests are organized. The state allocates certain functions—such as interest representation and consultative participation—thereby creating a unified and bureaucratic network. Even spontaneous and oppositional movements are incorporated into this scheme by being dependent on state funding.[30]

In France, migrant organizations are primarily not based on single ethnicities but are rather built of cross-ethnic membership (as in the case of SOS Racisme) or represent cross-national ethnic groups (such as the Maghrebian organisation France-Plus) and are usually located on the national level. As with the key Turkish organizations in Germany, migrant organizations in France have traditionally established close links with parties on the left as a consequence of migrating for labor purposes and thus forming part of a French working class. Although France has relaxed its views on ethnic organizations, these are relatively scarce (at least compared to Germany and the Netherlands) as a consequence of the lack of recognition for ethnicity in French citizenship discourse and the dominance of four particular cleavage lines in the post-war era: class, religion (traditionally between secular and clerical), foreign policy (protectionism versus EU integration) and form of governance (presidential versus parliamentary).[31] This has led to migrants being predominantly organized and unified with respect to specific political issues. These tend to be related to ethnicity and cultural–religious concerns, functioning outside of mainstream politics, and as such emerge as a response to the particular political climate and environment. In this respect, they very much correspond to how interests and discontent are generally manifested in the French polity through what Mény calls "the periodic eruption of violence and protest that contradict or counterbalance choices expressed through the ballot box." [32] The reasons for this, Mény suggests, can be found in the institutional setup of French society that through its exclusivity has not managed to channel violent social protests into peaceful and formal expressions. Parties, unions, and interest groups have had difficulties to effectively organize group activity as a consequence of the extremely varied electoral rules. This has led to fragmented formation of wings and factions within parties and has made it difficult to set up alliances. Therefore, in order to be heard, contenders must resort to extreme measures, such as violent demonstrations or large-scale strikes, which have been proven to pay off. This is due to the paradoxical nature of the French state, which is haughty, all-powerful, and disdainful but when faced with violent protests tends to become ready to concede and forgiving since there is no other way out.[33]

Outcomes of Institutions: How do They Structure Political Behavior?

Organized migrant interests and the way in which they mobilize are thus often understood to be a consequence of the particular organizational models provided by the host society. These models and institutions not only have an effect on the way these claims are made (conventional/non-conventional) but also, as Ireland has argued, direct them towards particular levels (host state, supra-state, or homeland-oriented).[34] This point is furthermore acknowledged by Soysal: "Host societies shape the collective organization of migrants by providing (or not) certain resources for and models of organizing…certain host society institutions and policies encourage collective identity and organization." [35] In other words, the presence or absence of particular opportunities for political engagement provides them with certain political cues from which they define their goals and strategies in relation to the host society.

The emphasis on mobilization as a response to the political environment provides a different focus compared to the two previously dominating paradigms regarding the relationship between migrants/minorities and collective action. The first suggests a class-based approach, where the underprivileged structural and socioeconomic position of migrants has a direct consequence for their degree of mobilization and underlying motives. According to this line of thought, economic divisions within the working class are seen as racialized under the structural crisis of advanced industrial capitalism that transforms a common race or ethnicity into a class of its own and serves as a common identity for political participation and as a form of emerging, but false, class consciousness. This precarious situation can only be overcome by cooperating with the indigenous working class through trade unions and labor parties, where the race category becomes subordinate to the more general class category. The second explanation—the ethnicity/race paradigm—takes an opposite stance, advocating that the ethnic class is not so much a display of false consciousness but rather a continuous form of collective action independent from class. Here, shared experiences, such as racism and discrimination, distinguish migrants from the host society's population.[36]

However, the ultimate causes of behavior—class and ethnicity—are taken as given and not related to particular country contexts. Both approaches assume that migrants will tend to behave in a similar fashion regardless of the political institutional framework.[37] In contrast, the political opportunity approach suggests that collective action is determined by external events—the availability of resources and opportunities made available by changes in the institutional setting. The key issue here is that the opportunity approach places group mobilization in a political context and provides an explanation as to why mobilization takes a certain appearance and when and why it is successful rather than why it originally emerges. Furthermore, this model predicts that the amount and type of group formation are a direct outcome of the particular structure of political institutions and the construction of political power in a given society. [38] Thus, it is when changes occur in the external opportunities that group action and formation are more likely to be observed. If powerful groups change their attitudes against politically marginalized groups, these groups should respond to this opening by increasing group action, founding new organizations, and using these as channels for mobilization. This perspective originally builds on the resource mobilization theory of collective action, which focuses on the perceived cost and benefits of alternative strategies and the need for resource mobilization prior to mobilization. The impact stemming from the shift from local to national power structures on organizational forms and types of collective action makes an important addition to the understanding of the social and political terrain that forms the condition for the emergence and success of modern movements.[39]

It is, however, important to note that migrant organizations are also qualitatively different from other types of voluntary organizations in terms of their aims and functions. In terms of organizational aims, migrant associations can be said to serve four characteristic purposes. First, migrant organizations can act as a link between the sending country and the receiving one in that they can provide advisory services for future migrants. This means that the organization could potentially act as an intermediary or an alternative for the complex bureaucracy. They can also have a cushioning function; that is, they can "soften" the shock of transition by offering a setting in which immigrants can meet fellow nationals and speak their own language. Organizations can also maintain the interaction among immigrants. This is especially relevant for migrants who lack informal ties, and therefore they may attempt to forge formal ties so as to retain some form of bonding.[40]

Second, organizations can function as an alternative or complement to the state in terms of integration and adaptation to the new society. If an organization or a number of them are able to set up well-functioning relationships with authorities responsible for integration policies, migrant associations can potentially facilitate integration. This could include providing information about the host country in the native language or acting as a link between migrants and different socioeconomic areas of society and/or the political world. In this way organizations allow migrants to practice the ways of the host society in an ethnic setting. As such, they can thus be used as a "training school" for further political participation in the host society.

Third, migrant associations, if part of an established network, can serve as a unified voice for their particular ethnic group in relation to the host society. Organizations can be used to translate the group's consensus on certain subjects. The extent to which immigrants cluster in organizations is also an important indicator for measuring the extent of a collective (or collectively expressed) identity. The character, number, and size of organizations indicate the extent to which immigrants intend to profile themselves as different or are seen by others as different. Organizations can thus be viewed as an expression of the collectively felt identity of their members. They can be defensive (as a response to exclusion) or offensive (stemming from a choice of immigrants to set themselves apart from others). Furthermore, one should make a distinction between organizations that aim at enforcing the ethnic identity and those that encourage integration. Offensive organizations will often have as their goal the retaining of an identity, whereas defensive organizations have strategy rather than identity as their main goal, where strategy can either be stressing or eliminating difference. [41] The concentration of migrants and their home country-based social networks are viewed as crucial to their organizing on the basis of ethnic attributes. Finally, migrant organizations can play an important role for the maintenance of a linkage between the ethnic group and the country or region of origin, especially in a diaspora situation. Also, they can serve as contact points between ethnic communities in different settlement countries. This last characteristic has been particularly dominant among Turkish communities residing in different European countries.[42]

However, Ostergaard-Nielsen suggests that the way in which Turks organize is not always dependent on host society institutions but more related to their socioeconomic position in the host society, developments in Turkey, and developments in European-Turkish relations.[43] This situation, Ostergaard-Nielsen continues, is exemplified by the multitude of Turkish organizations in Germany that display a vast variety of political backgrounds and affiliations. In part, they reflect the political affiliation of the Turkish migrants ranging from radical left- and right-wing nationalist to more mainstream and moderate organizations.[44] In addition, there is also a large body of religious organizations such as those of the Alevis, which developed in response to discrimination by the Sunni majority. Similarly, the Turkish Sunnis have developed a number of organizations around a secular form of Islam in the same vein as practiced by the Turkish state. This in turn has given rise to competing organizations formed by Milli Görü, which by and large opposed the division of church and state. However, as argued above, whether Turkish organizations are more engaged in homeland or host society issues will be influenced by the structural conditions and opportunities available for participation. In Germany, naturalization has traditionally been restrictive, which has excluded many Turks from the mainstream political arena, thus giving rise to two main types of political engagements, either in the transnational activities described by Ostergaard-Nielsen or as trying to push for change in their status in Germany. At the same time, local conditions, as discussed by Yurdakul, may allow for more inclusive participation in terms of cooperation with German authorities to improve processes of integration.[45]

In the Netherlands, Turks have also imported their homeland politics to Dutch organizational life, generating similar left-right and religiously oriented associations. However, it was not until the early 1980s that Dutch authorities began to seriously consider Turkish organizations in the same vein as the more established Surinamese counterparts. The new policy that was introduced aimed at promoting and preserving cultural identities, to emancipate their constituencies, and to represent community interests. Furthermore, these new policies opened up a much more favorable funding climate for Turkish organizations in the Netherlands and also gave these organizations an enhanced status and legitimacy. [46] Although Turks in many European countries have been described as being ideologically split and having difficulties uniting,[47] van Heelsum's study on Turkish associations in the Netherlands finds that despite political and religious cleavages a significant number of Turkish associations are in fact interconnected with each other through a cohesive network of interlocking board members. [48] These changes in the way in which Turkish organizations were viewed by the Dutch authorities very much correspond to the opportunities set out in Dutch citizenship policy, which aimed at inclusion and emancipation through civil society engagement.

In comparison, migrant (as well as non-migrant) associations in France have a weaker civil society position where the French state has been prone to advocate and fund general organizations that cater to a cross-section of the population. Voluntary organizations have become more involved in local and regional level decision-making as equal partners but are at the same time in a weak position in which they are subject to local authorities or government agencies to "ok" them and then admit them within their orbit.[49] However, this situation changed in the early 1980s when following the abolishment of legal restrictions on migrant associations the opportunities for starting up migrant organizations increased, although these organizations often lack national representation and do not tend to represent a united front. Turkish associations in France also differ numerically in relation to those in Germany and the Netherlands due to Turks being a relatively small migrant group. This has created a different scenario in France in which the ideological (left-right) and religious (secular-Islamic) splits are less prevalent, and instead a linguistic-national split has surfaced between the Turks and the numerically superior North African migrants.[50]

Conclusion

The political institutions of nation-states continue to have an impact on the way that migrant groups are able to mobilize politically in the host society. The political opportunity approach helps in understanding why migrant mobilization takes different expressions, modes, and courses of action. Focusing on how states do, or do not, provide particular institutional channels for participation allows us to identity the possibilities that migrants have to exercise influence in the host society. The Turks in the Netherlands have since the 1980s enjoyed a situation of fairly inclusive state policies, although the exact level of influence still needs to be evaluated. This has allowed organized Turkish interests to participate on a par with native Dutch interests and other ethnic minority groups. In contrast, the lack of a formal platform or arena in the host society can either redirect participating groups (such as the Turks in Germany) towards a supra-national level or towards the sending country, but it can also spark mobilization for increased cultural rights and group specific recognition (as in France).

However, it should be pointed out that there are some key changes underway with regard to how European states view citizenship and, especially, how they view ethnic political participation. Citizenship has moved away from being a primarily legal term expressing the relationship between the individual, the state, and the territory to also be a prominent feature in the integration debate. European states are now at a stage where they have to decide whether citizenship is a tool for integration or whether to go down the North American route and use citizenship as a reward to be handed out to "successfully integrated" migrants. The debate around citizenship has also shifted away from being primarily about rights and opportunities towards an emphasis on active citizenship and its key role for social cohesion. The reemphasis of citizenship can be explained with reference to two particular events. First, it is an effect of immigration developing into a security issue. Migration, it is argued, has become a security concern and can pose new types of threats to the state (or even to Western democratic values more generally). This process has further meant that issues relating to migration have started to move beyond the established rules of the political game and are now framed as issues that require either special measures or are considered to be above politics. As a security threat, the state can thus justify the use of extraordinary measures—for example, giving state institutions increased powers to remove citizenship. Second, as a reaction to perceived failures of multicultural politics. The reasoning behind these arguments suggest that on the one hand, becoming a citizen should mean more than merely acquiring a new passport, and references are made to factors such as lack of social cohesion and problems of ethnic segregation. On the other, critics suggest that multiculturalism has had an isolating effect and contributed to extremism, which is a point that has been particularly prominent in the Netherlands.

These developments are likely to have an impact on the type of mobilization that occurs and on the relationship that particular migrant groups have with the host society. Current trends could point towards a direction in which "ethnically exclusive" participation will become increasingly more difficult for groups such as the Turks since host societies will be more concerned with migrants showing that they are properly integrated and participating in and through mainstream channels. An indicative development can be found in the increasing use of integration "tests" that states are introducing as a requirement for naturalization. Although many states believe that additional integration courses and tests are beneficial, it remains unclear as to exactly how these new measures are to achieve "better integration" and what the connection to national identity is. However, these integration requirements may not solely serve as a way to filter out unwanted citizens but could also aim to facilitate the political participation of migrants as citizens-to-be by providing them with necessary skills such as language and information on migrants' rights and responsibilities.

Notes

1. See Karen Phalet and Mark Swyngedouw, "National Identities and Representations of Citizenship: A Comparison of Turks, Moroccans and Working-class Belgians in Brussels," *Ethnicities,* Vol. 2, No. 1 (2002), pp. 5–30.; Irene Bloemraad, Anna Korteweg and Gökçe Yurdakul, "Citizenship and Immigration: Multiculturalism, Assimilation and Challenges to the Nation-State," *Annual Review of Sociology*, Vol. 34, No. 8 (2008), pp. 1–27.
2. Gökçe Yurdakul, "State, Political Parties and Immigrant Elites: Turkish Immigrant Associations in Berlin," *Journal of Ethnic and Migration Studies,* Vol. 32, No. 3 (2006), pp. 435–53.
3. Yasmine Soysal, *Limits of Citizenship: Migrants and Postnational Membership in Europe* (Chicago: University of Chicago Press, 1994).
4. Ruud Koopmans and Paul Statham, "Migration and Ethnic Relations as a Field of Political Contention: An Opportunity Structure Approach," in Ruud Koopmans and Paul Statham (eds.),*Challenging Immigration and Ethnic Relations Politics* (Oxford: Oxford University Press, 2000), pp. 13–56.
5. Pontus Odmalm, "One Size Fits All? European Citizenship, National Citizenship Policies and Integration Requirements," *Representation,* Vol. 43, No.1 (2007), pp. 19–34.
6. M. Crul and H. Vermeulen, "The Second Generation in Europe," *International Migration Review,* Vol. 37, No. 4, (2003), pp. 965–86.
7. Marco Giugni and Florence Passy, "Migrant Mobilization between Political Institutions and Citizenship Regimes: A Comparison of France and Switzerland," *European Journal of Political Research*, Vol. 43, No. 1 (2004), pp. 51–82.
8. Gamze Avci, "Comparing Integration Policies and Outcomes: Turks in the Netherlands and Germany," *Turkish Studies*, Vol. 7, No.1 (2006), pp. 67–84.

9. Simon Green, "Divergent Traditions, Converging Responses: Immigration and Integration Policy in the UK and Germany," *German Politics*, Vol. 16, No. 1 (2007), pp. 95–115.
10. Pontus Odmalm, *Policies and Political Participation: Inclusion or Intrusion in Western Europe?* (Basingstoke: Palgrave, 2005).
11. Jean Tillie and Boris Slijper, "Immigrant Political Integration and Ethnic Civic Communities in Amsterdam," in Seyla Benhabib, Ian Shapiro and Danilo Petranovich (eds.), *Identities, Affiliations, and Allegiances* (Cambridge: Cambridge University Press, 2007).
12. See Koopmans and Statham, "Migration and Ethnic Relations as a Field of Political Contention," p. 30.
13. Rogers Brubaker, *Citizenship and Nationhood in France and Germany* (Cambridge, MA: Harvard University Press, 1992).
14. Adrian Favell, *Philosophies of Integration: Immigration and the Idea of Citizenship in France and Britain* (Basingstoke: Palgrave, 1998).
15. See Koopmans and Statham, "Migration and Ethnic Relations as a Field of Political Contention."
16. See Odmalm, "One Size Fits All."
17. Christian Joppke, "Transformation of Citizenship: Status, Rights and Identity," *Citizenship Studies*, Vol. 11, No. 1 (2007), pp. 37–48.
18. Koopmans and Statham, "Migration and Ethnic Relations as a Field of Political Contention."
19. Giugni and Passy, "Migrant Mobilization between Political Institutions and Citizenship Regimes."
20. Riva Kastoryano, "Transnational Participation and Citizenship: Immigrants in the European Union," *Transnational Communities Working Paper Series* (Oxford: Oxford University, 1998), taken from http://www.transcomm.ox.ac.uk/working%20papers/riva.pdf.
21. Jan Rath, "Political Participation of Ethnic Minorities in the Netherlands," *International Migration Review*, Vol. 17, No. 3, pp. 445–69 (1983).
22. Sydney Tarrow, *Power in Movement: Social Movements, Collective Action and Politics* (Cambridge: Cambridge University Press, 1994); see also Herbert P. Kitschelt, "Opportunity Structures and Political Protest: Anti-nuclear Movements in Four Democracies," *British Journal of Political Science*, Vol. 16, No. 1 (1986), pp. 57–85; Doug McAdam, "Conceptual Origins, Current Problems, Future Directions," in Doug McAdam, John D. McCarthy and Mayer Z. Zald (eds.), *Comparative Perspectives on Social Movements: Political Opportunities, Mobilising Structures, and Cultural Framings* (Cambridge, MA: Cambridge University Press, 1996), pp. 23–41; Sydney Tarrow, *Power in Movement: Social Movements and Contentious Politics* (Cambridge: Cambridge University Press, 1998); and Charles Tilly, *From Mobilization to Revolution* (New York: Random House, 1978).
23. Phillippe C. Schmitter, "Interest Intermediation and Regime Governability in Contemporary Western Europe and North America," in S. Berger (ed.), *Organizing Interests in Western Europe* (Cambridge: Cambridge University Press, 1981), pp. 287–327.
24. David P. Conradt, *The German Polity* (New York: Addison-Wesley Longman, 2001).
25. Soysal, *Limits of Citizenship*.
26. Koopmans and Statham, "Migration and Ethnic Relations as a Field of Political Contention."
27. See Maria Berger, Christian Galonska and Ruud Koopmans, "Political Integration by a Detour? Ethnic Communities and Social Capital of Migrants in Berlin," *Journal of Ethnic and Migration Studies*, Vol. 30, No. 4 (2004), pp. 491–507; and Koopmans and Statham, "Migration and Ethnic Relations as a Field of Political Contention."
28. Soysal, *Limits of Citizenship*.
29. Yurdakul, "Citizenship and Immigration."
30. Soysal, *Limits of Citizenship*.
31. Kristoffer Wahlbäck, "Frankrike," in R. Lindahl (ed.), *Utländska Politiska System* (Lund: Dialogos, 1991), pp. 56–88. ("France"; "Foreign Political Systems").
32. Yves Mény, "France," in J.M. Colomer (ed.), *Political Institutions in Europe* (London: Routledge, 1996).
33. See also William G. Andrews and Stanley Hoffman, *The Impact of the Fifth Republic on France* (New York: State University of New York Press, 1981).

34. Patrick Ireland, *The Policy Challenges of Ethnic Diversity: Immigrant Politics in France and Switzerland* (Cambridge, MA: Harvard University Press, 1994).
35. Soysal, "Citizenship and Immigration," (1994), p. 86.
36. Stephen Castles and Godula Kosack, "From Aliens to Citizens: Redefining the Status of Immigrants in Europe: How the Trade Unions Try to Control and Integrate Immigrant Workers in the German Federal Republic," *Race*, Vol. 15, No. 4 (1974), pp. 497–514; John Rex, Sally Tomlinson and David Hearnden, *Colonial Immigrants in a British City: A Class Analysis* (London: Routledge, 1979).
37. Koopmans and Statham, "Migration and Ethnic Relations as a Field of Political Contention."
38. Sydney Tarrow, "States and Opportunities," in Doug McAdam, John D. McCarthy and Mayer N. Zald (eds.), *Comparative Perspectives on Social Movements: Political Opportunities, Mobilizing Structures, and Cultural Framings* (Cambridge, MA: Cambridge University Press, 1996), pp. 41–61.
39. Kitschelt, "Opportunity Structures and Political Protest."
40. Hector Cordero-Guzmán, "Immigrant Aid Societies and Organizations," in J. Ciment (ed.), *Encyclopedia of American Immigration* (Armonk, ME: Sharpe, 2001), pp. 334–40.
41. Floris Vermeulen, "Organisational Patterns: Surinamese and Turkish Associations in Amsterdam, 1960–1990," *Journal of Ethnic and Migration Studies,* Vol. 31, No. 5 (2005a), pp. 951–73.
42. Maria Schrover, *Immigrant Organisations in the Netherlands: Then and Now* . Paper presented for the workshop "Paths of Integration: Similarities and Differences in the Settlement" (IMIS Osnabrueck, June 19–21, 2003).
43. Eva Ostergaard-Nielsen, "Trans-state Loyalties and Politics of Turks and Kurds in Western Europe," *SAIS Review of International Affairs,* Vol. 20, No. 1 (2000), pp. 23–38.
44. See also Yurdakul, "Citizenship and Immigration."
45. Ibid.
46. Floris Vermeulen, *The Immigrant Organising Process: The Emergence and Persistence of Turkish Immigrant Organisations in Amsterdam and Berlin and Surinamese Organisations in Amsterdam, 1960–2000* (Amsterdam: IMES, 2005b).
47. For an example, see Lale Yalcin-Heckman, "The Perils of Ethnic Associational Life in Europe: Turkish Migrants in Germany and France," in Tariq Modood and Prina Werbner (eds.), *The Politics of Multiculturalism in the New Europe* (London: Zed Books, 1997).
48. Anja van Heelsum, "Political Participation and Civic Community of Ethnic Minorities in Four Cities in the Netherlands," *Politics,* Vol. 25, No. 1 (2005), pp. 19–31.
49. Alistair Cole, *French Politics and Society* (Hemel Hempstead: Prentice Hall, 1998).
50. Yalcin-Heckman, "The Perils of Ethnic Associational Life in Europe."

Turkish Associations in the United States: Towards Building a Transnational Identity

ŞEBNEM KÖŞER AKÇAPAR

McGhee Center for Eastern Mediterranean Studies, Georgetown University, Washington, DC, United States of America

ABSTRACT   *Migrant associations have always been an important feature of migrant communities, assuming a significant role towards identity formation and integration in the host society. Such organizations also create an important transnational link between countries of origin and settlement. Using the example of Turkish associations in the United States and their institutionalization process, this essay argues that organizational dynamics of immigrants are greatly affected by the general attitude towards immigrants in the host country and homeland policies regarding emigrants (macro level), their relations with other ethnic groups already resident in the host country (meso level), and the status of immigrants and some of their pre-migration characteristics (micro level).*

Introduction

Migrant organizations help in understanding the diversity and dynamics within immigrant communities.[1] Migration scholars are interested in a number of questions related to immigrants, such as their political incorporation, voting tendencies, and organizational behavior. Why are immigrant organizations established and how do they change over time? What is the relationship between immigrants' backgrounds and the nature of migrant associations? Should maintaining strong associational links lead to increased political participation? Do immigrant organizations serve as a bridge between cultures or not? Why do immigrants vote for certain parties and not others? Why do some political parties include more immigrants in their lists than others?

There is also a growing interest in immigrant organizations by homeland and hostland politicians. Governments of home countries have an impact on immigrant organizations, as they have a vested interest in maintaining links with former migrants for as long as possible. There is an increasing importance placed on immigrants and the establishment of immigrant communities in the home countries not only because they send remittances to the homeland and are seen as potential voters but also—as evident in the case of Turkish immigrants living in Western Europe—because immigrants have usually carried their homeland conflicts and politics with them, thus creating transnational issues. [2] Immigrants also create or recreate a national/ethnic identity, often transcending the nation-state and establishing a transnational link between countries of origin and settlement. In that sense, they may even attempt to influence the foreign policy of the host country towards the home country.[3] Governments of host countries also have a great impact on the establishment of such ethnic organizations, as they may choose to prohibit, ignore, or encourage immigrant organizations or part of their activities. [4] Depending on the general acceptance of immigrants and immigration policies in the host country, migrant organizations are sometimes seen as agents of integration, thereby providing a form of positive "social capital" facilitating adaptation and assistance. [5] Furthermore, they are more easily monitored and more convenient to deal with, as has been seen in the attitudes of host governments towards major Muslim organizations in Western Europe after September 11. Yet due to their involvement with homeland and community interests, migrant associations may be regarded as a hindrance to assimilation. After all, in the event of political tensions, wars, and even during soccer games between home and host countries, the major question is about the real allegiance of immigrants.

Despite this growing interest in migrant organizations, there is little scholarly research on Turkish immigrants and the social networks they have established in the United States. So far, only one article has been devoted to the history, diversity, political participation, and transformation of organizational behavior among Turkish-Americans due to their often negotiated and changing identities.[6] However, migrant associations have always been an important feature of migrant communities in the United States. [7] This paper will explore the role of associations in creating a transnational identity over time by taking the example of Turkish migrant organizations in the United States. Therefore, different patterns of Turkish migration to the United States, including the early flows, current trends, and demographics will be examined. Moreover, it will provide information on the organizational attitudes of Turkish-Americans and the history of various Turkish-American associations and how they have changed over time to serve the needs of a more diversified and growing Turkish-American community.

The essay argues that organizational dynamics of Turkish immigrants are greatly affected by a number of factors at three different levels. At the macro level, these organizational dynamics are affected by the general attitude towards immigrants in the host country and the homeland policies regarding Turkish-Americans as an emerging diaspora. At the meso (relational) level, they are affected by the migrants' relationship with Americans in general and more hostile ethno-religious groups, like the Armenian and Greek diasporas, in particular. At the micro level, they are affected by the status of the migrants (permanent or temporary, belonging to a particular social, religious, and professional group).

The information in this paper was gathered using available secondary data, on-site observation, and inquiry over three years in different major cities in the United

States as well as primary data from semi-structured and in-depth interviews with the representatives and members of Turkish-American associations. An anthropological research strategy was adopted to gather primary data. For example, life histories were collected through repeated interviews, and participant observation was practiced during reunions, association meetings, and gatherings.

Patterns of Turkish Migration to the United States

Immigration from Turkey to the United States can be classified according to three groups. The first includes the early flow of immigrants from the Ottoman Empire and the Turkish Republic. The first migratory flows were made up primarily of non-Turkish and non-Muslim citizens of the empire and occurred largely due to economic and political problems.[8] According to official US statistics, 93.51 percent of the 22,085 immigrants registered as Turks between 1900 and 1925 were young and illiterate males.[9] World War I and a number of laws restricting the entry of immigrants affected the flows negatively.[10] The second wave of immigration took place between 1950 and 1980, and it was a more skilled migration, as many professionals and graduate students were involved. As opposed to the male-dominated first flows, there were many young women and accompanying families during this period. Since the 1980s, the flow of Turkish nationals to the United States has taken many different forms, including an increasing number of students and professionals as well as clandestine migrants who provide unskilled and semi-skilled labor.

Early Flows from Turkey to the United States (1820–1950)

According to official US statistics, Turkish migration to the United States was insignificant until 1900.[11] A very small number of Turkish Muslims came to America between 1820 and 1860. During the last 15 years of Sultan Abdülhamid's rule (1876–1915) many immigrants whose country of last residence was recorded as Turkey came to the United States (see Table 1). By the early 1900s, larger numbers of Turks immigrated to the United States and settled in New York City, Chicago, Detroit, Philadelphia, and San Francisco.[12]

By 1910, the number of immigrants from the Ottoman Empire was divided into two categories: Turkey in Asia [13] and Turkey in Europe.[14] These early immigrants were mostly non-Muslim Ottoman citizens carrying Ottoman passports, namely Sephardic Jews, Greeks, Armenians, Bosnians, Albanians, Serbs, Assyrians, Christian Arabs, and Bulgarians, and they identified themselves by ethnicity and/or religion.[15]

Although some figures on early migration from Turkey have been made available they do not accurately reflect the whole Turkish population. One of the reasons for the lack of accuracy of the data is that many immigrants were registered by American authorities under ethnic and/or religious affiliation. Therefore, it was impossible to distinguish the country of origin for all immigrants. Some Turkish immigrants also anglicized their names and declared themselves as Armenians or Christians in order to gain easy access to the United States.[16] The estimates on the number of Turkish

Table 1. Turkish Immigration to the United States (1820–1950)*

Year	Number of Immigrants
1820	1
1821–1830	20
1831–1840	7
1841–1850	59
1851–1860	83
1961–1870	131
1871–1880	404
1881–1890	3,782
1891–1900	30,425
1901–1910	157,369
1911–1920	134,066
1921–1930	33,824
1931–1940	1,065
1941–1950	798
Total	**362,034**

*By Region and Selected Country of Last Residence.
Source: 2004 Yearbook of Immigration Statistics, Office of Immigration Statistics, U.S. Department of Homeland Security.

Muslim immigrants during this initial period are rather confusing. Some scholars estimate that less than 10 percent of all people who emigrated from the Ottoman Empire and Turkey between 1820 and 1950 were Muslim Turks.[17] Some others note that the number of Muslim Turks entering the United States between 1900 and 1920 is estimated to be around 45,000 and 65,000[18] or between 15,000 and 20,000.[19]

A majority of Turks entered the United States via the ports of Providence, Rhode Island; Portland, Maine; and Ellis Island. [20] French shipping agents, the missionary American college in Harput,[21] French and German schools, and word of mouth from former Armenian migrants were major sources of information about the New World for those who wished to emigrate. [22] There were also reports of a considerable amount of illegal migration from Anatolia, as young men were trying to escape conscription as well as poverty, [23] and emigration from the Ottoman Empire was forbidden.[24] Some of the reasons for this prohibition on exit might be explained as the lack of desire to lose young men and tax income as well as the fear of damage to Ottoman prestige abroad, as most of the would-be emigrants were poor and uneducated.[25] Because of two different approaches of citizenship in the Ottoman Empire and in the United States [26] relations between the two countries were negatively affected until the beginning of the twentieth century. In particular, problems arose when naturalized former Ottoman citizens returned to their homeland and claimed property and inheritance, as they were neither recognized as foreign subjects nor as Ottoman citizens.[27] Nevertheless, almost 70,000 former citizens of the Ottoman

Empire returned home after acquiring American citizenship within the first quarter of the twentieth century.[28]

Early Turkish migrants were mainly from Southeastern Anatolia and from the lower socioeconomic classes.[29] Most of these Turkish Muslim immigrants had difficulties in adjusting to American society. First of all, more than half of the Turkish immigrants were illiterate and did not know English. The majority of them were farmers and shepherds who had never seen a big city. They came from the villages and small towns of Harput, Dersim, Siverek, Rize, Samsun, Trabzon, Giresun, Antep, and Elazığ.[30] Second, as they regarded themselves as temporary residents they often had little or no interest in adaptation to American society. The main concern among this wave of male-dominated economic migrants was to save enough money and return home. [31] Moreover, their numbers, ethnic social capital, and prior civic involvement were not sufficient to establish organized communities, although they maintained their linguistic and religious identity, which centered around coffeehouses.[32] While living in the United States they mainly identified themselves with their "millet" or religion and with their region. Islam and hemşerilik (coming from the same town) was one of the most powerful elements in identity and communal life in America among early Turkish migrants. [33] Even those married to native-born Americans of European heritage retained their cultural and religious beliefs while assimilating into the larger society at the same time.[34]

The majority of the first Turkish Muslim migrants lived in urban areas and worked in the industrial sector, taking the most difficult and lower-paying jobs in leather factories, tanneries, the iron and steel sector, and the wire, railroad, and automobile industries, especially in New England, New York, Detroit, and Chicago. [35] They trusted each other in finding jobs and a place to stay. Many of them stayed in boarding houses for men. Sometimes there was cooperation between ethnic Turks and other Ottomans, like Greeks, Jews, and Armenians, and sometimes ethnic conflicts were carried to some parts of the United States, such as in Peabody, Massachusetts, where there was tension between Greeks, Armenians, and Turks.[36]

The flow of immigration to the United States was interrupted first by the Restrictive Immigration Act of 1917, which limited entries into the United States based on literacy, and then by World War I. [37] Subsequently, the Johnson-Reed Quota Act of 1924—also known as National Origins Act—restricted large-scale Turkish immigration to the United States. Between 1931 and 1940, immigration from Turkey to the United States decreased tremendously, to a low of 1,065, mainly due to restrictions in the American immigration law, the Great Depression, and the attraction of the newly established Turkish Republic.[38]

Unlike other ethnic groups, most of the early Turkish migrants returned to their homeland. The rate of return migration was exceptionally high among Turkish Muslims after the establishment of the Turkish Republic in 1923. [39] The founder of the Turkish Republic, Mustafa Kemal Atatürk, sent ships from Turkey, such as Gülcemal, to the United States to take these men back to Turkey without any charge.[40] Educated Turks were offered jobs in the newly created Turkish Republic, whereas other unskilled workers were encouraged to return, as the male population

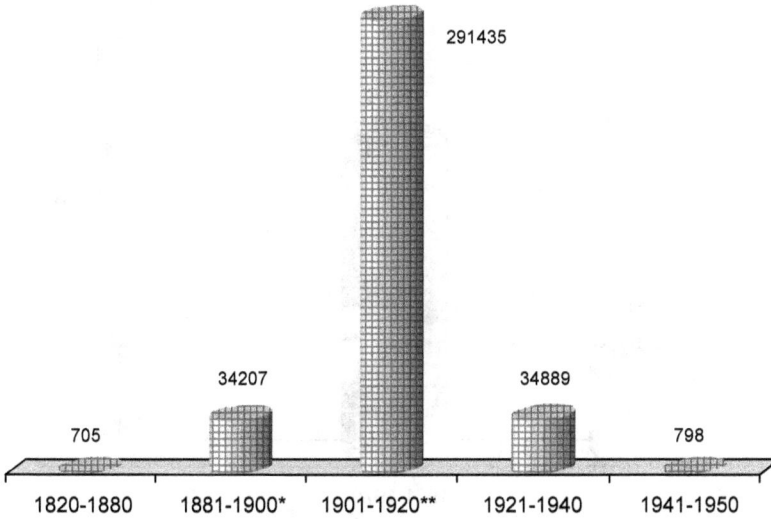

Figure 1. Turkish Immigration to the United States (1820–1950).
Source: U.S. Immigration and Naturalization Service Statistical Yearbook (2004)*

was depleted due to World War I and the Turkish War of Independence. [41] A new Turkish identity was recreated after the proclamation of the Turkish Republic in 1923. A smaller number of early migrants who remained in the United States were not able to assume this identity and were largely assimilated into American society, some of them not even registering Turkish surnames after the adoption of the Surname Law in 1934 in Turkey.[42]

Migration of Professionals (1951–1980)

After World War II immigration from Turkey resumed, and more than 3,500 people came to the United States from Turkey between 1951 and 1960. In the 1960s, 10,000 people entered the United States from Turkey, followed by another 13,000 in the 1970s.[43] According to research carried out by the National Science Foundation (NSF), between 1956 and 1970, 907 Turkish engineers and 594 Turkish medical doctors came to the United States.[44]

As of late 1940s, but especially in the 1960s and 1970s, Turkish immigration to the United States changed its nature from one of unskilled to skilled migration. It is estimated that at least 2,000 engineers and 1,500 physicians have emigrated to the United States.[45] Because of restrictive immigration laws and the annual quota in place until 1965, the rate of Turkish immigration between 1940 and 1950 was around 100 a year; however, the number of Turkish immigrants to the United States increased to 2,000 to 3,000 per year after 1965 due to the liberalization of US immigration laws.[46] As a result, there was a substantial increase in the number of special-

13399

10142

3519

1951-1960   1961-1970   1971-1980

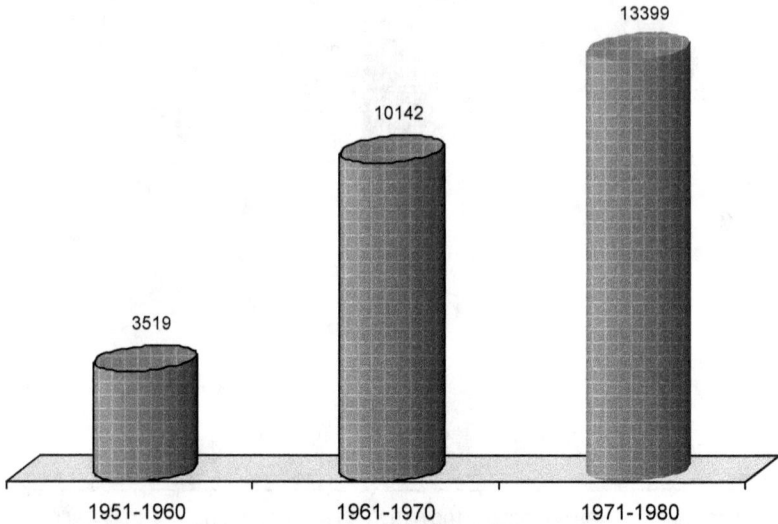

Figure 2. Turkish Migration to the United States (1951–1980).
Source: U.S. Immigration and Naturalization Service Statistical Yearbook (2004).

ists and professionals emigrating to the United States from Turkey, and the number of people coming from Turkey increased by more than threefold during the period of 1961 to 1970. The migratory flows within this period from Turkey to the United States were largely motivated by educational and professional reasons, as well as by economic considerations. Most Turkish people entering to the United States at that time were owners of small- to medium-scale businesses, physicians, engineers, and scientists. The general profile of Turkish men and women immigrating to the United States in the 1950s and 1960s depicted someone young, college-educated with a good knowledge of English, and with a career in medicine, engineering, or another profession in science or the arts. [47] Together with this skilled migration, several hundred semi-skilled workers, especially tailors, came from Turkey with their families to work in places like the Bond Clothing Company in Rochester, New York, between the late 1960s and early 1980s.[48]

Apart from the skills of incoming Turkish people to the United States, another characteristic differentiating the earlier flows with the second wave was that return migration was minimal.[49] Although some people returned to Turkey, they came back to the United States and integrated into larger society because of limited job opportunities and economic and political problems in Turkey at that time. Despite the lack of reliable figures, it is estimated that in the late 1970s there were fewer than 100,000 Turks in the United States. This group included naturalized citizens, permanent residents, long-term illegal aliens, and some members of the second and third generations. In 1970, the US Census reported 54,534 foreign-born and American-born people of foreign and mixed parentage from Turkey. In the same census,

24,000 people listed Turkish as their mother tongue.[50] They settled mainly in urban areas such as New York City, Chicago, Detroit, [51] Los Angeles, Philadelphia, San Francisco, Maryland, Virginia, and Connecticut.[52]

Immigration of Different Groups: Professionals, Students, and Semi-skilled/ Unskilled Workers (1980–2008)

After 1980 there was an increase in the number of skilled migrants, as migration of students, scholars, and professionals coming from Turkey to the United States reached its highest numbers. However, the highly skilled and educated profile of the Turkish-American community has changed in recent years, as another group of Turkish immigrants in the country includes unskilled or semi-skilled Turkish labor workers. They usually work in restaurants, gas stations, hair salons, construction sites, and grocery stores, although some of them have obtained American citizenship or green cards and have opened their own ethnic businesses. [53] It is reported that some of these workers arrived via cargo ships and then left their ships illegally, whereas some others overstayed their visas. Obviously, it is difficult to estimate the number of undocumented Turkish immigrants in the United States who overstayed their visas or jumped off a ship.[54] This trend in migration is called the "Germanification" of Turkish-Americans because of their resemblance in many ways to Turkish guest workers in Germany.[55] More than 20,000 Turks live in Passaic County, New Jersey. There are also large communities living in Long Island around Huntington-Riverhead and in Brooklyn. Some of these migrants are related to each other and some come from the same towns and villages; *hemşerilik* is an important concept in terms of social cohesion.[56]

With permanent residency awarded through the US Lottery system (Diversity Immigration Visa Program), there is social and economic diversity among Turkish immigrants, as they come from all socioeconomic and educational backgrounds. Many of them were only able to find work well below their educational level—at least during the initial years of their residency.

In the 2000 US Census, the five states with the largest populations of foreign-born residents from Turkey were New York, California, New Jersey, Florida, and Massachusetts. Combined, these five states constituted 60.7 percent of the total foreign-born population from Turkey in the United States. There is also a fast-growing Turkish population in Philadelphia.[57]

Based on informal estimations by Voice of America-Turk, Micallef states that there are approximately 200,000 Turkish-Americans. [58] According to the OECD's conservative estimations, the number of Turkish people in the United States was given as 220,000 in 2003. [59] The US Census Bureau's statistics in 2005 show that 165,000 people in the United States declared Turkish ancestry, [60] out of which 35,000 lived in the Northeast; 15,000 in the Midwest; 28,000 in the South; and 22,000 in the West. [61] Turkish-American organizations estimate that there are around 300,000 people of Turkish origin—of whom 15,000 to 20,000 live in the greater Washington, DC, area; 100,000 around New York City; and large numbers in Texas, Chicago, and California. The Turkish Foreign Ministry has no precise figures for total numbers of Turkish citizens living in the United States. However, the Turkish consular offices in Washington, New York City, Los Angeles, Houston, and Chicago estimate that there are almost 350,000 Turks in the United States. According to the US Immigration and Naturalization Service (INS), 465,771 Turkish immigrants entered to the United States between 1820 and 2004. However, as noted earlier, these figures may include those ethnic and religious minorities of the Ottoman Empire. Today, it is estimated that around 4,000 Turkish immigrants enter the United States each year. [62] In this age of globalization, internationalization of education, and other opportunities, the number of Turks entering the United States in non-immigrant categories, including as temporary workers and trainees (H visas), students and their families (F and M visas), intra-company transferees and their families (L visas), and exchange visitors and families (J visas), is also increasing every year, and it underlines the prevalence of circular and professional migration between the two countries. Many Turks who initially went to the United States to study and work for a brief period of time stayed on. They became citizens (see Figure 3 for naturalizations between 1994 and 2007) and invested in the host country. Some of them are in intercultural marriages with other ethnic groups and Americans, and some others even changed their names to common American names. More and more children are born in the United States, and they have started to be politically active as well. However, among young and middle-aged profes-sionals there are also those who return to Turkey due to increasing job opportunities in the private sector in Istanbul and because of worsening economic conditions in the United States. [63]

Early Turkish Associations in the United States

It is often argued that unlike other non-Muslim Ottoman subjects and ethnic groups that migrated to the United States, early Turkish migrants failed to create successful organizations to help their community integrate better in America. Many reasons

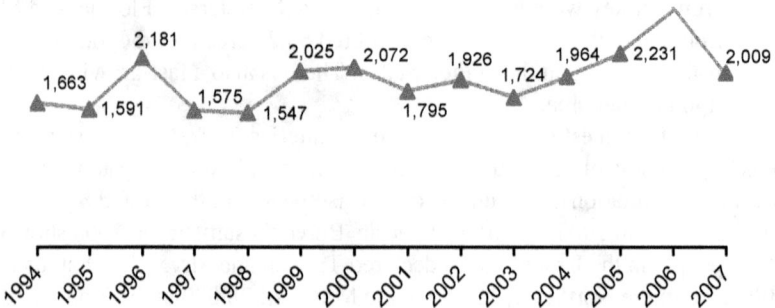

Figure 3. Naturalized Turkish People in the United States (1994–2007).
Source: 2007 Yearbook of Immigration Statistics, U.S. Department of Homeland Security (www.dhs.gov/immigrationstatistics).

cited for the perceived failure of organizational attitudes include lack of leadership, temporariness, lack of interest in adjusting to the larger society, economic downturn and the Great Depression, and the pull factor of newly established modern Turkey at that time. Regardless, Turkish early migrants founded the first Muslim housing cooperatives and associations between 1909 and 1914. After World War I, though the number of Turks in the United States decreased by half, the ones who stayed became more organized. In Chicago, Detroit, New York, and Massachusetts they established clubs and convened once a week. [64] More than 25 associations were established, and newsletters, called *Hemşehri, Sedai-Vatan,* and *Birlik,* were published. Two associations at that time, the Turkish Aid Society (Turk Teavün Cemiyeti) in New York and the Red Crescent (Hilali Amber), were collecting money not only for funeral services and other community affairs but also to help the Turkish National War.[65] In 1923, Fuat Umay, the general secretary of the Turkish Society for the Protection of Orphans at the time, visited New York and several other cities and collected around $100,000 from Turks living in the United States for Turkish orphans.[66] The first lobbying effort by the small Turkish community took place when Turks in America, with the sponsorship of Turkish Welfare Association in New York, prepared a memorandum addressed to the US Administration and Congress leaders calling them to work in collaboration with the new Turkish Republic.[67]

In 1933, Turks in the United States established the Cultural Alliance of New York and the Turkish Orphans' Association, gathering to collect money for orphans in Turkey who had lost their parents in the Turkish War of Independence (1919–1923).[68] They also channeled money and materials back to Turkey through the Red Cross, who turned it over to the Red Crescent, their Muslim organization, to help victims of earthquakes and floods.[69]

It was also documented that there was cooperation between these early Turkish associations and Sephardic Jewish associations in New York and Chicago. The Sephardic Jews who immigrated to the United States from Turkey established the American Sephardic Committee for the Turkish Earthquake Relief in the 1940s and collected money to be sent to Turkey for reconstruction. [70] However, neither the second generation nor the newcomers in the 1950s and 1960s were as eager to continue the ethnic associations established by the first generation.[71]

In the late 1950s, many Turkish associations sporadically published their own periodicals, such as *Yankı, Türk Dünyası,* and *Anavatan. Türk Evi,* a monthly in English and Turkish, was published between 1970 and 1978.[72] Although there were nearly 100 Turkish-American clubs and organizations in the late 1970s, including some university student associations, they were either not well-organized or they had just a few active members.[73]

"Divided They Stand?": Turkish-American Organizations Today

By the end of 2008, there are more than 200 Turkish-American associations all around the United States. Some of the earlier organizations either disappeared

altogether or changed their names, status, and even the profile of membership. [74]
Many Turkish-American migrant organizations have similar structures, as they are
run on a volunteer basis with a board of directors elected by a membership paying
annual dues. One of the umbrella organizations of Turkish-Americans, the Assembly of Turkish American Associations (ATAA), was co-founded by two local
cultural associations, the American Turkish Association of Washington, DC (ATA-
DC) and the Maryland American Turkish Association (MATA) in 1979 in an effort
to create a more politically oriented Turkish-American organization at the national
level. It has over 60 component associations in the United States, Canada, and
Turkey and has 8,000 members all over the United States. The president of ATAA,
Nurten Ural, is a businesswoman of Crimean Turkish background who first
migrated to Turkey with her parents and then moved to United States when she was
a small child. The president-elect for the 2009–2011 term is a second-generation
Turkish-American.

Another umbrella organization, the Federation of Turkish American Associations
(FTAA), which started in 1956 with two associations, namely the Turkish Cypriot
Aid Society and the Turkish Hars Society, hosts over 40 member associations in
2008. The Federation of Turkish American Associations (FTAA) is located in the
Turkish House in the vicinity of the United Nations. The Turkish House, which was
bought by the Turkish government in 1977 as the main office for the consulate-
general, also serves as a center for cultural activities: there is a Saturday school for
Turkish-American children, and it also houses the Turkish Women's League of
America. It was established with the aim of uniting and supporting the community
and serves as an umbrella organization for smaller Turkish associations. The FTAA
and ATAA compete for member associations, their representative power, and recognition. The FTAA boasts of bringing together different groups of people from different backgrounds—educated, less educated, secular, and religious alike—and
criticizes ATAA as being elitist. The president of FTAA claimed that it was the only
grassroots organization among Turkish-Americans and stated that they did not pay
attention to socioeconomic and cultural differences, as the most important thing was
serving the interest of Turkish-Americans and working towards a common objective,
uniting against the Greek and Armenian lobby and making Turkish-American voices
heard by the American authorities.[75] The ATAA, on the other hand, takes advantage
of its location in Washington, DC, close to the circles of power and the US Congress
and criticizes the FTAA for not being assertive and hard-working enough in explaining the issues that are important to the Turkish-American community. In past years
there were internal struggles in both organizations concerning leadership and criticism about their activities and involvement in home-country politics instead of in
adopting a more host-country oriented integrationist approach.

While the number of local cultural organizations, which are mainly involved in
organizing parties and events for their members, has increased since the late 1990s,
some other community-oriented organizations have been established as well. [76]
Some Turkish-American associations, often in collaboration with the growing
number of non-governmental organizations in Turkey, send remittances home,

which are used to finance community projects such as building hospitals and schools and may reduce poverty and foster development in certain areas.

"Social remittances"[77] are also important in the sense that closer contacts with Turkish-American organizations would help Turkey benefit from a flow of ideas, know-how, and the exchange of information. Transnational business and scientific networks have a huge potential in this regard. As members of the Turkish-American community who work as investors and entrepreneurs have knowledge of both countries they can significantly contribute to the private sector development in Turkey, either directly by engaging in business ventures and investments themselves or by establishing a link between companies and facilitating trade. For example, the biggest scientific organization of Turkish-Americans, the Turkish American Scientists and Scholars Association (TASSA), aims to build a bridge between the United States and Turkey. Established in 2004, this organization arose as a response to the "brain drain" debate in Turkey and has started to encourage "brain circulation" between Turkey and the United States by facilitating scientific exchange and short-term circular movements of highly-skilled Turkish Americans.[78]

With the third wave of migration from Turkey to the United States and the diversification of Turkish-Americans, religion has become a more important identity marker. Especially after 1980s, some religious organizations, Islamic cultural centers, and mosques were founded to serve the needs of Turkish people with even more diverse backgrounds living in the United States. Adherence to Islam separates the members of this last group of Turkish immigrants from the second wave. Although religion and Islam had almost no place among the secular associations formed by people coming from a certain educational and sociocultural background in the 1960s and 1970s, there are now more and more Turkish-Americans who define themselves as Turks, Americans, and Muslims.[79] Moya states "religion often incites the formation of separate associations within the same national group." [80] Turks are no exception. Followers of Fethullah Gülen [81] formed one local cultural organization, the American Turkish Friendship Association (ATFA), in 2003 and one intercultural organization, called the Rumi Forum, in 1999, which invites speakers to inform the public about Islam and Turkey. The Gülen community established mosques and interethnic private schools in New York, Connecticut, and Virginia and a college called Virginia International University in Fairfax County, VA. The members of ATFA are a mixed group of blue-collar and white-collar workers, and they are sometimes described as the "other Turks" among highly-skilled and secular Turkish-Americans. It is interesting how the migrant organizations such as ATFA and the Rumi Forum helped change the image of Fethullah Gülen from a controversial Islamic scholar in Turkey to that of a leader of "moderate" Islam who supports interfaith dialogue in the United States. The President of ATFA commented on their position regarding their "otherization":

There might be people who call us the "other" Turks. But we are in *gurbet* (a foreign land). Therefore, I do not think it is appropriate to ignite clashes among Turks. We all have the same objectives but follow a different path. We introduced ourselves to the Turkish American associations in the area. We met their representatives personally. A person is afraid of something he does not know. We don't see anyone as the 'other' and we do not describe ourselves as the 'other.' Our aim is to ease the lives of Turks who moved to the United States and help them integrate without losing their cultural heritage.[82]

Followers of Süleyman Hilmi Tunahan, a Naqshbandi-Mudjadidi *shaykh* and a preacher who died in 1959, otherwise known as *Süleymancılar*, also formed many mosques and cultural centers along the East Coast. [83] Apart from these two groups, the Turkish General Directorate for Religious Affairs appointed imams to 12 Turkish mosques in the United States. There is also a community center project around the mosque in Lanham, MD, on 15 acres of land, which was bought by the Turkish Foundation of Religious Affairs. Unlike the mosques in Turkey that serve merely as places of worship, the community center is designed not only to serve the religious needs of Turkish-Americans living in greater Washington, DC, area but like other places of worship in America, it will be a cultural institution with secular functions—a preschool for children, a research center for scholars, a conference room, and an adult education center.[84]

The Changing Role and Dynamics of Turkish Migrant Organizations in the United States

Not only do immigrant organizations form a "transnational space," linking the country of origin to that of destination, they also become places of belonging, strengthening solidarity among their members and connecting the first generation with the newly arrived.[85] As the Turkish-American community grows and diversifies in time, it has developed the capacity to generate a more "differentiated organizational structure."[86] The early Turkish-American Associations were founded mainly for cultural reasons, such as to celebrate *bayrams*, to reinforce the religious and *hemşeri* identity, and to transfer aid to those who were left behind. The early immigrants not only lacked a unifying religious identity among other Muslims, especially Arabs, because of differences in practice and language, but also lacked a "clear-cut national identity to distinguish them from other Ottoman and non-Ottoman groups who defined themselves in ethnic terms, with their religious identity serving as an ideological-cultural base."[87] Despite some local organizational efforts, however, these early Turkish associations in the United States generally reflected the first generation's lack of desire to integrate fully into the American society. As Bilge notes:

The type of voluntary associations they (earlier immigrants) established not only reflected their preference for insulation against outsiders, but also actively served to thwart their acculturation and assimilation into the American mainstream.[88]

In time, these early associations that merely focused on preserving culture in a foreign land have ceded their place to more organized migrant associations.

Maintaining a transnational link between host and home countries and creating an economic, cultural, and political connection while fostering relations between the two benefits "transmigrants" who happen to live in both places at the same time due to globalization, dense business, professional, scientific, and social networks, and family ties. There is also more and more circular movement among Turkish-Americans. Turkish-Americans have established a wide range of networks through associations to serve the needs of a diverse community. Business organizations aim at creating more trade between Turkey and the United States while at the same time attracting investors on both sides and facilitating business exchanges. There are also many professional and scientific organizations, mosques and Islamic cultural centers, Turkish student associations at major universities, community initiatives, women's groups, local cultural associations, advocacy groups, and political action committees (see Appendix 1 for a comprehensive list of Turkish American organizations).

The turning point for the changing nature of Turkish-American associations from those that organized picnics and cultural events to those with a more political agenda coincided with the hostile efforts of other ethnic groups, the Greek and Armenian lobby. After the mid-1970s, due to a series of events—the Turkish intervention in Cyprus, the American military embargo targeting Turkey, accusations from the members of Greek and Armenian diaspora, and the Armenian Secret Army for the Liberation of Armenia's [89] massacres targeting Turkish diplomats in the United States and elsewhere—Turks living in the United States felt for the first time the need to mobilize politically and to influence American policies in favor of their homeland. They also felt the need to unite and educate the American public about Turkey and defend Turkish issues vis-à-vis Greek and Armenian organizations.[90]

The secretary of ATAA stated that due to a number of hostilities against the Turkish-American community in 1974 and negative news in the media about Turkey, many Turkish-Americans became proactive and started to educate themselves and their American friends. She further stated that:

At that time, in the mid-1970s, we became sensitive to the political issues. Everybody was united and felt that we should do something about this, but there was a lot of shyness and fear in the Turkish community. The Turkish community in the US then wanted to be out of any political involvement. Like other major cities, we also had a cultural association in Washington, DC and the understanding was that since the charter was a non-profit and non-political association, we should not touch political issues. First, we started to respond by writing letters to editors of newspapers but politically we were very weak. Then the movie *Midnight Express* came out and it made a huge damage to the Turkish image in the USA and we started to be on the defensive. We were also attacked by Greeks and Armenians and they accused us of committing genocides. Greeks victimized themselves as a result of our Independence War. In 1979, the Armenian terrorism started. ASALA was killing people all throughout the world. But the media response was very lukewarm. For a while, even the founders of ATAA were under FBI protection, as we were being threatened.[91]

Taking advantage of their pre-migration characteristics, such as socioeconomic background and knowledge of the host country's language, this second wave of professional, educated, and secular Turks living in the United States formed a politically oriented organization in defense of the homeland. Turkish government officials also realized the potential of Turks in the United States and encouraged them to form such organizations that were long overdue. Additionally, migrant organizations are positively viewed in the United States, and they assert an influence on American politics. However, lack of political and civic participation in the homeland, their temporary status in the host-land, their limited numbers, the lack of effective leaders in the migrant community, and limited funds available to Turkish-American migrant organizations obstructed their professional engagement with political structures. Differences of political and civic participation between Turkey (more collective) and the United States (more individual) was also a challenge for many Turks during the initial period of institutionalization.

The third wave of migration from Turkey has changed the characteristics of Turkish immigrants in the United States. Although some of these Turkish-Americans may not speak the language well, they are quite expressive and assertive. Some of them started their own small businesses and became very successful businessmen in no time. Now that many Turkish-Americans have realized they are in the United States to stay, they have organized differently. There is also the second generation of Turkish immigrants who were born in the United States, and there is the challenge of teaching them at least the basics of their native language. Some migrant organizations have Turkish language classes for children on Saturdays. Instead of celebrating special events with smaller groups, many organizations are involved in organizing fairs and parades.[92] Rather than focusing solely on Turkey and Turkish issues, the new generation of community leaders understands the differences, and they are more involved in their community's problems, international politics, and global challenges.

The evolution of Turkish-American organizations has been quite different from that of Turkish organization established in Western Europe. Many Turkish associations in Western Europe were initially oriented only towards Turkey, their religion, and Turkish political parties for many years, although after the 1980s some associations raised their voice to address issues in the host country. [93] Only after Turkish immigrants in Western Europe become much more involved with the politics in the host country after gaining the rights to vote and be elected have they assumed a binational identity. Some Turkish immigrants in the United States, on the other hand, despite being skilled, educated, and making more money than average Americans, did not have an upper hand in creating effective migrant organizations. Yet they did have the advantage of being accepted in the wider society much more easily than those in Europe thanks to citizenship laws, more positive attitudes towards cultural differences and immigration in general, and a different interpretation of integration in the United States. While Turkish immigrants in the United States established self-defense organizations like their compatriots in Western Europe, there was one major difference: theirs were not aimed against hostile segments of the host society but rather against other ethnic minorities or diasporas. As for their religious identity, unlike the Turkish immigrants in Western Europe, the religious identity of Turkish-Americans came to the fore much later despite a long migration history. Whereas Turkish immigrants in Europe are mainly explored in terms of their Muslim identity, the identity construction of Turkish-Americans as a Muslim ethnic group has yet to be investigated in depth.[94] It is interesting to note that so far there are no Alevi orga-nizations in the United States. Despite the existence of a small Alevi community, Alevism is not an identity marker in the New World as it is in Germany. [95] The reasons of migration and pre-migration characteristics play an important role in different attitudes towards homeland and organizing after migration. The vast major-ity of Turkish immigrants in the United States did not leave Turkey because of polit-ical persecution, unlike some Turkish immigrant communities in Europe, so they do not have an ambiguous attachment to the homeland. Turkish-Americans felt the need to establish more effective organizations when they realized they were perma-nent rather than temporary, when there was support from the home country to unite to defend their interests regarding foreign policy, when they realized that it is American policy that supports migrant organizations, and they can indeed exert some power, and when they felt a threat from other migrant organizations and ethnic groups in the United States, such as Armenian and Greek-Americans.

Although Turkish-Americans are establishing a bigger Turkish caucus in the US Congress, they are still keeping behind the main decision-making processes.[96] There are only a couple of Turkish-Americans holding elected office as of 2008.[97] In 2005, the second-generation Osman (Oz) Bengur was the first candidate (Democrat from Maryland's 3rd district) of Turkish origin to run for Congress in US history. In 2008, Rifat Sivislioglu was running for DuPage county board in Chicago, IL as a second generation Turkish-American. Although he did not win, he directed a vigorous campaign (www.VoteRifat.com) and won the support of Turkish-Americans and other immigrant groups in his district. He also raised money for his campaign through Turkish-American organizations. He suggested that Turkish-Americans should be more active in political campaigns from an early age and start at the local level.[98]

Conclusion

This essay discussed various Turkish-American organizations and how they have developed over time due to host and home countries' attitudes towards immigrants and their organizations, other ethnic groups living in the United States, and chang-ing dynamics and characteristics of the community. Although Turkish-American associations grew larger in size by attracting more members and have become more diverse in years, they still had limited financial and human capital and the political, sociocultural, and even personal divisions within the larger Turkish-American community continue to be a major obstacle in raising a stronger voice. There is, however, an increasing "immigrant political transnationalism"[99] among the Turkish-American community. Turkish-Americans have started to become much more involved politically and to make an impact as a group both in the United States and in Turkey. Some Turkish-Americans with dual citizenship make demands of active political participation in Turkey. The former president of FTAA, Egemen Bağış, has been serving in the ruling Justice and Development Party (AKP) in Turkey since 2002 and has assumed the role of chief negotiator of Turkey in accession talks with the EU. Political circles in Turkey attach growing importance towards Turkish immigrants and the establishment of Turkish communities abroad. First, Turkish immigrants were given the right to have dual citizenship in 1981, and Law No. 5749, paving the way for the possibility to vote while residing outside the country, was accepted by the Turkish parliament and put into force on March 22, 2008. Turkish-Americans are no longer seen as a part of "brain drain" who deserted their homeland to seek better economic and professional benefits but as people with skills and education who can help the interests of their homeland. Politicians from Turkey, including President Abdullah Gül, Prime Minister Recep Tayyip Erdoğan, and other ministers usually have meetings with representatives of Turkish-American organizations in Washington, DC, and New York when they make official visits to the United States.

As regards host country politics, apart from the Turkish Caucus and efforts to influence American politics towards Turkey through a number of organizations, there is growing political involvement and activism among Turkish-Americans, especially with the founding of political action committees. [100] Immigrant organizations also provide a space "where civic skills of immigrants can be improved, and where they can learn American ways of organizing, including fundraising." [101] For the 2008 elections, Turkish-Americans raised over one million dollars for the Democratic and Republican congressional, state, and local candidates. [102] New generations of Turkish-Americans are growing up, they speak English as native speakers, and they assume the role of mediators between two cultures. Some Turkish-American organizations, like the Turkish Coalition of America, offer internship opportunities in the US Congress for Turkish-Americans with the aim of enhancing the participation of the community in American political life and to prepare them as political leaders.[103]

It is estimated that around 100,000 Turkish-Americans voted in the November 2008 presidential elections, and divisions in the community over which candidate to support were quite apparent. [104] There were many Turkish-Americans supporting Republican candidates; there were also many who supported Democrats over Republicans for the same reasons as any American, such as the economy, the Iraq War, healthcare, and energy policies. Some Turkish-Americans actively participated in Senator Hillary Clinton's campaign, while some others have either supported President Barack Obama from the very beginning or changed sides after Hillary Clinton lost. While some members of the community established groups such as Turkish Americans for Obama, some Turkish-Americans raised their concern just before elections about vice presidential candidate Joe Biden, regarding his earlier remarks supporting the Armenian genocide resolution, partition of Iraq, and sanctioning an embargo on Turkey after the 1974 intervention in Cyprus. [105] After the elections, major Turkish-American organizations, such as ATAA and Turkish Coalition of America congratulated Barack Obama regardless for whom they voted:

> The TCA and the Turkish American community across the nation look forward to working with the new President and his Administration in the issues facing our country, Turkey and the world. As Turkish Americans, we look forward to a new era between the United States and Turkey. We pledge our full support to advance this relationship to benefit both two nations and, indeed, peace and security in the world.[106]

Nevertheless, the Turkish-American community is dynamic. There is an established Turkish-American community that has been living in the country for more than 40 years. There are transient individuals, such as graduate students and professionals, who might decide to settle in the United States permanently and join already established networks or to move to a second host country or even return to Turkey after long years of living in the United States. There are recent migrants with fewer skills and less education. There are secular Turks who have been living in the United States since the 1970s and who still shy away from Islam and have difficulty in understanding the establishment of a "new elite" in urban centers and in Turkish politics since the late 1980s who would like to adopt an American form of secularism in Turkey. There are immigrants who define themselves as Turkish, Muslim, and American. However, there is collaboration among these different groups in the recent years, as they tend to unite against the Armenian and the Greek lobbies. Turkish-American organizations are also joining forces with Turkic organizations in creating a transnational Turkish identity. Through the extensive use of the Internet and an increasing number of web portals, they are also creating "virtual communities," and through naturalizations and double citizenship, they have become one of the emerging diasporas in the United States.

Notes

1. Marlov Schrover and Floris Vermeulen, "Immigrant Organizations," *Journal of Ethnic and Migration Studies*, Vol. 31, No. 5 (2005), pp. 823–32.
2. John Friedman, *The Prospect of Cities* (Minneapolis: University of Minnesota Press, 2002); Nedim Ögelman, "Documenting and Explaining the Persistence of Homeland Politics Among Germany's Turks," *International Migration Review*, Vol. 37, No. 1 (2003), pp. 163–93; Nedim Ögelman, "Immigrant Organizations and the Globalization of Turkey's Domestic Politics," in Rey Koslowski (ed.), *International Migration and the Globalization of Domestic Politics* (London: Routledge, 2005).
3. Héctor R. Cordero-Guzman, "Community-based Organizations and Migration in New York City," *Journal of Ethnic and Migration Studies*," Vol. 31, No. 5 (2005), pp. 889–909.
4. Schrover and Vermeulen, "Immigrant Organizations," p. 823.

5. Douglas Massey *et al.*, *Return to Aztlan: The Social Process of International Migration from Western Mexico* (Berkeley: University of California Press, 1987); quoted in Cordero-Guzman, "Community-based Organizations and Migration in New York City," p. 907, see note 3.

6. See Prof. Kemal H. Karpat's article, "The Turks Finally Establish a Community in the United States," *International Journal of Turkish Studies*, Vol. 12, Nos. 1 & 2 (2006), pp. 167–86.

7. See for example Elizabeth C. Babcock, "The Transformative Potential of Belizean Migrant Voluntary Associations in Chicago," *International Migration*, Vol. 44, No. 1 (2006), pp. 31–53; Roger Waldinger, Eric Popkin and Hector A. Magana, "Conflict and Contestation in the Cross-border Community: Hometown Associations Reassessed," *Ethnic and Racial Studies* , Vol. 31, No. 5 (2008), pp. 843–70; Caroline B. Brettell, "Voluntary Organizations, Social Capital, and the Social Incorporation of Asian Indian Immigrants in the Dallas-Fort Worth Metroplex," *Anthropological Quarterly*, Vol. 78, No. 4 (2005), pp. 853–83; Alejandro Portes, Cristina Escobar and Alexandria W. Radford, "Immigrant Transnational Organizations and Development: A Comparative Study," *International Migration Review*, Vol. 41, No. 1 (2007), pp. 242–81; José Itzigsohn, "Immigration and the Boundaries of Citizenship: The Institutions of Immigrants' Political Transnationalism," *International Migration Review*, Vol. 34, No. 4 (2000), pp. 1126–54; Gerald Gamm and Robert D. Putnam, "The Growth of Voluntary Associations in America, 1840–1940," *Journal of Interdisciplinary History*, Vol. 29, No. 4 (1999), pp. 511–57; Anna Karpathakis, "Home Society Politics and Immigrant Political Incorporation: The Case of Greek Immigrants in New York City,"*International Migration Review*, Vol. 33, No. 1 (1999), p. 55–78.

8. See Justin McCarthy, *The Ottoman Peoples and the End of the Empire* (New York, Oxford, 2001).

9. Barbara Bilge, "Turks", in David Levinson and Melvin Ember (eds.)*American Immigrant Cultures: Builders of a Nation* (Gale Group, 1997); quoted in Rifat N. Bali, *Anadolu'dan Yeni Dünyaya: Amerika'ya İlk Göç Eden Türklerin Yaşam Öyküleri* [From Anatolia to the New World: Life Stories of First Turks Migrated to the United States of America] (Istanbul: İletişim Yayınları, 2004), p. 264.

10. Bali, *Anadolu'dan Yeni Dünyaya,* p. 28.

11. David M. Reimers, *Other Immigrants: The Global Origins of the American People* (New York: New York University Press, 2005), p. 215.

12. Richard B. Turner, *Islam in the African-American Experience* (2nd edition) (Bloomington: Indiana University Press, 2003), p. 120.

13. Karpat states that although statistics on immigration from Turkey in Asia started to be kept as of 1869, they were most of the time unreliable and a very limited number of people were recorded. For example, it was recorded that between 1867 and 1881 only 74 Asian Ottomans entered the United States and no information was provided for the ten-year period after 1885. By 1910, the number of Ottomans from Asia was given as 59,729 (K. Karpat, "The Ottoman Emigration to America, 1860–1914," *International Journal of Middle East Studies*, Vol. 17, No. 2 (1985), p. 181.

14. Garbi Schmidt, *American Medina: A Study of the Sunni Muslim Immigrant Communities in Chicago,* Vol. 8 (Lund, Sweden: University of Lund, Department of History of Religions, 1999), p. 40.

15. Gönül. Pultar, "Shadows of Cultural Identity: Issues of Biculturalism Raised by the Turkish American Poetry of Talat Sait Halman," in Ruth Hsu *et al.* (eds.), *Re-placing America: Conversations and Contestations* (Honolulu: University of Hawaii and the East-West Center, 2000), p. 131; Talat S. Halman, "Turks," in Stephan Thernstrom (ed.), *Harvard Encyclopedia of American Ethnic Groups* (Cambridge, MA: The Belknap Press of Harvard University Press, 1980), p. 992; Yvonne Y. Haddad, *Not Quite American? The Shaping of Arab and Muslim Identity in the United States* (Waco, TX: Baylor University Press, 2004), p. 3; Roger Daniels, *Coming to America: A History of Immigration and Ethnicity in American Life* (2nd ed.) (New York: Perennial, 2002).

16. Barbara Bilge, "Voluntary Association in the Old Turkish Community of Metropolitan Detroit," in Yvonne Y. Haddad and Jane I. Smith (eds.), *Muslim Communities in North America* (Albany: State University of New York Press, 1994), p. 385; Karpat, "The Ottoman Emigration to America," p. 182.

17. Berrak Kurtuluş, *Amerika Birleşik Devletleri'ne Türk Beyin Göçü* [Turkish Brain Drain to the USA] (Istanbul: Alfa, 1999), p. 53.

18. Frank Ahmed, *Turks in America: The Ottoman Turk's Immigrant Experience* (Greenwich, CT: Columbia International Press, 1993), p. 11; see also Kemal Karpat, "The Turks in America," *Turcs d'Europe... et d'Ailleurs, Les Annales de l'Autre Islam* [Turks in Europe and Elsewhere, Annals of Other Islam], No. 3 (1995), p. 223; John J. Grabowski, "Prospects and Challenges: The Study of Early Turkish Immigration to the United States,"*Journal of American Ethnic History,* Vol. 25, No. 1 (2005), p. 86.

19. Kemal Karpat, "The Turks Finally Establish a Community in the United States,"*International Journal of Turkish Studies*, Vol. 12, Nos. 1 & 2, (2006), p. 169.

20. Ahmed, *Turks in America*, p. 14; Bilge, "Voluntary Association in the Old Turkish Community of Metropolitan Detroit," p. 386.

21. See Işil Acehan, *Outposts of an Empire: Early Turkish Migration to Peabody, Massachusetts* (unpublished master's thesis submitted to the Department of History, Bilkent University, May 2005, accessible at http://www.thesis.bilkent.edu.tr/0002829.pdf) on the role of American consulate in Harput and American missionaries there in the increased number of Armenians and Muslims alike at that time.

22. İlhan. Kaya, *Shifting Turkish American Identity Formations in the United States,* unpublished dissertation, Florida State University (2003), pp. 48–9; Bali, *Anadolu'dan Yeni Dünyaya*, p. 339.

23. Karpat, "The Ottoman Emigration to America," p. 182; Bali, *Anadolu'dan Yeni Dünyaya*, p. 25.

24. Karpat, "The Ottoman Emigration to America," p. 187.

25. Ibid., p. 186.

26. Ottoman Empire followed the principle of *jus sanguinis* whereas the United Stated adhered to the *jus soli* principle.

27. Karpat, "The Ottoman Emigration to America," pp. 189–91.

28. Leland J. Gordon, *American Relations with Turkey 1830–1930* (Philadelphia: University of Philadelphia Press, 1932) quoted in Bali, *Anadolu'dan Yeni Dünyaya*, p. 31.

29. Karpat, "The Ottoman Emigration to America."

30. Ahmed, *Turks in America*, p. 10–11; Kaya, *Shifting Turkish American Identity Formations in the United States*, p. 48.

31. Ahmed, *Turks in America*, p. 12.

32. Ahmed notes that coffeehouses were foreign to American culture until the arrival of Turks, and the highest concentration of coffeehouses in New England were along Walnut Street in Peabody: *Turks in America*, p. 66. However, coffeehouses did not only function as "clubhouses" for men, but they were also used as informal employment agencies, charity organizations, and public places where people used to meet to celebrate religious holidays: Bilge, "Voluntary Association in the Old Turkish Community of Metropolitan Detroit," pp. 392–93.

33. Ahmed, *Turks in America*, p. 75; Bilge, "Voluntary Association in the Old Turkish Community of Metropolitan Detroit," p. 381; Grabowski, "Prospects and Challenges," p. 87.

34. Ahmed, *Turks in America*, p. 15.

35. Ibid., p. 12.

36. Acehan, *Outposts of an Empire*; Ahmed, *Turks in America*; R. N. Bali, "From Anatolia to the New World: The First Anatolian Immigrant to America,"*International Journal of Turkish Studies,* Vol. 12, Nos. 1 & 2 (2006), pp. 53–69; Karpat, "The Turks Finally Establish a Community in the United States."

37. Schmidt, *American Medina*, p. 40; Haddad, *Not Quite American?*, p. 4.

38. Kaya, *Shifting Turkish American Identity Formations in the United States*, p. 51.

39. Halman states that almost 86 percent of the 22,000 Turks who entered to the United States between 1899 and 1924 returned to Turkey: "Turks," p. 993. Ahmed also confirms that only fewer than 20 percent stayed after 1923: *Turks in America*, p. 80.

40. Ahmed, *Turks in America*, p. 81.

41. Halman, "Turks," p. 993.

42. Grabowski states that through the Red Crescent, a Turkish organization operating in the United States at that time, some Turks who remained registered surnames in accordance with the surname law adopted in 1934 in Turkey: "Prospects and Challenges," p. 97.

43. Reimers, p. 216.
44. Turhan Oğuzkan, "The Scope and Nature of Turkish Brain Drain," in Nermin Abadan-Unat (ed.), *Turkish Workers in Europe, 1960–1975: A Socio-economic Reappraisal* (Leiden: E.J. Brill, 1976), pp. 74–103.
45. Halman, "Turks," p. 993.
46. Kaya, p. 2.
47. Ahmed, *Turks in America*, p. 85.
48. Ibid., p. 86.
49. Halman, "Turks," p. 994.
50. Ibid., p. 992.
51. See Bilge's article on the Turkish community of metropolitan Detroit and adjacent Ontario and patterns of intermarriages between Turkish and Americans. Barbara Bilge, "Turkish-American Patterns of Intermarriage," in Barbara C. Aswad and Barbara Bilge (eds.), *Family and Gender among American Muslims: Issues Facing Middle Eastern Immigrants and their Descendants* (Philadelphia: Temple University Press, 1996), pp. 59–106.
52. Halman, "Turks," p. 994; Kurtuluş, Amerika, *Birleşik Devletleri'ne Türk Beyin Göçü*, p. 55.
53. Kaya, p. 58.
54. In 1996, the INS estimated that their numbers were fewer than 30,000. See Reimers, p. 216.
55. Uğur Akıncı, "Germanification of Turkish Americans" (www.theturkishtimes.com/archive/02/05_15), quoted in Kaya, p. 58, see note 22; also quoted in Roberta Micallef, "Turkish Americans: Performing Identities in a Transnational Setting,"*Journal of Muslim Minority Affairs*, Vol. 24, No. 2 (2004), p. 240.
56. There is unskilled chain migration to the United States from the Black Sea region in Turkey, mainly from Yağlıdere, Giresun (Müzeyyen Güler, "Turkish Immigrants in the United States: Men, Women, and Children," *International Journal of Turkish Studies*, Vol. 12, Nos. 1 & 2, (2006), pp. 145–65, and from Yuva, Giresun (Lisa DiCarlo, "Migration from Giresun to the United States: The Role of Regional Identity," *International Journal of Turkish Studies*, Vol. 12, Nos. 1 & 2, (2006), pp. 133–43. Hemşerilik is an important concept in choosing the United States as a destination country among immigrants.
57. Reimers, p. 216, see note 11.
58. Micallef, "Turkish Americans," p. 233.
59. Unpublished OECD's SOPEMI Report on Turkey, Prepared by Ahmet İçduygu 2004 .
60. According to the US Census Bureau, ancestry refers to a person's ethnic origin or descent, roots or heritage, or the place of birth of the person, the person's parents, or ancestors before arrival in the United States.
61. See www.census.gov/compendia/statab/tables/0850051.pdf.
62. Kaya, p. 2.
63. Şebnem Köşer Akçapar, "Do Brains Really Go Down the Drain? Turkish Highly Skilled Migration to the U.S. and the Brain Drain Debate in Turkey," *Revue Européenne des Migrations Internationales* (REMI), Vol. 22, No. 3 (2007), pp. 79–108.
64. Ahmed, *Turks in America*, p. 65.
65. Karpat, "The Turks in America," p. 234.
66. See Mehmet Fuat Umay, *Cumhuriyetin KuruluşYıllarında Bir Devrimci Doktorun Anıları [Memoirs of a Revolutionary Doctor in the Early Years of the Republic]*, prepared for publication by Cahit Kayra (Istanbul: Türkiye İş Bankası Kültür Yayınları, 2006).
67. Birol Akgün, *The Turkish Yearbook*, Vol. 31 (2000), pp. 99–117.
68. Micallef, "Turkish Americans."
69. Ahmed, *Turks in America*, pp. 60–61.
70. Joseph M. Papo, *Sephardim in Twentieth Century America* (California, 1987); quoted in Bali, *Anadolu'dan Yeni Dünyaya* (İstanbul: İletişim Yayınları, 2004), p. 98.
71. Bilge, "Voluntary Associations in the Old Turkish Community of Metropolitan Detroit," p. 400.
72. Halman, "Turks," p. 995.

73. Ibid., p. 994.
74. For example, Anadolu Club, which was established on Long Island mainly by doctors and engineers as a professional society, is now located in New Jersey and has a wide range of members, from white collar to blue collar workers and organizes a wide range of activities from cultural gatherings and collecting social aid to fostering US-Turkey relations.
75. Personal communication, April 2006.
76. For example, HasNa offers conflict resolution and professional skills training in Southeast Turkey and Cyprus. Turkish-Americans also invest directly or indirectly in health and education services in Turkey through migrant associations. The American Turkish Society (ATS) invests in Turkey and supports projects in collaboration with non-governmental organizations in Turkey. At the same time, ATS initiated a teacher exchange program and a fellowship for the training of young Turkish physicians in the United States. Other projects by Turkish-American organizations involve opening micro-enterprise training courses for Turkish rural women. Turkish Children Foster Care, Bridges of Hope Project, and Washington Turkish Women's Association, through fundraising and donations from their members, help Turkish students with financial difficulties and support public schools in Turkey and donate computers and other material and assist them to build libraries and science labs.
77. Term taken after Peggy Levitt, "Social Remittances: A Conceptual Tool for Understanding Migration for Development," *Working Paper No. 96.04* (Cambridge: Harvard Center for Population and Development Studies, 1996), available at: http://www.hsph.harvard.edu/hcpds/wpweb/96_04.pdf.
78. Şebnem Köşer Akçapar, "Highly Skilled Migration from Turkey to the United States," in Kemal Kirişçi and Ahmet İçduygu (eds.), *Land of Diverse Migrations: Challenges of Emigration and Immigration in Turkey* (Istanbul: Bilgi University Publications, 2009).
79. One exception is the Turkish Society of Rochester, NY. This association was formed by a group of tailors brought to Rochester towards the end of 1960s. They also established their mosque and provided other religious services, such as funerals, and participated in interfaith dialogue. The association also offers social and educational services to its members.
80. Jose C. Moya, "Immigrants and Associations: A Global and Historical Perspective," *Journal of Ethnic and Migration Studies*, Vol. 31, No. 5 (2005), p. 846.
81. Fethullah Gülen has been living in Pennsylvania since 1999 due to medical and political reasons. In October 2008 he was approved for permanent residence or a green card after years of rejection by American authorities.
82. Personal communication with the author, June 2008.
83. Some of the mosques and cultural centers affiliated with the Süleymancılar in the United States are: Fatih Mosque in Brooklyn, NY; Süleymaniye Mosque in Deer Park, NY; Osmaniye Mosque in Moriches, NY; Selimiye Mosque in Boston, MA; Yeni Dünya in Clifton, NJ; Muradiye in Chicago, IL; Hamidiye in Rochester, NY; Aziziye in Bear, DE; and Mevlana in Bristol, PA (see Karpat, "The Turks Finally Establish a Community in the United States," p. 177). The attaché for religious affairs at the Turkish Embassy in Washington, DC, stated that there is cooperation between Süleymancılar and Diyanet even more than Gülen's group (personal communication, October 2008).
84. See www.taccenter.org for details.
85. See Moya, "Immigrants and Associations," p. 849, see note 80.
86. See e.g. Floris Vermeulen, "Organizational Patterns: Surinamese and Turkish Associations in Amsterdam, 1960–1990," *Journal of Ethnic and Migration Studies*, Vol. 31, No. 5 (2005), p. 959; Moya, "Immigrants and Associations," p. 852, see note 80.
87. Karpat, "The Turks Finally Establish a Community in the United States," p. 170.
88. Bilge, "Voluntary Association in the Old Turkish Community of Metropolitan Detroit," p. 400.
89. ASALA is short for the Armenian Secret Army for the Liberation of Armenia, and it is recognized as a terrorist organization that was mainly active between the 1970s and 1980s.
90. See Karpathakis, "Home Society Politics and Immigrant Political Incorporation" for a discussion of Greek immigrant incorporation into the American political system and how the "Americanization process" among Greek migrants was brought about by political concerns in the home country through migrant organizations, see note 7.

91. Personal communication with Dr. Oya Bain, October 2005.
92. The Turkish fair in Washington, DC, is organized on the first Sunday of October; the Turkish American Day Parade is organized on the occasion of the May 19 celebrations of the Youth and Sports Festival in New York City; the Children's Festival is organized in the greater DC area to mark April 23 celebrations in Turkey. These festivals change their nature in a migration setting, as they become a symbol of Turkish-American identity and presence in the New World. The Children's Festival organized by ATA-DC and celebrated by Turkish-Americans on the occasion of April 23, 2007, became an international one and included other ethnic groups in the greater Washington area.
93. Ali Gitmez and Czarina Wilpert, "A Micro-Society or an Ethnic Community? Social Organization and Ethnicity amongst Turkish Migrants in Berlin," in J. Rex, D. Joly, and C. Wilpert (eds.), *Immigrant Associations in Europe* (Brookfield: Gower, 1987), pp. 86–125; Vermeulen, "Organizational Patterns," p. 956, see note 86.
94. İlhan Kaya, "Identity and Space: The Case of Turkish Americans," *Geographical Review*, Vol. 95, No. 3 (2005), pp. 425–40.
95. See article by E. Özyürek in this special issue.
96. There are 80 members of the Turkish caucus; 43 of them are Democrats.
97. One is a judge in Houston, TX, and the other is a trustee in Naperville in DuPage County, IL. Another example is given by K. Karpat, *Studies on Turkish Politics and Society: Selected Articles and Essays* (Boston, MA: Brill, 2004), p. 622. (Orhan Yirmibe ş served as mayor of Delavan, in southern Wisconsin. He entered to the United States in the late 1940s as an economics student and stayed in the United States and became a businessman).
98. Personal communication during ATAA's annual convention, May 2008.
99. See Itzigsohn, "Immigration and the Boundaries of Citizenship.", see note 7.
100. Political action committees are organizations created by certain interest groups, including immigrants, to collect funds for contributing to election campaigns of their preferred political candidates. One political action committee is TC-USA PAC in Washington, DC, and the other is Turkish PAC in Texas. These are bipartisan organizations created by Turkish-Americans supporting political candidates and encouraging them to participate more in the US political process.
101. See Brettell, "Voluntary Organizations, Social Capital, and the Social Incorporation of Asian Indian Immigrants in the Dallas-Fort Worth Metroplex" on a similar discussion regarding Indian immigrant organizations in the United States, see note 7.
102. This does not include any donations to presidential candidates.
103. See the website of the Turkish Coalition of America (www.turkishcoalition.org) for further details.
104. See the article in Turkish *Newsweek* published on November 1, 2008: "Balancing Hearts and Heads: Turkish Americans Typically Vote Republican. This Time, They Are Divided over which White House Candidate Should Get Their Ballot." Available at: http://www.newsweek.com/id/166813.
105. Just a couple of days before 2008 elections in the United States, Turkish PAC announced that "it is not supporting Obama-Biden ticket on the premises that if they are elected, their actions are expected to result in further deterioration of the already-fragile friendship and cooperation between Turkey and the U.S." (www.turkishpac.org).
106. See full text online at http://www.tc-america.org/obama_com.html.
 * Peak immigration years were between 1904 and 1908, and 1910 and 1914. Between 1881 and 1914, 29,019 people were registered as entering to the United States from Turkey in Asia whereas 156,782 of them were from Turkey in Asia between 1901 and 1920. (See K. Karpat, "The Ottoman Emigration to America, 1860–1914," *International Journal of Middle East Studies*, Vol. 17, No. 2 (1985), Appendix I and IX).

Appendix 1. List of Turkish-American Organizations

Local Political Organizations (Advocacy and Lobbying Groups)*

* 501 (c) 4 tax code, tax exempt, advocacy and endorsing candidates allowed.
Turkish American Alliance for Fairness (www.taaf-org.net)
Turkish Americans for Informed Policy (TAFIP)
Georgia Turkish American Advocacy Group (www.gtaag.org)
American Turkish Council (ATC), Washington, DC (www.americanturkishcouncil.org)

Political Action Committees

Turkish American Political Action Committee, Houston, TX (www.turkishpac.org)
  Turkish Coalition USA Political Action Committee (www.tc-usa-pac.org)

Local Social/Cultural/Philanthropic/Educational/Business Associations*

* 501 (c) 3 tax code, tax exempt, contributions are tax deductible, no upper limit for contributions by donors, limited lobbying activity.

American Turkish Society (ATS) (www.americanturkishsociety.org)
Ari Foundation (www.arifoundation.org)
Istanbul Center (www.istanbulcenter.org)
Turkish American Friendship Council (www.theatfc.org)
American Friends of Turkey (AFOT) (www.afot.us)
Turkish Coalition of America (TCA) (www.turkishcoalitionofamerica.org)
Turkish American Association for Cultural Exchange (www.taace.org)
Turkish American Cultural Association of Alabama (TACA-AL)
Turkish American Association of Arizona (TAA-AZ) (website: www.taaaz.org)
Turkish American Cultural Association of Southern New England (TACA-SNE)
Turkish American Cultural Society of Colorado (TASCO) (www.tacsco.org)
Turkish American Association of Southern California (ATA-SC) (www.atasc.org)
Turkish American Association of California (TAAC) (www.taaca.org)
Florida Turkish American Association (FTAA)
Turkish American Cultural Association of Florida (TACAF) (www.tacaf.org)
Turkish American Cultural Association of Georgia (TACA-GA) (www.tacaga.org)
Turkish American Society of Georgia
Turkish American Friendship Association of Hawaii (TAFA-HI)
Turkish American Cultural Association (TACA-Chicago) (www.tacaonline.org)
Turkish American Association of Greater Kansas City (www.taakc.org)
Turkish American Association of Louisiana (TAAL)
Turkish American Cultural Society of New England (TACS-NE) (www.tacsne.org)
Maryland American Turkish Association (MATA) (www.atamd.org)

Turkish American Cultural Association of Michigan (TACAM) (www.tacam.org)
Turkish American Association of Minnesota (TAAM) (www.taam.org)
Turkish American Cultural Alliance of St. Louis (TACA-St. Louis) (www.tacastl.org)
American Turkish Association of North Carolina (ATA-NC) (www.ata-nc.org)
Turkish American Association of New Jersey (Turk Ocagi)
Turkish American Community Center in New Jersey
Turkish Society of Rochester (TSR) (www.tsor.org)
Syracuse Turkish Association
Anadolu Club (www.anaoluclub.org)
Young Turks Cultural Aid Society (www.youngturks.org)
Young Turks of America Cultural Aid Society in NYC
Turkish American Association of Central Ohio (TAACO) (www.taaco.org)
Turkish American Society of Northeastern Ohio (TASNO)
Turkish American Association in Ohio
Turkish American Association of Oklahoma (TAA-OK)
Pittsburgh Turkish American Association (PTAA) (www.ptaa.org)
Turkish American Friendship Society of the United States (TAFSUS) (www.tafsus.net)
American Turkish Association of Houston (ATA-Houston) (www.atahouston.org)
Turkish American Association of Northern Texas (TURANT) (www.turant.org)
Turkish American Cultural Association of Washington (TACAWA) (www.tacawa.org)
American Turkish Association of Washington DC (ATA-DC) (www.atadc.org)
Ataturk Society of America (ASA), Washington, DC (www.ataturksociety.org)
Turkish American Association of Milwaukee (TAAM)
American Turkish Association of Milwaukee in Wisconsin
Turkish American Association for Cultural Exchange (www.taace.org)
Turkish American Cultural Association of Long Island (TACA-LI) (www.tacali.org)
Turkish American Cultural Alliance of Chicago (www.tacaonline.org)
Rumi Forum (www.rumiforum.org)
Turkish Cultural Foundation (www.turkishculturalfoundation.org)
Orange County Turkish American Association (OCTAA)
American Turkish Association of San Diego (ATA-SD)
Turkish American Association of San Antonio (www.taa-sa.org)
Istanbul Sports, Cultural and Educational Association (www.istanbulspor.net)
American Turkish Friendship Association (ATFA) (www.atfa.us)
Turkish Hars Society
Maryland Turkish Inhabitants (MARTI) (www.themarti.org)
International Turkish Society Federation (ITSF)
American Turkish Veterans Association (ATVA)
Turkish American Alliance for Fairness (TAAF)
Hudson Turkish American Cultural Association (HUTACA) (www.hutaca.org)

Anatolia Cultural Center (www.anatoliaculturalcenter.org)
Galatasaray Fan Club
Besiktaş Fan Club
Fenerbahçe Fan Club
Kardelen Turkish Dance Ensemble (www.kardelendance.com)
Bridges of Hope Project (www.bridgesofhopeproject.org)
Friends of Anatolia (www.friendsofanatolia.org)
Anatolian Artisans (www.anatolianartisans.org)
Turkish Children Foster Care (TCFC) (www.turkishchildren.org)
Turkish Folk Dance Troupe (www.turkfolkdc.org)
Moon and Stars Project (www.moonandstarsproject.org)
Bosphorus Art Project
HasNa (www.hasna.org)
Turkish Philanthropic Fund (www.tpfund.org)
Turkish Educational Foundation (www.tef-usa.org)
Turkish Fine Arts Ensemble
Institute of Turkish Studies (ITS) at Georgetown University
Turkish   American Scientists and Scholars Association (TASSA) (www.
tassausa.org)
Turkish-American Business Forum (FORUM) (www.forum.org)
Turkish American Business Connection (www.tabc-us.org)
Turkish   Industrialists' and Businessmen's Association (TÜS   İAD)   USA
(www.tusiad-us.org)
Turkish-US Business Council of DEIK, Washington, DC (www.deik.org.tr)
Turkish American Chamber of Commerce, Industry and Maritime (TACCIM)
(www.taccim.org)
ITKIP Association USA (Istanbul Textile and Apparels' Exporters' Association in
NY) (www.itkibusa.org)
Turkish American Chamber of Commerce (TACC) (www.Turkishcommerce.org)
Turkish American Chamber of Commerce and Industry (TACCI) (www.turkishus-
chamber.org)
Florida Turkish American Chamber of Commerce (www.flturkishcommerce.org)

Youth/Student/Alumni Associations

Intercollegiate Turkish Student Society (ITTS)
Turkish American Youth Association
Assembly of Turkish Student Associations, Washington, DC (www.atsadc.org)
Istanbul Technical University Alumni Association Intl, Inc. (www.itumuk.com).
Middle East Technical University Alumni Association
Boğaziçi University Alumni Association
Robert College Alumni Association
Istanbul University Alumni Association of USA (www.iumezusa.org)

Professional Organizations

Turkish American Physicians Association (TAPA)
Turkish American Medical Association (TAMA)
Association of Turkish American Scientists (ATAS)
Turkish American Neuropsychiatric Association (TANPA)
The Society of Turkish American Architects, Engineers, and Scientists (MIM)
(www.m-i-m.org)
Turkish American Physicians Association
American Association of Teachers of Turkic Languages (AATT) (www.princeton.
edu/~turkish/aatt)

Religious Organizations and Mosques

United American Muslim Association, Brooklyn, NY
Fatih Mosque, Brooklyn, NY
Osmaniye Mosque, Moriches, NY
Selimiye Mosque, Boston, MA
Yeni Dünya Mosque, Clifton, NJ
Muradiye Mosque, Chicago, IL
Hamidiye Mosque, Rochester, NY
Aziziye Mosque, Bear, Delaware
Mevlana Mosque, Bristol, PA
American Turkish Islamic and Cultural Center, Forest Hills, NY
Turkish American Eyüp Sultan Islamic Center, Brooklyn, NY (Directorate General
of Religious Affairs)
Turkish American Muslims Cultural Association, Levittown, PA (TAMCA) and
Yunus Emre Mosque (Directorate General of Religious Affairs)
Turkish American Islamic Foundation, Lanham, MD
Turkish American Community Center (www.taccenter.org) (Directorate General of
Religious Affairs)
Mimar Sinan Mosque, Sunnyside, NY (Directorate General of Religious Affairs)
Delaware Valley Muslim Association and Selimiye Mosque, Burlington, NJ (Directorate General of Religious Affairs)
Murat Mosque, Monroeville, NJ (Directorate General of Religious Affairs)
Connecticut Turkish Islamic Cultural Association and Mevlana Mosque, New
Haven, CT (Directorate General of Religious Affairs)
Ulu Mosque, Paterson, NJ (Directorate General of Religious Affairs)

Women's Groups

Florida Turkish American Association, Women's Club
Washington Turkish Women's Association (WTWA)
Turkish Women's League of America (TWLA)

Boston Anneleri (www.angelfire.com/ab7/bostonanneleri)
Daughters of Ataturk (www.DofA.org)
Turkish American Women Scholarship Fund (TAWSF) (www.tawsf.org)
Turkish American Ladies League (TALL) (www.tallglobal.org)

Umbrella Organizations

Federation of Turkish American Associations (FTAA) (www.ftaa.org)
Assembly of Turkish American Associations (ATAA) (www.ataa.org)

Virtual Organizations and Networks

Mezun (www.mezunusa.com) web portal
Tulumba (www.tulumba.com) online store
Laz Bakkal (www.LazBakkal.com) online store
Taste of Turkey (www.tasteofturkey.com) online store
Turks.us (www.turks.us)
Turkish Forum (www.turkishforum.org/tr/)

Turkic Associations

Azerbaijan Society of America (www.usazeris.org)
Azerbaijani-American Council (www.aac.azeris.org)
U.S. Azeris Network (www.usazeris.org)
Karacay Turks Mosque and Cultural Association
Crimean Turks Mosque, Brooklyn, NY
Solidarity of Balkan Turks of America
U.S. Council for Human Rights in the Balkans, Inc.
Turkestanian American Association
Uyghur American Association
Kazak-Tatar Association
Turkish Cypriot Cultural and Educational Association, New Jersey
Turkish Cypriot Aid Society
Association of Balkan Turks of America (Brooklyn, NY)
American Association of Crimean Turks (Brooklyn, NY)
The Melungeon Heritage Association in Virginia (www.melungeon.org)

Turkish American Media Organizations, Newspapers, Periodicals, TV Broadcasts

Turkish Times (ATAA's newspaper published biweekly in English)
USA Turkish Times (first weekly Turkish newspaper in the United States)
(www.usaturkishtimes.com)

Zaman America
Hürriyet America (www.hurriyetusa.com)
Turk of America (www.turkofamerica.com)
Mezun Life (monthly magazine of mezun.com)
Turkuaz Magazine (www.turkuazmagazine.com)
The Turkish American (quarterly magazine of ATAA)
Voice of Ataturk
Bonbon (monthly magazine for Turkish-American children) (www.bonbonk-ids.com)
Turk North America (www.turknorthamerica.com)
Forum—The Turkish American Newspaper (www.forumgazetem.com)
Turkish New York (www.turkishny.com)
Turkish Journal (online Turkish newspaper) (www.turkishjournal.com)
Turkish American Hour (weekly Turkish TV show in Fairfax, VA, and Washington, DC (www.turkishamericanhour.org)
Voice of Anatolia TV in New York City, NY
Voice of Turkey in Rochester, NY

Immigrant Associations in Canada: Included, Accommodated, or Excluded?

SAIME OZCURUMEZ

Department of Political Science, Bilkent University, Ankara, Turkey

ABSTRACT   *Concurring with the view that political opportunity structures and citizenship regimes affect participatory patterns of immigrants through shaping associational activity and mobilization of immigrant groups, this essay examines the evidence from the case of Turkish immigrant associations in Canada to delineate and analyze variables other than institutional context and citizenship regimes that constrain collective participation. It focuses on the impact of history of immigration by Turks to Canada (Montreal and Toronto), trajectory and scope of associational activity, group size and heterogeneity, and political participation. It concludes that collective mobilization and participation by immigrant groups are constrained by intra-group characteristics alongside the institutional context of the receiving country.*

Introduction

In studying different patterns of ethnic mobilization and participation across varying citizenship regimes scholars and policymakers have identified a need to facilitate participation of immigrant groups in different political systems for enhancing democratic inclusiveness in liberal democracies. This view has come to constitute the conventional wisdom in the literature not only on ethnic mobilization and participation but also on democratic inclusiveness. Participation of these groups as such, however, does not follow uniform patterns across receiving societies. By examining participatory patterns of ethnic groups at various levels of government across Europe (local, regional, national, supranational) some scholars suggest that participation by immigrants in fact reflects varying institutional structures, repertoires, and channels available in national as well as supranational contexts.[1]

   This essay concurs with the view that domestic institutions such as political opportunity structures and citizenship regimes of receiving countries affect participatory patterns of immigrants through shaping associational activity and mobilization of immigrant groups. This study, however, introduces a caveat and a set of conditions for the conventional expectations in this regard. The literature claims that more open political opportunity structures and more inclusive citizenship regimes are likely to result in increased levels of participation by immigrant groups and ethno-cultural communities. However, the evidence from the case of Turkish immigrant associations in Canada points to the limits of such expectation as it suggests that there remain variables other than institutional context and citizenship regimes that constrain collective participation. In fact, these findings are even more intriguing when compared to the evidence from the activities of Turkish immigrant associations in different European receiving countries. From a comparison of the associational activities of Turkish immigrants in Canada with those in Germany and France[2] the following propositions can be derived. First, the smaller the number of individuals and the more dispersed the group across the receiving country the more constrained participatory efforts remain. Second, the more available integration mechanisms offered by the receiving country the less likely is the service provision and advocacy by immigrant associations. Third, the more emphasis on multiculturalism and diversity in the receiving country the higher the likelihood of emphasizing cultural representation and participation on the part of immigrant groups and, at the same time, the less likely the emphasis on political participation. Fourth, the more heterogeneous the immigrant community the less likely political participation proper and the more likely diversified associational activities. Fifth, the wider the perception of discrimination towards and/or adversarial politics targeting the immigrant group the more likely collective mobilization and activism.

In order to test the empirical validity of these propositions this study analyzes the origins, organization, role, and practice of immigrant associations established by Turkish communities in Canada in general and in Toronto and Montreal in particular. This study brings new insights to the literature on participation of immigrant associations. Despite the ever-growing political science and sociological research on Turkish immigrants and their associations in Europe, there is a striking gap in the literature concerning the organization of Turkish immigrants in North America in general and in Canada in particular. [3] While this may be due to the sheer size of the Turkish migrant population in Europe in contrast to North America, a comparison between these groups in Europe and North America would shed crucial light on how different dynamics of domestic institutional contexts play out in these two very different settings.

Through a case study of associations of Turks in Canada this essay will examine the dynamics between the domestic institutional context (featured by political opportunity structures as well as the citizenship regime of the receiving country) and organized activities of immigrants around culture, religion, business, and politics. Empirical research for this study is based on interviews with executive members of Turkish immigrant associations in Canada between 1998 and 2004, participant observation in a subset of these associations in Montreal, and an analysis of community print media. Since Canada is often cited as a country committed to multiculturalism with considerable respect for diversity, what does the evidence from the associational activities of Turkish communities in Canada demonstrate with respect to the impact of inclusive channels for organized participation of immigrants in the Canadian social, political, and cultural system? In addressing this question, this article argues that contrary to expectations, more open participatory channels or inclusive citizenship policies do not automatically translate into increased political participation and ethnic mobilization. However, domestic institutional contexts as such *do* promote a vigorous associational life organized for particularly cultural ends and at different levels.

First, this article will introduce the Canadian sociopolitical context as a multicultural society and will identify the available channels for associational activity. Second, there is a brief overview of patterns of immigration from Turkey to Canada. Third, the associational life of Turkish immigrants in Canada, particularly those in Montreal and Toronto, is examined so as to assess how the domestic institutional context affects participatory patterns of this particular group. The article ends with concluding remarks.

Canada as a Mosaic: A Multicultural Polity

Canada is often cited as a relatively open country for immigrant/legally resident populations and their organized activities for a set of reasons. First, Canada has been committed to multiculturalism and diversity since the early 1970s, attributing equality to all Canadian citizens without regarding any difference on the basis of race, ethnic origin, language, or religious affiliation. This overall approach is supported by a set of official commitments through the Canadian Charter of Rights and Freedoms, the Canadian Human Rights Act, the Employment Equity Act, the Official Languages Act, the Pay Equity Act, and the Multiculturalism Act. Provinces and territories also have laws, human rights commissions, and programs that promote diversity. Such deep-seated commitment, however, does not imply that Canada is without its challenges in terms of fighting against racism and discriminatory practices. It is also in a constant need of reforms around how its increasing diversity could be successfully accommodated. In fact, there is perennial research conducted to overcome the increasing challenges that accompany the richness of diversity along different policy areas such as health and education. Second, the political system as a whole, including the activities of political parties and the general approach to associational life by ethno-cultural communities, point to continued efforts to include organized immigrant interests at different levels of government ranging from the local to the federal. Accordingly, there is an abundance of associations organized and run by ethno-cultural communities with aims covering a variety of policy questions. Among these associations are those that are organized for promoting equitable access to health and social services for all immigrant communities in different provinces (such as ACCÈSSS, Alliance des Communautés Culturelles pour l'Égalité dans la Santé et les Services Sociaux, in Quebec), facilitating gender equality for women of different ethnic backgrounds (for example, South Asian Women's Associations), and providing services to specific ethno-cultural communities (like Chinese Family Services). Such vivid associational life, however, should not suggest a substantial decrease in terms of the problems encountered by ethno-cultural communities; it merely confirms that organized representation of ethnic communities is part of how the system in Canada works with its linguistic, religious, and cultural diversity.

This approach is founded and continuously questioned, reshaped, improved, and kept alive due to Canada's long tradition of balancing equitable representation and participation of both French and English speaking peoples as well as its commitment to aboriginal peoples. An example of how the commitment to consultation of diverse groups at the provincial level plays out within an overarching paradigm of diversity is also reflected in the consultative bodies that are established with the aim of allowing for representation of ethno-cultural communities in the health policy process, such as the Community Engagement Program of the Vancouver Health Authority. Moreover, topics such as mental health, interpretation services in critical service provision, education, and addressing problems of the aging population in Canada that cut across all ethno-cultural communities are addressed with the inclusion of ethno-cultural groups in the debates. Again, such inclusion should not imply effective participation and/or substantial contribution to the end result; it reiterates that the system in Canada is based on a broad commitment to awareness and incorporation of its diversity in policy processes at different levels by a range of practices across the country.

Such commitment is reflected in the practices that concern facilitation of integration processes of newcomers. Provinces such as Quebec, Manitoba, and British Columbia design and administer their own settlement programs. Most of the immigrants who arrive in Canada settle in the three major cities—Toronto, Montreal, and Vancouver—and the ethnic composition of the population in these cities reflects Canada's current and future diversity (see Figures 1, 2, 3, 4 and 5), among which the Turkish community takes its place. As permanent residents, individuals (most of whom are qualified as "skilled workers" selected under the immigration programs) and their dependents preparing for integration into Canadian society may enjoy a diversified set of language courses as well as integration courses where they settle. These services are provided in all provinces mainly by immigrant-serving organiza-

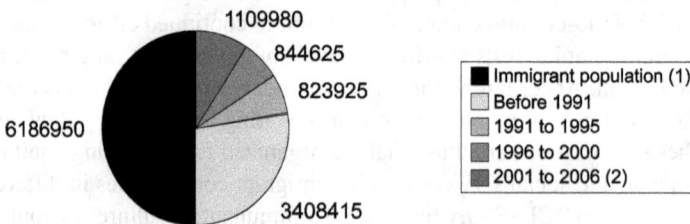

Figure 1. Foreign-born immigrants.
Source: Statistics Canada.

(1) Immigrants are persons who are, or have ever been, landed immigrants in Canada. A landed immigrant is a person who has been granted the right to live in Canada permanently by immigration authorities. Some immigrants have resided in Canada for a number of years, while others are more recent arrivals. Most immigrants are born outside Canada, but a small number were born in Canada. Includes immigrants who landed in Canada prior to Census Day, May 16, 2006.

(2) Includes immigrants who landed in Canada prior to Census Day, May 16, 2006.

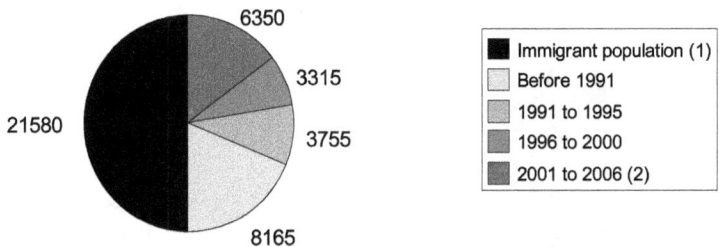

Figure 2. Turkey-born immigrants in Canada.
Source: Statistics Canada.
(1) Immigrants are persons who are, or have ever been, landed immigrants in Canada. A landed immigrant is a person who has been granted the right to live in Canada permanently by immigration authorities. Some immigrants have resided in Canada for a number of years, while others are more recent arrivals. Most immigrants are born outside Canada, but a small number were born in Canada. Includes immigrants who landed in Canada prior to Census Day, May 16, 2006.
(2) Includes immigrants who landed in Canada prior to Census Day, May 16, 2006.

tions.[4] In order to advance integration in key areas, labor market initiatives such as the "Canadian Immigration Integration Project" promote interaction among all stakeholders including government agencies as well as a wide range of NGOs, foundations, and immigrant-serving organizations. They facilitate labor market integration particularly for newcomers from China, India, and the Philippines.[5] Another example is the large-scale METROPOLIS research project, which works on comparative research and public policy concerning immigration and diversity.[6]

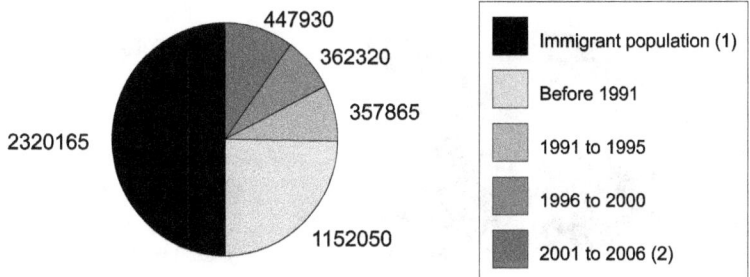

Figure 3. Foreign-born immigrants in Toronto, Ontario.
Source: Statistics Canada.
(1) Immigrants are persons who are, or have ever been, landed immigrants in Canada. A landed immigrant is a person who has been granted the right to live in Canada permanently by immigration authorities. Some immigrants have resided in Canada for a number of years, while others are more recent arrivals. Most immigrants are born outside Canada, but a small number were born in Canada. Includes immigrants who landed in Canada prior to Census Day, May 16, 2006.
(2) Includes immigrants who landed in Canada prior to Census Day, May 16, 2006.

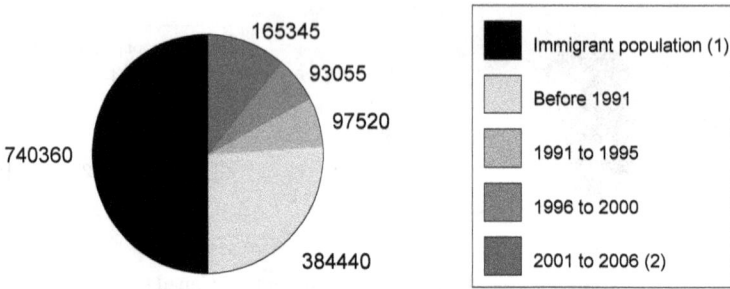

Figure 4. Foreign-born immigrants in Montreal, Quebec.
Source: Statistics Canada.
(1) Immigrants are persons who are, or have ever been, landed immigrants in Canada. A landed immigrant is a person who has been granted the right to live in Canada permanently by immigration authorities. Some immigrants have resided in Canada for a number of years, while others are more recent arrivals. Most immigrants are born outside Canada, but a small number were born in Canada. Includes immigrants who landed in Canada prior to Census Day, May 16, 2006.
(2) Includes immigrants who landed in Canada prior to Census Day, May 16, 2006.

This approach of continuous facilitation of integration of permanent residents is complemented by a relatively open citizenship regime that enables permanent residents to acquire citizenship within three consecutive years of residence in Canada as regulated by the Citizenship Act or by birth for the children of permanent residents. A basic level of familiarity with one of the official languages and passing the citizenship test are the basic conditions through which the permanent residents will

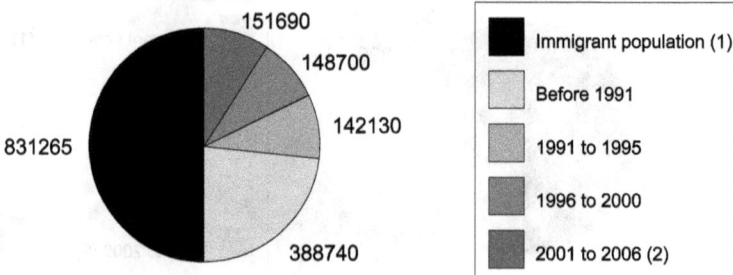

Figure 5. Foreign-born immigrants in Vancouver, British Columbia.
Source: Statistics Canada.
(1) Immigrants are persons who are, or have ever been, landed immigrants in Canada. A landed immigrant is a person who has been granted the right to live in Canada permanently by immigration authorities. Some immigrants have resided in Canada for a number of years, while others are more recent arrivals. Most immigrants are born outside Canada, but a small number were born in Canada. Includes immigrants who landed in Canada prior to Census Day, May 16, 2006.
(2) Includes immigrants who landed in Canada prior to Census Day, May 16, 2006.

begin to practice the political rights. In contrast to most European cases, such a process of citizenship acquisition suggests a comparatively uncomplicated and less demanding transition from non-citizen status to citizen status with political rights and privileges.

Such straightforward channels for access to citizenship, however, need not be interpreted as increased and expanded levels of participation in politics by ethno-cultural communities in Canada. Although acquisition of voting rights and being able to stand for elections are in fact open for these groups through acquisition of citizenship, such access does not necessarily translate into active participation or representation in politics at local, provincial, and federal levels. [7] An interesting feature of the national party system in Canada is that for the selection process of the candidates, the major parties allow the participation of legally resident non-citizens. Such participation in party politics encourages parties to seek members from ethnic communities and also to engage with ethnic groups that have large social networks. This form of political interaction opens avenues for political mobilization by ethnic groups as well as a role for the representatives of ethnic groups that includes possibilities for immigrants of Turkish origin. In this way, through the political process the votes of new Canadian citizens become increasingly important for political parties at the national level party system. Thus the parties develop strategies to include such groups that benefit both sides to a certain extent. For example, parties in Quebec, especially the Liberal Party, made specific attempts to attract ethno-cultural communities into the political system by highlighting the multicultural agenda and its commitment to diversity, which they cited as likely to be challenged by a nationalist Bloc Quebecois and Parti Quebecois. [8] The Turkish community in Montreal, for example, actively supported several candidates running in the most recent Quebec elections in March 2007.

In this overall structure of relative openness to diversity supported by legal regulation, policy initiatives, and practices concerning consultation of ethno-cultural communities as well as a relatively uncomplicated citizenship regime it would be expected that Turks in Canada would engage with no difficulty in the social, political, and cultural realm in Canada through both their individual and collective efforts. However, evidence presented in the next sections suggests that such participation is neither automatic nor immediate. The next section introduces the brief history of immigration of Turks to Canada. It provides an overview of their organizations, activities, participatory efforts, and mobilization to examine how the Turkish immigrant associations take part in Canadian cultural diversity.

The Turkish Community and their Organizations in Canada

A Brief History of Turks in Canada

Identifying the size of the Turkish community in Canada for the past and the current period is not an easy task. This is partly due to the difficulty in defining who constitutes an immigrant of Turkish descent in the Canadian context. In Canada, the term

Turk or Turkish applies to immigrants and descendants of immigrants who claim Turkish identity or cultural ties to Turkey and occasionally is not limited to those who arrived from Turkey or holding Turkish citizenship. This method of self-identification is also reflected in the cooperation among different associations. Moreover, the Canadian census also relies on self-identification, rendering estimations of numbers of Turks more difficult.

Leaving methodological challenges aside, according to the official statistics provided by Statistics Canada, which classifies ethno-cultural communities on the basis of place of birth and languages spoken, there were approximately 50,000 individuals of Turkish origin in Canada in 2006 (see Figures 6, 7, and 8). The immigration inflow from Turkey has taken place in different waves from different parts of the country, mainly in the post-World War II period. In the period between 1960 and 1970 most incoming immigrants of Turkish origin were skilled professionals with mostly urban backgrounds. These individuals, some of whom continue to actively participate in associational life in Canada, are representatives of the modernized and westernized generation of Republican Turkey. [9] During this period, students who arrived to acquire professional degrees, mainly in engineering and medicine, chose to live in Canada and are represented in the executive committees of both the immigrant associations and the elite of the contemporary Turkish community.

The motives behind immigration inflows to Canada are similar with respect to immigration to most advanced industrialized countries. These include a search for better economic and educational opportunities and a better life for the next generation than what the immigrants would be able to secure in their country of origin for almost all periods beginning with the 1960s. The critical period after which immigration from Turkey diversified is the 1980s. Immigration from Turkey to Canada

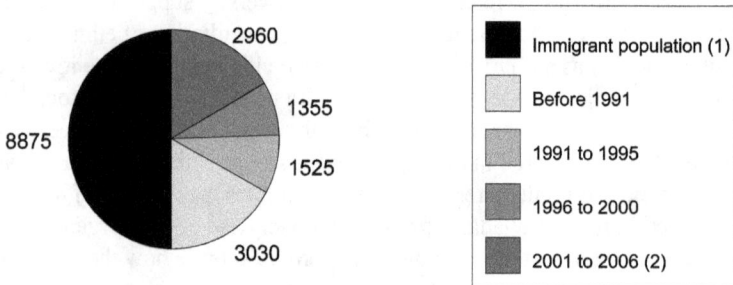

Figure 6.   Turkey-born immigrants in Toronto, Ontario.
Source: Statistics Canada.
(1) Immigrants are persons who are, or have ever been, landed immigrants in Canada. A landed immigrant is a person who has been granted the right to live in Canada permanently by immigration authorities. Some immigrants have resided in Canada for a number of years, while others are more recent arrivals. Most immigrants are born outside Canada, but a small number were born in Canada. Includes immigrants who landed in Canada prior to Census Day, May 16, 2006.
(2) Includes immigrants who landed in Canada prior to Census Day, May 16, 2006.

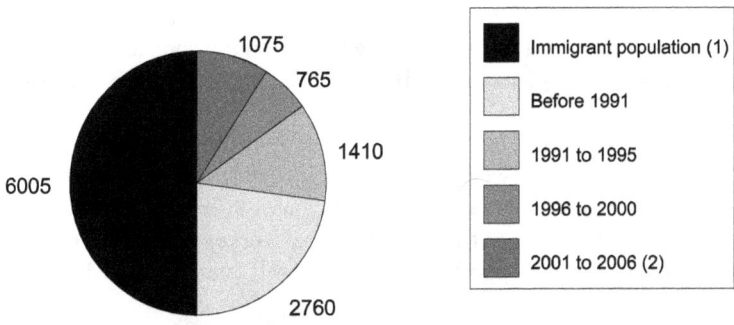

Figure 7. Turkey-born immigrants in Montreal, Quebec.
Source: Statistics Canada.
(1) Immigrants are persons who are, or have ever been, landed immigrants in Canada. A landed immigrant is a person who has been granted the right to live in Canada permanently by immigration authorities. Some immigrants have resided in Canada for a number of years, while others are more recent arrivals. Most immigrants are born outside Canada, but a small number were born in Canada. Includes immigrants who landed in Canada prior to Census Day, May 16, 2006.
(2) Includes immigrants who landed in Canada prior to Census Day, May 16, 2006.

diversified in two major ways during this period. Those from rural parts of Turkey began to arrive in Canada (for example, a substantive number of individuals from Denizli arrived in Montreal in 1986). Moreover, due to the political turmoil in Turkey and the Cyprus conflict, increasing numbers of asylum seekers also chose to live in Canada in the same period. During these periods Canada did not require

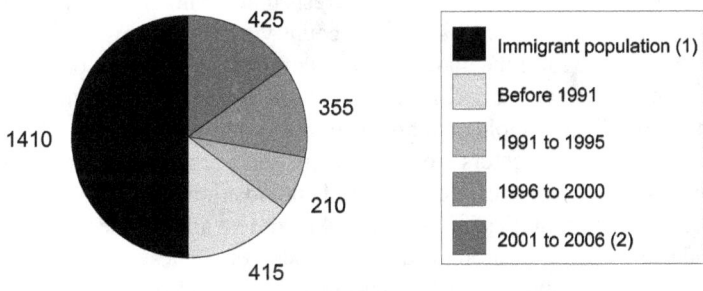

Figure 8. Turkey-born immigrants in Vancouver, British Columbia.
Source: Statistics Canada.
(1) Immigrants are persons who are, or have ever been, landed immigrants in Canada. A landed immigrant is a person who has been granted the right to live in Canada permanently by immigration authorities. Some immigrants have resided in Canada for a number of years, while others are more recent arrivals. Most immigrants are born outside Canada, but a small number were born in Canada. Includes immigrants who landed in Canada prior to Census Day, May 16, 2006.
(2) Includes immigrants who landed in Canada prior to Census Day, May 16, 2006.

entry visas from Turkish citizens. These individuals first started to settle in Montreal, Toronto, and Vancouver and began to form the core communities that would constitute the membership of different associations that they subsequently established.

Immigration from Turkey to Canada continued in different categories post-1980, mostly consisting of skilled workers and some investors who arrived with their families, as well as continued family reunification of those who arrived in the preceding period. They arrived from all regions of Turkey and settled mostly in the major cities with more job opportunities for themselves and better educational facilities for their children. Immigrants of Turkish origin do not constitute a large percentage of the immigrant population in these cities when compared to other ethno-cultural communities and are significantly smaller when compared to Turks in different European countries. Despite constituting a relatively small and diverse group, the community unites mainly around the ideal of upholding and promoting of Turkish cultural values and cuisine around which most associations form. More-over, these associations are present in many cities, occasionally engaging in service provision and advocacy, albeit with limited scope, which will be discussed in detail in the next section as the organization and mobilization of the Turkish community in Canada is reviewed.

Why Engage in Associational Activity? Promoting Community Culture

The literature on engaging in associational activity identifies various sociological, psychological, and political reasons for establishing associations by ethno-cultural communities. Among the most common motives are filling the gap for   *service provision* of services that are either not provided or not adequately provided by the receiving country, or *advocacy* for interests that are not met by the receiving country. A need to maintain ties with the country of origin as well as the cultural and linguistic heritage form the main objectives of most associations of Turks in Canada. Such an objective seems to run through the entire community, surpassing the otherwise mixed sociological profile of the community that reflects cleavages across socioeconomic sectors, political inclinations, urban-rural backgrounds, and secular-religious tendencies. Such a mixed composition is common to almost all ethno-cultural communities in Canada, and in almost all of these communities there is a tendency to organize around cultural associations. These associations focus on forming folk music and folklore groups and celebrate national holidays with events or community meetings.

An early organization called the Canadian Turkish Friendship Association (Türk Kanada Dostluk Cemiyeti) was formed in 1964 in Toronto. Until the late 1980s, this association also assisted with integration activities and provided some services to immigrants of Turkish origin. In 1976, the Turkish Culture and Folklore Society of Canada (Türk Kültür ve Folklor Derne ği) was founded, which was followed by the Anatolian Folk Dancers (Anadolu Halk Oyuncuları) in 1982. These associations emphasizing Turkish cultural heritage multiplied across Canada wherever Turkish communities lived. Examples of these organizations are the Association of Canadian Turkish Cypriots (Mississauga), the Canadian Association for Solidarity of Turks from Bulgaria (Mississauga), the Turkish Canadian Association of London, and the Canadian Turkish Cultural Association of Hamilton.

In Montreal, where a substantial number of Turks have settled, Association Culturelle Turque du Quebec (Quebec Turk Kültür Derneği) was founded in the late 1970s. In 1993, another group called Association Culturelle et Amicale (Quebec Kültür ve Dostluk Derneği), also known as Turquebec, was founded, and this association also engages in cultural activities such as folklore dancing mainly for children, organization of performances for Children's Day, and participation in Canada Day parades and Quebec Day parades. To a limited extent, the association organizes information sessions for their members in particular and the Montreal Turkish community in general on practical issues including taxes, home ownership, health, and financial management presented by volunteers from among the community in different professional positions.

In the late 1980s, the emphasis on representing Turkish culture for all associations took a dramatic turn for at least some members of the community. As the asylum seekers began to arrive in large numbers from Turkey, mostly seeking economic betterment rather than escaping political persecution, the presence of Turks in Canada began to catch the attention of the general public and policymakers from a very different angle. In addition to being a welcome addition to Canadian diversity, the mass arrival of individuals from Turkey around 1986 brought up questions about whether these individuals had legitimate claims to settle in Canada on the basis of asylum procedures. Immigration and Citizenship Canada intended to send many of these individuals back to Turkey. This resulted in the "Protest March from Montreal to Ottawa" to raise the voice of those who wished to stay. As a result, some of them were able to stay while others had to return to Turkey, only to come back and settle in Canada after a number of years. This group formed the core membership for Association Culturelle Turque du Quebec. The march also constituted the first and most extensive political mobilization by Turks in Canada, which surely pointed to how the community would be ready to organize in the presence of adversarial politics. Subsequent instances of street protests and mobilization—albeit much more limited than the march—took place while the Turkish community protested against the discussions in the Canadian parliament on the Armenian issue.[10]

Despite these instances of political mobilization, the primary emphasis on cultural representation of Turkey remained the main focus of the earlier associations. Such focus partially originated from, first, the emphasis in Canada on community values and cultural diversity that promotes such organizational patterns for ethno-cultural communities. Second, it is also a product of the characteristics of those who arrived in Canada in the 1960s who (due to their professional and language skills, urban backgrounds, and education) did not feel the need for extensive service provision or advocacy due to the low barriers to integration they faced in the Canadian labor market or to social, cultural, and political life in Canada in general. In the following decades the emphasis on culture as the main motive for founding associations continued. This is not to suggest that such a unity around promoting Turkish culture resulted in unification around associations, which will be addressed further in the section on the attempts to form and sustain an umbrella association. In fact, the socioeconomic and lifestyle differences emanating from the country of origin are reflected in the nature of different associations. Despite a relatively small community in Montreal, Quebec, two associations function to represent different sections of the community, though they occasionally collaborate for different activities ranging from folklore events to celebrating national holidays or hosting artists from Turkey. One of these associations, Turquebec, is composed of mostly professionals with urban backgrounds, and it emphasizes cultural activities and political advocacy in Canadian politics concerning Turks as well as Turkey-related matters. The other, the Association Culturelle Turque du Quebec, is composed of those with mostly rural backgrounds focusing on mostly service provision, including offering courses in English and French and Turkish history, especially for children; facilitating the conducting of religious practices; and organizing activities for celebrating religious and national holidays. The executives of the associations as well as the communities come together for special events such as regular *iftars* during Ramadan or dinners organized for celebrating the proclamation of the Turkish Republic. They also coordinate and mobilize for advocacy on matters relating to adversarial politics originating from the country of origin, which will be examined below. However, the within-group differences remain such that they continue to exist and operate through separate associations. The diverse preferences and different organizational challenges within the group are not limited to the experiences of the Turkish community living in Montreal. In order to respond to the specific needs of a community that is ever-changing and diversifying, new associations such as the Turkish Society of Canada (founded in 2006) or the more recent Turkish Community Heritage Centre of Canada (TCHCC, or Kanada Türk Toplumu De   ğerleri Merkezi, KTTDM, founded in February 2008), were established to promote Turkish culture and to provide services for language training and integration into the labor market—services that are becoming increasingly critical for Turks in Canada, similar to most other communities.[11]

When reviewing the activities of the associations in the past decade or so clearly the most visible and successful community projects reflect commitment to cultural representation of Turks in Canadian multicultural society. Among these are the building of the Peace Garden in the Botanical Gardens of Montreal, the Tulip Festival in Ottawa, the regular concerts given by Turkish Classical Music Groups around Canada, and the organization of Children's Day performance in collaboration with other ethno-cultural communities. All these efforts confirm the commitment to emphasizing culture and peace in relations with other communities in Canada. These relations went through testing times, especially when the Canadian and Quebec legislatures decided to debate the Armenian issue. Leaving aside the protest march in 1986, popular reactions against the passing of the bills in both parliaments and lobbying have constituted the most extensively organized activity for the Turkish community and their associations in Canada. The emergence of such issue, which the community perceived as a serious threat to their existence and the future of their descendents, gave way to the idea of forming an umbrella association—which itself presented various challenges with respect to mobilization and participation of Turks in the Canadian political system.

Culture Plus Business: Winning Formula?

As noted in the section on the brief history of immigration of Turks to Canada, those who arrived as landed immigrants from Turkey often had professional qualifications that generally helped them to find jobs within a relatively short period of time in the Canadian labor market. However, it is still possible to observe mixed experiences in the Canadian labor market, which is similar to the European cases and which also resemble the evidence from the labor market experiences of most ethno-cultural communities in Canada. Partly due to the points system adopted for determining permanent residence status most of these individuals were skilled professionals (including but not limited to medical doctors, engineers, computer scientists, finance specialists, etc.) who were fluent at least in one of Canada's official languages. As with members of all other ethno-cultural communities, being employed as a landed immigrant/newcomer to Canada did not necessarily mean that the individual was employed in his/her own profession immediately after arrival (or in certain cases ever), particularly for those arriving with medical degrees. In some cases, these individuals either engaged in retraining for another profession or pursued the requirements of retraining for having the equivalence for credentials of their own profession. In others, they engaged in entrepreneurial activities such as joining the retail sector, the restaurant sector, child care services, real estate agencies, moving and storage business, immigration, and/or legal consultants among a wide range of possibilities.

Echoing the cases of Turks in Europe, there are successes as well as disappointing stories for skilled workers as well as for entrepreneurs in the Turkish community. On the one hand, there are extremely successful businessmen in different sectors of the economy who joined the business elite of Canada. On the other hand, there are newcomers who experienced substantial difficulties with respect to integration into the labor market and were forced to accept part-time or contract work, which is usually low-paid and lacking social security benefits. Some semi-skilled workers in the community have also concentrated in certain sectors and have been substantially affected by the structural changes in the economy. In Montreal, for example, a good number of women who worked as seamstresses and in the textile industry suffered from the restructuring of the Quebec textile industry whereby job losses adversely affected many women in the Turkish community working in this sector. Despite these difficulties, Turkish immigrants have not been represented in labor unions and there is virtually no active involvement in advocating causes for better job opportunities, particularly through the associations. The ethno-cultural community networks are occasionally used for finding first-time jobs; however, there is no study that documents how this is reflected in the employment experience or entre-preneurial prospects.

However, the community does cooperate for business and employment interests. First, there are three major sources of information compiled on businesses as well as job opportunities in Canada within the community: the regular ads in the Turkish community media, *Golden Directory Canada (Altin Rehber Kanada)*, and *Referans*. Second, there are two prominent business associations: the Turco-Canadian Chamber of Commerce and Industry in Montreal and the Turkish Canadian Business Council in Toronto, both of which act as contact points for business between Turkey and Canada as well as being platforms of exchange for business-men within the community. A remarkable feature of these institutions is that they also act as sponsors for cultural activities as well as steering interest groups in terms of promoting political participation and lobbying around matters that concern Turks in Canada as well as issues relating to relations with Turkey. In other words, they constitute a clear example of how community business interests also become a part of the cultural and political mobilization of the group, particularly in order to over-come financial difficulties. However, similar to the cultural interests, business inter-ests also have not resulted in a combined effort to unite the Turkish communities across Canada.

Religion Unites or Divides, or Both?

Another noteworthy aspect of the Turkish community in Canada is that despite small numbers the community displays significant diversity with respect to religious affil-iation and attitudes toward religion. Those who identify as Turks subscribe mostly to Islam but also to Christianity and Judaism. Additionally, within each group there are those who are regularly practicing and conservative while there are others who are more secular and distant to religion. However, religious diversity within the commu-nity is not reflected in associational life. Those who organize around religion reflect and promote Islamic values and practices. Hence, some associations have emerged that provide religious services such as space for prayers or facilities for meetings and *iftars* during Ramadan. The Canadian Turkish Islamic Heritage Association (Kanada Türk Islam Kültür Derne ği), founded in 1983, and the Canadian Turkish Islamic Foundation (Kanada Türk İslam Vakfı), founded in 1987, both in Toronto, are among these associations. More recently, the Canadian Interfaith Dialogue Center (Kanada Dinlerarası Diyalog Merkezi), founded also in Toronto, engages in activi-ties with other Muslim communities in Toronto in particular and across Canada in general. In Montreal, Association Culturelle Turque du Quebec acts as an associa-tion that facilitates religious practice with a sizable community center and mosque. The center has a local imam similar to the one in Toronto and offers courses on Islamic principles, especially for children. However, in terms of associational life, although it is commonplace to conceive of Turkish immigrant associations as part of the larger Islamic community in Canada, religion does not provide strong cohesion within the group to ensure higher levels of solidarity.

An Umbrella Association: A Blessing or a Challenge for Participation?

Similar to most other associational activities of Turkish communities in Europe and ethno-cultural communities across advanced industrialized societies, the Turkish community in Canada also made several attempts at establishing and sustaining an umbrella association. This association would serve as a contact point and a platform for exchange of ideas for identifying the needs of the community and would enable a single and strong channel for articulation of interests. These attempts resulted in the founding of the Federation of Canadian Turkish Associations (FCTA, Kanada Türk Dernekleri Federasyonu) on 1 June 1985 with headquarters in Toronto. As of the start of 2009, 17 associations from all across Canada were members of the FCTA.[12] The federation underlines a commitment to unity among Turks in accordance with Atatürk's principles as well as a dedication to democracy, secularism, and social justice while respecting individual rights. [13] Moreover, the federation, similar to most other Turkish associations, highlights the goal of representation of Turkish culture and Turks in Canada and aims at facilitating relations with Canadians and all other ethnic communities, which is reflected in its membership (including, for example, the Canadian Turkish Cultural Association of Hamilton and the Turquebec Association Culturelle et Amicale). As the discussion above regarding the ambiguity around who could be categorized as part of the Turkish community in Canada, the membership of the FCTA reflects the diversity within the Turkish community. Among the members of the FCTA, for example, are the Canadian Association for Solidarity of Turks from Bulgaria, the Canadian Azerbaijani Turkish Cultural Association, and the Canadian Turkmen Center.

Activities of FCTA display characteristics of both service-providing and advocacy organizations for immigrants. In terms of service provision, FCTA pursues different projects: the Employment List (İş Listesi) promotes exchange of job and trading opportunities; Turkish Classes (Türkçe Sınıfı) aims to meet the needs of the Turkish community for education in the native language; and the Communication List (İletişim Listesi) functions to promote exchange of information among Turks in Canada on different topics. In order to promote advocacy for the rights of the Turkish community, several projects are also pursued, such as Defend Turks (Koru Turk), which aims to collect information on any form of discrimination or problems of equality experienced by Turks in Canada and to provide reference sources on various topics that relate to debates and issues emanating from challenges and issues originating from Turkey. The documents and reference literature produced through this project are expected to inform Turks across Canada about advocacy activities in particular. To that end, the FCTA draws on references from the Assembly of American Turkish Associations on the Armenian issue, terrorism, and the Cyprus issue.[14] In order to inform the Turkish community about history and facts so as to expand lobbying efforts to the grassroots level.

Moreover, the FCTA aims to promote democratic participation of Turks in Canadian politics at the federal, provincial, and local levels both for encouraging voting by and standing in elections of Turks across Canada. Nevertheless, success in achieving these objectives is far from being as extensive as the ones pursued by Turks across Europe. The FCTA is usually subject to criticism reflected in the community media, and the community expects it to be much more proactive in pursuing the stated objectives.

Accordingly, similar to the evidence in most European cases, the Turks in Canada also experience three major difficulties among others in sustaining ethno-cultural mobilization and participation under an umbrella organization. First, there is a significant discrepancy between the expectations of the community from the umbrella associations and what these associations can deliver. Expectations of more activism by the FCTA for the community are not matched by action due to the voluntary, not-for-profit characteristic of this association limiting its realm of activity due to constraints of human and financial resources. Such difficulty persists despite availability of funding opportunities, which are offered by various governmental agencies in Canada. Second, accountability and credibility of the umbrella association is consistently questioned. Such skepticism emanating from the community is reflected in negative reporting about the executive members and the associations themselves in various community media. [15] Third, members of associations, including those of the umbrella organization, are divided along the lines of how close they would like to situate themselves and their activities vis-à-vis the country of origin as well as its representatives. Such tension leads to concerns of how and to what extent the community in Canada should cooperate with Turkish authorities or engage in matters emanating from issues in Turkish foreign policy. Despite rendering associational activity and ethnic mobilization as problematic, a common concern seems to prevent the dissolution of all these associations in general, which is that Turks in Canada would like to raise the next generation in an environment in which peaceful relations with all other ethno-cultural communities are paramount. However, this goal did not serve to trigger or sustain substantial political participation. It is in recent times that the community began to engage in political participation, albeit to a limited degree.

Media Linking Associational Lives

In terms of communication within the community concerning political matters, the print media serves as an extensive channel for sharing information on community matters as well as Canadian politics. For example, the monthly newspaper printed in Montreal since 1994, *Bizim Anadolu / Notre Anatolie / Our Turkey,* reports regularly on political affairs in Canada, including elections and changes in legislation in addition to community activities and other news related to the community with content presented in three languages (Turkish, French, and English). *Bizim Anadolu* is distributed widely across Canada and the United States. Similar content is provided by *CanadaTurk*, which is another widely read publication acting as a news channel on topics ranging from politics and economics to community news across Canada. A survey conducted in March 2008 by this newspaper to observe the political tendencies of the Turkish Canadian community in terms of political parties at the federal level attests to increasing activism and awareness within the community concerning political participation. Additionally, Turkuaz TV broadcasts from Toronto weekly on community news and cultural events.

Political Participation: A Tale of Testing Limits?

Despite a long presence in Canada, relatively widespread associational activity, and largely open access to citizenship all facilitating the use of political rights, political participation and ethno-cultural mobilization by the Turkish community have generally remained rather limited. Such a finding is in stark contrast to the activities of the Turkish community in Europe. There have been exceptional instances to these relatively lower levels of participation and mobilization such as those when Turks engaged in protest during the "March to Ottawa" for promoting their demands for asylum in 1986 and in the 2000s when immigrant groups mobilized against the bills that were brought to the federal parliament concerning the Armenian issue. Some of the reasons for the limited nature of collective action are rooted in the size and dispersed nature of the Turkish community across Canada, internal group dynamics stemming from group heterogeneity, different expectations of members of the group from the political system, and other challenges faced by groups such as limited financial resources and experience within the political system in Canada. However, such challenges do not completely rule out options of or activities around political participation; they repeatedly act as reminders of the limits of political participation, even in a relatively open domestic institutional context.

The Turkish Community's efforts at ethno-cultural mobilization and political participation exploiting access channels available in the Canadian system can be classified around a set of activity themes and levels of government targeted. The activity themes generally relate to the topics that originate from political and other affairs of the country of origin, Turkey. As a result, similar to most other communities, the instances when diverse groups within the Turkish community unite and act include occurrences of natural disasters, threats or episodes of adversarial politics, and promotion of Turkish culture. In terms of the levels of government targeted, it is interesting to observe that the Turkish community conducts activities at different levels of government (local, provincial, and federal), as is the case in various federal settings in Europe.

First, with respect to natural disasters, the 1999 earthquake in the İzmit-Istanbul area mobilized all Turks in Canada in that they engaged in various activities ranging from fundraising to clothing and food drives from within the community and Canadian sources to assist those in need in the home country. Similar to these efforts, during the earthquake in Pakistan they mobilized to help those in need in that country, reinforcing their emphasis on peaceful intercultural relations.

Second, with respect to threats or episodes of adversarial politics, the Cyprus issue and the Armenian issue seem to be the key themes that are perceived to constitute sources of adversarial politics and around which Turkish communities in Canada mobilize to articulate their voice to have the Turkish views and opinions heard in the Canadian debate. These activities range from letter-writing to key

public officials and the media in Canada to organizing and participating in information seminars on these matters. Though far from being classified as well-designed
lobbying activities, and limited to the efforts of a few dedicated and capable individuals, the voice of the Turkish community joins the Canadian debates as a result of
these ventures. These endeavors overcome within-group heterogeneity as the
community aims to invest in peaceful relations among ethno-cultural communities
in Canada.

Third, in addition to instances of natural disasters and adversarial politics, among
the central themes that trigger mobilization is, again, culture. One of the most striking
examples at the local level has been the founding of the Peace Garden in Montreal in
2000, organized and led mainly by the community elite and supported through the
dedicated work of fundraising and coordinated activities by a large majority of the
Turkish community in Montreal. Such an initiative serves to point to two important
characteristics of the community and marks a new era in terms of how and why the
community organizes and plans to organize in the coming years. First, this initiative
is an indicator that the community could unite and act on the cultural/political cause
of marking the Turkish community's place among the ethno-cultural communities in
Canada through a permanent art exhibition in an ultimately multicultural space in the
city. Second, while collaborating for this project, the Turkish Community in Montreal
not only began to overcome differences among themselves but also financial difficulties, including those involved in engaging in fundraising activities, giving opinions
on the design and form of monuments, and collaborating with the municipal authorities in the host society as well as with architects and officials from the country of
origin.

In terms of the levels of government targeted, in addition to the cultural activities
at the municipal level mentioned above there remain other activities at the provincial
and federal levels, again, mainly around issues of adversarial politics. An example
from the federal and provincial levels is the mobilization of the Turkish community
for protests through writing letters and electronic mail and visits to members of
parliament to protest the passing of a bill on the Armenian issue both at the federal
parliament in Ottawa and at the provincial parliament in Quebec. The efforts brought
the entire community together and encouraged them to participate as stakeholders in
the debate and to demand what they believed to be the right policy move. They
engaged in researching and printing pamphlets and handbooks on the issue, introducing the Turkish side of the debate to different politicians, members of parliament, and
policymakers. In fact, the mobilization around this issue goes back to the late 1980s,
when the Turkish embassy was attacked in 1985 during the hostilities perpetrated by
terrorists against Turkish officers in Europe. Though the outcome of the lobbying
activities of the Turkish community has not satisfied their expectations and demands,
this mobilization effort served as an invaluable learning experience for engaging in
politics. Such attempts also pointed to the perceived needs of the community
with respect to developing the methods and instruments employed, planning for the
timing of the activities, and designing the strategies adopted when articulating their
community's demands. This experience also led to the strengthening of internal ties

within the umbrella organization, the FCTA. Additionally, increasingly younger generations participate in internships in the parliaments and serve at the municipality level or join government offices, which may prove significant assets for the community.

Moreover, in the 2007 provincial elections in Quebec the Montreal Turkish community mobilized and actively worked in the campaigns of the candidates they supported and joined the promotion of membership drives as well as other activities in the campaigns of political parties. Different members of the community worked in a dedicated manner for weeks and have secured experience and visibility for the Turkish community as part of the politically mobilized and aware ethno-cultural groups in the province. The outcomes of such efforts have been closer relationships with representatives in parliament, for example with those in the Liberal Party.[16]

This brief examination of the content and extent of political participation and associational life of the Turkish community in Canada helps to identify several similarities to and differences from political participation and associational activities toward political ends when compared with those of other ethno-cultural communities in Canada on the one hand and also of Turks in Europe on the other. First, the Turkish community in Canada organizes for political action usually around helping those in need as a result of natural disasters and against adversarial politics requiring lobbying in Canadian politics. Under these circumstances, the Turkish community mobilizes with considerable levels of solidarity and dedication toward having their voices articulated. Such exceptional circumstances facilitate unified effort and allow for overcoming collective action problems.

Second, in contrast to Turks in Europe, the Turkish community in Canada experiences integration and immigration challenges at relatively lower levels, and these challenges are generally directed at individual members of the group rather than the group as a whole. This is partially due to the immigration and integration experience of Turks in Canada, which enables them to integrate into the labor market and social/cultural life of Canada as opposed to isolationist tendencies, which would highlight differences among themselves and the people in the receiving country from other ethno-cultural communities or from Canadian-born. Moreover, the Canadian citizenship regime, which allows for relatively uncomplicated acquisition (which is in stark contrast to most European cases), alleviates most of the legal barriers to active political involvement. Last but not least, the more recent attempts at political participation suggest that the Turkish community is indeed interested in and is likely to engage in continued efforts due to the accumulated knowledge around the workings of the political system and networks in Canada. The activism of the 2000s may be attributed to the increase in numbers of Turks in Canada, availability of financial resources, or awareness of possibilities of fundraising as well as resentment due to consequences of limited action in the past decades as well as accumulated experience with the lobbying efforts for a variety of reasons and ends. The accumulated experience also strengthens within-group cohesion and cooperation and serves to surface challenges and opportunities of working together to promote the interest of the community and the representation of the country of origin in Canada. In parallel, interviews with community leaders also suggest that perceptions of "increasing levels of threat" or "adversarial politics" in the contemporary period might have contributed to the increased involvement of the associations in politics.

Conclusion

The conventional wisdom in the literature emphasizing the centrality of the inclusive citizenship regime and relatively open political opportunities would expect the Canadian domestic institutional structures to substantially facilitate political mobilization and engagement of ethno-cultural communities. According to these expectations, collective mobilization of Turks in Canada would be more frequent and systematic than their compatriots in Europe. The evidence presented in this study, however, shows that political participation of these groups is a recent phenomenon that is in its incipient stages. Various factors account for this outcome.

First, it seems that due to the fact that Turks exist in smaller numbers in Canada and that they are distributed across the country yet only concentrated in major cities their participatory activity remains limited. This is also reflected in difficulties of sustaining an umbrella association that consistently and effectively acts on behalf of Turks across Canada. Second, instead of engaging in self-help organizations for providing services to facilitate integration, most members of the Turkish community seem to have relied on institutionalized integration channels offered through the Canadian system. Hence organizational activity for service provision remained limited and relatively under-organized for decades and therefore did not breed learning effects for extensive service provision for language courses or job searching skills, unlike their counterparts in Europe. Third, since the early period of Turkish immigration to Canada, the immigrant associations have traditionally emphasized cultural objectives over political ones. The limited emphasis on political participation with the exception for rare circumstances in times of adversarial politics can best be explained by the Canadian emphasis on multiculturalism and celebration of diversity.

Finally, two major factors hinder substantive political participation. Group heterogeneity (differences in socioeconomic background carried over from the country of origin, attitudes toward religion, reasons for migration, and the like) renders cooperation for collective demands difficult. It is only through resentments (in cases of difficulties with labor market integration, perceptions of injustice and discrimination in cases of political initiatives directed at their community, and so on) that the community engages in collective mobilization during peak times of the controversy and not a as a result of sustainable socialization into the political system of the receiving country.

Notes

1. See Yasemin Nuhoglu Soysal, *Limits of Citizenship: Migrants and Postnational Membership in Europe* (Chicago: University of Chicago Press, 1994); Patrick Ireland,*The Policy Challenge of Ethnic Diversity: Immigrant Politics in France and Switzerland*(Cambridge, MA: Harvard University Press,

1994); Gokce Yurdakul, "State, Political Parties and Immigrant Elites," *Journal of Ethnic and Migration Studies*, Vol. 32, No. 3 (2006), pp. 435–53; and Saime Ozcurumez, "Immigrants and Participation beyond the Nation-state," in Oliver Schmidtke and Saime Ozcurumez (eds.), *Of States, Rights and Social Closure: Governing Migration and Citizenship* (New York: Palgrave, 2008), pp. 257–78.

2. Saime Ozcurumez, "Immigrants and Participation beyond the Nation-state."

3. See Sirma Bilge, "Présence turque au Canada: parcours migratoires et elements d'un diagnostic sociologique," ["Turkish Presence in Canada: Migratory Trajectories and Elements of a Sociological Analysis,"] in Altay Manço (ed.) *Turquie: vers de nouveaux horizons migratoires* [*Turkey: Towards New Migratory Horizons?*] (Paris: l'Harmattan, 2004), pp.179–208, as a rare exception focusing on their activities.

4. See for a comprehensive list http://www.cic.gc.ca/english/resources/publications/welcome/wel-20 e.asp#qc.

5. See http://ciip.accc.ca/Default.aspx?DN=784,783,32,Documents.

6. See http://canada.metropolis.net/.

7. Among others for Toronto, see Myer Siemiatycki and Engin Isin, "Immigration, Diversity and Urban Citizenship in Toronto," *Canadian Journal of Regional Science,* Vol. 20, Nos. 1–2 (1998), pp. 73–102; and Myer Siemiatycki and Anver Saloojee, "Ethnoracial Political Representation in Toronto: Patterns and Problems," *Journal of International Migration and Integration*, Vol. 3, No. 2, (2002), pp. 241–73; for Montreal see Carolle Simard, "Ethnic Minority Political Representation in Mont-real," *Working Paper No. 8* (Concordia-UQAM Chair in Ethnic Studies, 1999).

8. Carolle Simard, "Ethnic Minority Political Representation in Montreal"; and Livianna Tossutti and Tom Pierre Najem, "Minorities and Elections in Canada's Fourth Party System: Macro and Micro Constraints and Opportunities," *Canadian Ethnic Studies,* Vol. 34, No. 1 (2002), pp. 84–111.

9. See also Sirma Bilge, "Présence turque au Canada."

10. The debate over what transpired during World War I between Turks and Armenians of the Ottoman Empire remains as a cleavage between the two contemporary communities who live in Canada, and as a theme around which political mobilization by both communities takes place.

11. Reported in *Bizim Anadolu*, March 2008.

12. See http://www.canturkfed.net/tr/home_tr.html.

13. See Article 2 of By-Law of the FCTA describing its purpose. FCTA's by-law is online at http://www.canturkfed.net/en/home_en.html.

14. The Cyprus issue constitutes of the debate on decades-long conflict over the island's status after the partitioning of the island in 1974 and how the conflict should be resolved.

15. See 'Surveys' section of Canada Turk's website at http://www.canadaturk.ca/anketler.asp. Retrieved on 10 April 2008.

16. In fact, Massimo Pacetti, a member of the federal parliament for the Liberal Party, repeatedly acknowledges the contributions of the Turkish community in his speeches and meetings (*Bizim Anadolu*, November 2007).

Islam, Conflict, and Integration: Turkish Religious Associations in Germany[1]

GÖKÇE YURDAKUL & AHMET YÜKLEYEN
*Berlin Graduate School of Social Sciences, Humboldt University Berlin, Germany, **Department of Sociology and Anthropology, University of Mississippi, United States

ABSTRACT *A comparison of the two largest Turkish Islamic organizations in Germany, Diyanet İşleri Türk İslam Birliği and Islamische Gemeinschaft Milli Görü ş, challenges the dichotomous categorization of Muslim organizations as "good" or "bad." On the one hand, the Turkish state supports Diyanet İşleri Türk İslam Birliği, which promotes Islam in private life as a source of individual piety and loyalty to the Turkish state. On the other hand, Milli Görüş, which originally supported political Islam in Turkey, is now working to gain public recognition of Islam in Germany. Relying on extensive fieldwork data and interviews with the executive members of these two organizations, this essay concludes that a comparative approach to their views on immigrant integration in general and the headscarf debate in particular shows that they both have ambivalent approaches to Muslim incorporation in Europe.*

Introduction

Religiously oriented associations have always been popular among Turkish immigrants in Germany, increasingly so in the aftermath of September 11. More specifically, after the terrorist attacks, the Muslim characteristics of their community gained popularity among Turkish expatriates as a form of immigrant political mobilization and representation, and many Turkish immigrant associations began to articulate their political demands along religious lines. At the same time, German politicians and the German mass media began to look more closely at Islam in general and at German Muslim communities in particular. Gathering places of Muslims, such as mosques and religious associations, were targeted for state inspections and were referred to in flashy newspaper headlines as "shelters for terrorists."[2] While many Muslim associations opened their doors to the members of the majority population to demonstrate their "innocence"[3] others felt threatened by police raids and journalistic hype and consequently minimized their interactions with German society.

In essence, two forms of Muslim communities and two representations of Islam were shaped in the aftermath of September 11: a state-supported Islam on the one hand and Islam as a threat to the state on the other. In a 2004 book, Mahmoud Mamdani refers to this split as "good Muslim, bad Muslim," pinning the label's origins on American President George W. Bush:

> After an unguarded reference to pursuing a 'crusade,' President Bush moved to distinguish between 'good Muslims' and 'bad Muslims.' From this point of view, 'bad Muslims' were clearly responsible for terrorism. At the same time, the president seemed to assure Americans that 'good Muslims' were anxious to clear their names and consciences of this horrible crime and would undoubtedly support 'us' in a war against 'them.' But this could not hide the central message of such a discourse: unless proved to be 'good,' every Muslim was presumed to be 'bad.' All Muslims were now under obligation to prove their credentials by joining a war against 'bad Muslims.'[4]

Employing Bush's terminology, the "good Muslim, bad Muslim" distinction is explored by looking at two types of Turkish religious immigrant organizations in Germany, with a view to comparing their approaches to Muslim integration. [5] The first is the Religious Affairs Turkish Islamic Union (Diyanet İşleri Türk İslam Birliği, hereafter Diyanet İşleri), an association mainly supported by the Turkish state but also partly supported by German state institutions. The second is the Islamische Gemeinschaft Milli Görü ş (hereafter Milli Görüş), not supported by either state and considered a "threat" to both German and Turkish societies.[6]

These two associations have been chosen to represent the "good Muslim/bad Muslim" distinction at the associational level because they are considered the two major Turkish religious organizations in Germany, each having a distinct ideology and a large number of members. Diyanet İşleri controls 800 mosques in Germany alone, and Milli Görüş controls 514 mosques in Europe, most of which are located in Germany. Both have established a social service network over several decades in Germany; both have women's and youth groups, Koran reading courses, and funeral funds; and both try to attract the same Muslim clientele—second-generation Muslims in Germany.[7] By exploring the historical development and policies of these associations, the way by which Turkish Muslim associations define and enact diverse integration patterns and policies can be seen, specifically after September 11. To this end, the historical background of the two associations and their contentious relationship is reviewed. Their political positions in key debates in Germany are compared, with an emphasis on post-September 11 and the headscarf debate, which polarized opinion both inside and outside Muslim associations.[8] The relationships of religious associations with Turkish and German state authorities and political parties are analyzed, and divergences in their understanding of Muslim integration are examined.

Diyanet İşleri and Milli Görüş

Although Diyanet İşleri and Milli Görü ş share a common goal—to provide religious services to Turkish immigrants in Germany—they have different political perspectives. Diyanet İşleri was established in Germany in 1983 as a result of the Turkish parliament's decision to set up religious centers for Turkish immigrants in Europe. Contrary to the common belief that Diyanet İşleri is a formal representative of the Turkish state institution the Directorate of Religious Affairs, which is directly linked to the Prime Ministry, its members emphasize that they have only an informal agreement. [9] A religious attaché is appointed to the president of the association to serve a four-year term, and the imams sent to Germany are funded by the Turkish state. Other activities, such as youth groups, the mosque itself, and women's groups are funded by associational resources. In sum, Diyanet İşleri is careful not to make any statements in its internal or external affairs that would offend the official relations between the Turkish and German states.

Milli Görüş was present as an informal network in Europe even in the early 1970s. In Germany, it emerged as a diasporic association of the members of Milli Selamet Partisi (National Salvation Party), the banned party of Necmettin Erbakan, a former prime minister of Turkey and the spiritual leader of the Milli Görü ş ideology. Its ideology has been well-represented in the Turkish political arena by a series of religiously oriented political parties, such as Milli Nizam Partisi (National Order Party, founded in 1970 and banned from politics by the Constitutional Court in 1971); Milli Selamet Partisi (National Salvation Party, founded in 1972 and banned in the 1980 coup); Refah Partisi (Welfare Party, founded in 1983 and banned in 1998); Fazilet Partisi (Virtue Party, founded in 1997 and banned in 2001); and Saadet Partisi (Felicity Party, founded in 2001). During these various bans from political activities and the subsequent reestablishment of the party under different names, Milli Görüş was strengthened as a diasporic network of Turkish Muslims in Europe, specifically in Germany. Nevertheless, according to Hasan Damar, one of the founding members of Milli Görü ş, it was not that Erbakan came to Europe to organize them; rather, it was the other way around:

> We wanted to go back to our country and searched for ways. He [Erbakan] seemed to be the person who could develop our country with his heavy industrialization program, and this would allow us to return home. This is why we supported him.[10]

Regardless, Turkish labor migrants supported Erbakan to prepare Turkey for their return, and Erbakan needed their financial support to expand his line of parties. Both Diyanet İşleri and Milli Görü ş provide religious services to Turkish immigrants in Germany, but their constituencies are different, and this influences the organizations' priorities and rhetoric. The majority of Diyanet mosque members are first-generation migrants. The survey of the Center for Turkish Studies in Essen reports that the average age of Diyanet supporters in Germany is 41.8, whereas for Milli Görü ş followers this is 35.5. [11] Diyanet's message of Turkish national identity and unity resonates more with the first generation than with the younger generations, who are concerned with improving their living conditions in Germany.

Diyanet and Milli Görüş do not collaborate because of the dramatic differences in their political views. In fact, Diyanet members do not think very highly of Milli Görüş:

We supported the establishment of the DITIB [Diyanet   İşleri]. We didn't support the Milli Görüş, because we don't support their views. They have political views. Religion must be separated from politics. This is why we established the DITIB [Diyanet İşleri].[12]

In turn, Milli Görüş criticizes Diyanet İşleri:

The Diyanet is established in 1983. After the Kenan Evren's coup d'état, it is established against the rising Islamic trends in Europe…. Unlike the Diyanet, we are not staying quiet when there are changes in the society. We express our opinion for every matter. Our opinions are crystal clear. Our aim is not to provoke people, but we take a firm position. Other associations do not do that. And therefore, Milli Görüş causes allergy in the conservative milieu. They say 'ha, they have a certain discourse.'[13]

Even the women's groups have different tendencies. Although women have never been at the forefront of the Milli Görü ş movement, in the headscarf debate Milli Görüş actively defended a woman's right to wear a headscarf in public places. Diyanet and its women's groups, meanwhile, did not make any public statements concerning the debate.[14] The activities of the Diyanet women's groups are limited to Koran-reciting courses, German language courses, and sewing and literacy courses. Interestingly, Koran-reciting courses are funded by Turkish state authorities, whereas German language courses are paid for by the German state.

The differences between Diyanet İşleri and Milli Görü ş are not restricted to political ideology. Here, Milli Görü ş has a major disadvantage: it is listed by the Bundesverfassungsschutz (Germany's intelligence agency) as a "threat" to German democracy. It is considered part of a political Islam that prevents immigrants from achieving full integration into German society.[15] The Bundesverfassungsschutz also states that Milli Görüş pursues anti-integrative efforts, specifically through its insistence on the Islamic education of children. As proof, it cites statements appearing in Milli Görüş publications, noting the anti-German and anti-Semitic statements in *Milli Gazete*. The label "threat" largely restricts Milli Görü   ş activities and campaigns and places Milli Görü ş members under suspicion.[16] Thus, Diyanet is an attractive alternative for many second-generation Turks in Germany, who, after September 11, only want a secure atmosphere for prayer.

The Headscarf Debate

The major event that pitted Muslim associations against German state authorities was September 11. The terrorist attacks caused all Muslim associations to revise their policies and campaigns, and the religious, political, and cultural differences between Muslims and German society were closely scrutinized by state authorities. A key debate that appeared in the aftermath of September 11 concerned the removal of the Islamic headscarf from public places. Here, as elsewhere, the political positions of Diyanet, Milli Görü ş, and the Türkischer Bund Berlin-Brandenburg (Turkish Union Berlin-Brandenburg, TBB) have differed. While Diyanet is rarely present in the debate, refraining from making comments that might offend Turkish state authorities, Milli Görüş and the TBB have assumed an oppositional stance.

Turkish Muslim religious immigrant organizations, such as Milli Görü ş, argue that religious and cultural differences should be regarded as constitutional rights, and therefore, Muslim women should not be prevented from practicing their religion in the public sphere. In contrast, the social democratic-oriented immigrant organizations, such as the TBB, support the ban of all religious symbols from the public sphere, a position in line with the Turkish state's secularism. Despite its religious basis Diyanet commented only very briefly on the headscarf in German newspapers, downplaying the importance of the headscarf for Muslims in Germany. [17] In other words, Diyanet refrained from getting into arguments about the headscarf ban with German state authorities. However, Milli Görüş took a firm political position against the ban.

Meanwhile, the TBB issued a press release informing Germans of the differences between the traditional headscarf and the politicized headscarf and warned of the evils of the latter. They described the traditional headscarf as having a loose knot under the chin, leaving some of the front hair out; the political headscarf, also known as *türban* or *hijab*, is a conservative covering of the head, leaving no hair out, and is tightly wrapped around the neck. The TBB suggested that the former is eligible to "cross the border" from immigrant society to mainstream host society, but the latter must be eliminated from the public sphere.

Throughout the headscarf debate, the TBB consistently supported the idea that religion is a private matter and discouraged the wearing of religious symbols in the public sphere. In its role as cultural interpreter of a Turkish Islam that is unknown to many Germans, the TBB warned Germans that wearing religious symbols in the public sphere would hinder immigrant assimilation. Moreover, by calling the Muslim headscarf a threat to the religious neutrality of the German state, the TBB argued that one of the most important principles of German democracy was under scrutiny by Muslim communities.[18]

When the spokespersons of the TBB warned the Germans of the rise of Islamic fundamentalism they were referring to religiously oriented immigrant groups such as Milli Görüş.[19] Unlike the TBB, Milli Görü ş representatives and related associations argued that women should be allowed to wear headscarves in public places, a stance put forward in Milli Görü ş publications such as *Milli Görüş Perspektive*. Oğuz Üçüncü, secretary general of the Milli Görüş in Germany, says:

> The religious freedom of Muslim teachers who wear headscarves get restricted and their free entrance to jobs in the public service, which are their rights in the

constitutional law, become impossible. This nourishes prejudices against Muslims, encourages to further discrimination against Muslims in all social fields, and negatively affects integration efforts by Muslims. The essence of the judgment is that the state would have to declare neutrality. This principle of governmental action with a Muslim as a teacher is incompatible if she would want to wear a headscarf while teaching. Obviously the judge proceeds from a wrong understanding of the principle of neutrality.[20]

Üçüncü stresses that a headscarf ban will exacerbate discrimination against Muslim women and hinder Muslim integration. He juxtaposes two important concepts of democratic states—freedom of religion and state neutrality—and argues that in the court decision mentioned above the judge misinterpreted the state's neutrality in religious matters. Üçüncü says that state neutrality encourages religious plurality. Finally, taking exception to the court's finding that the wearing of a head-scarf by a teacher could lead to religious influence on students and to conflicts in the class, Üçüncü argues:

One of the aims of education is to make students think of other cultures and religion. This would be supported by a Muslim teacher who is wearing a head-scarf. Through this, she could help reducing prejudices and provide a better understanding.[21]

Like Üçüncü, Mustafa Yeneroğlu, the Milli Görüş lawyer in Cologne, takes a fiercely defensive position. In his interview with the author, he brought up the controversial connection between the headscarf and Islamic terrorism:

The decision of the constitutional court on the headscarf is wrong. Although it seems like the decision is an advantage [of wearing the headscarf in public places], when you look at other decisions of the Constitutional Court in religious matters, this one is a wrong decision. The Court left the freedom of religion, a matter of basic freedom, to the decision of federal-level parliaments. It left it to political initiatives... Whatever I say, in all the reports of the constitutional institutions, it is stated that 'these are fundamentalists, Islamists, radicals, extremists...they are terrorists.' This is how it is perceived.[22]

In these statements, it becomes clear that a main aim of Milli Görüş is to intro-duce some exclusively Muslim practices, such as the headscarf, into German political discussions.

As the above makes clear, a difference of approach and opinion among immigrant associations emerged during the headscarf debate: while Milli Görüş was bringing Muslim practices into open debate, the TBB was accusing Muslim associations of being Islamic fundamentalists, defining them as threats to German society, and Diyanet İşleri remained tellingly silent.

Approaches to Integration

The model that Milli Görüş draws for itself is social engagement with German society. Mustafa Yoldaş, chairman of the Schura, Rat der Islamischen Gemeinschaften (Council of Islamic Communities), is a prominent member of Milli Görü ş and explains his approach to integration in the following way:

> I have no problem with integration. However, many politicians expect assimilation instead of integration. I will tell you the difference. If integration is contributing to this society and being socially engaged with it, I am well-advanced in integration. I have been in Germany for 24 years, and I have been a German citizen for 11 years. I speak better German than Edmund Stoiber. I have been residing in Germany much longer than Angela Merkel. I have an academic career here. I donate blood every eight weeks. I am a member of the Red Cross. I have been to Africa three times with a project on interreligious dialogue. I don't think you can find anybody who voluntarily works as much as I do for the promotion of interreligious dialogue in North Germany. If this is integration, then I am integrated. But if what you want is to dye our hair blonde, wear blue contact lenses, then drink Hopfenbier, eat *bratwurst* and sing *Deutsche Volkslieder*, then you have to wait for a couple of centuries. I don't think this is going to happen.[23]

Diyanet's interpretation of Islam, often referred to as "official Islam" is more adaptable to the secular European public sphere, but its direct institutional connection to the Turkish state and promotion of loyalty to the Turkish nation can undermine German authorities' conception of integration. Diyanet presents Islam as a source of individual morality and piety, emphasizing religious rituals in private life. It avoids referring to the aspects of the Islamic law concerning political and public affairs in its publications and sermons. Although German authorities endorse "official Islam," the institutional structure of Diyanet raises concerns. It has direct links with the Turkish state and consolidates the national identity of its members, which contradicts promoting immigrant orientation towards integration into German society. Nevertheless, Diyanet leaders believe that having cultural, linguistic, and religious ties to countries of origin does not necessarily hinder the integration of Turkish immigrants. Moreover, Diyanet's control over a vast network of mosques makes it indispensable for German authorities to recognize Diyanet as a dialogue partner in Muslim affairs.

Diyanet also takes a proactive approach towards integration by promoting intercultural and interreligious dialogue through activities that include non-Muslim religious leaders and followers. It emphasizes Islam as the cultural component of being Turkish. It promotes dialogue with the majority society in order to introduce the cultural components of Islam and Muslim life. The major distinction in terms of integration politics between Diyanet and Milli Görü ş is their interpretation of Muslim life. Diyanet sees Muslim life as a cultural difference between the majority

84

and the Muslims, whereas Milli Görü ş takes a holistic approach to Muslim life in Germany. The latter wants to integrate specificities of Muslim life into the German public sphere and claim communal rights, such as Islamic education, ritual slaughtering of animals, and Muslim-only cemeteries. In effect, Milli Görü ş claims to establish Muslim community in the German public sphere through the recognition of communal rights. Diyanet İşleri claims to campaign for intercultural and interreligious dialogue, but most of its campaigns and policies promote Islam in private life as a source of individual piety and loyalty to the Turkish state and nation. It is paradoxical that while this organization promotes loyalty to the Turkish state and nation, this approach has not been considered as a hindrance to Turkish immigrant integration by the German state authorities and society.

Relations with the German State Authorities and Politics

Although most of its members are Turkish Muslims, the Milli Görü ş community wants to establish a multicultural Muslim community in Germany, inclusive of other Muslim groups, and to be officially recognized by German state authorities. However, this ideal does not find favor among German state authorities. Mustafa Yoldaş gives the following reasons for the apparent unwillingness to recognize Muslims as an institutionalized religious community:

> They want to prevent Muslims from institutionalizing in Germany. I mean, they do not want us to have an institutionalization like Jews and Christians. When we have *Körperschaft des öffentlichen Rechtes* [corporation of public law] status, we can have kindergarten, cemeteries, taxes, or membership payments. We can use these funds in the *Pflegeheim* [foster home] schools... They don't want that. Therefore, it does not matter if I have super ideas. We want institutionalization [of Islam]. I want the German government to support us. We don't want money, we want legal counterparts.[24]

A major reason why Milli Görü ş has been unable to find supporters among German authorities is that it is listed in the Bundesverfassungschutz as an "extremist" organization. Young Milli Görüş leaders believe this is a political game played by German politicians over Islamic politics. Mustafa Yenero ğlu, the leader of the legal office in the Cologne branch of Milli Görüş, puts it in the following words:

> A current minister said nonsense things [about Milli Görüş], I sued him, and I won. Then I sued him in four more cases.... He said things like 'Milli Görü is an enemy of Christians. Milli Görüş is happy for September 11.' He called me and asked to get together.... He said 'Can you drop the court cases?' I said 'Why?' He said 'Please take them back. I don't want to be openly renounced in society. You know I am a politician. I lost the previous court case, but I got a lot of applause from my supporters.... This is a democratic society, it is normal to give messages to our potential voters in order to carry the votes to

the ballot boxes. It is necessary for us to make popular statements in order to mobilize the masses (request you to take back your complaints from the court).' This is exactly how he says it...exactly....When he talks to me he says that he actually appreciates the Milli Görüş because we organize campaigns to facilitate integration [of Muslim immigrants].[25]

While noting that Islam and Muslim immigrants are represented as a potential threat to German society by German politicians in order to gain right-wing votes, Yeneroğlu points out the hypocrisy in German politics, stating that Milli Görü ş is painted as an icon of Islamic peril by German politicians.

Although Milli Görüş leaders cannot find supporters among German politicians and state authorities and are represented as a threat to the German society, they still make claims to the German state in a bid to create a sociopolitical space for Muslims in Germany. However, since it has no credibility, the organization must use different channels, associations, and representatives. One such association is the Islamische Föderation Berlin (IFB), which has the privilege of teaching Islam courses in German secondary education in the German language. [26] Burhan Kesici, a pedagogue at the IFB, explains their ambition in introducing the courses:

This is what we wanted to do for 24 years: to teach Islam courses in German schools. We realized this a couple of years ago.... First, we had a political struggle for six-seven years. Then we sued them. Because according to the German legal system, the state authorities have to legally recognize your asso-ciation. When they did not, we sued them. After 14 years of legal struggle, we won the court case.... But we experienced funny events, we had to tell them: 'Look we are Muslims, you have to accept that we are Muslims.'[27]

As a result of this legal struggle, IFB has gained the right to teach Islam as a reli-gion course in public schools. In 2002–2003, 1,607 students in Berlin (852 girls and 805 boys) took Islam as a religion course in Berlin: 74 percent were of Turkish nationality and 21 percent were Arabs. [28] In 2007–2008, the IFB claimed to have 4,600 students taking Islam as a religion course in public schools; according to this estimate, the number had tripled in five years.

Other than educational rights, the following have been introduced as legal court cases by Milli Görü ş: the right to ritual slaughter (decided positively in 2002), Muslim teachers' right to wear religious attire in schools (decided negatively in 2003), the right to have religious education (decided positively in 1984), Muslim girls' right to withdraw from swimming courses when both sexes are present (decided positively in 1993), the right to add Muslim names in conversion to Islam (decided positively in 1992), availability of Muslim services in social and medical institutions (under discussion), the right to burial according to Muslim rituals (under discussion), the right to the announcement of Islamic prayer (*ezan*) with speakers (not yet in court), the right to receive permission from the employer for daily prayer times (*namaz)* and for religious holidays (*dini bayram*) (not yet in court).[29]

Even though some of these cases have been successfully defended in the German courts, Milli Görüş specifically and Muslim associations in general face three major problems in claims-making. First, German state authorities do not legally recognize Milli Görüş or any other Muslim association as representing Muslims in Germany, nor do they give *Körperschaft des öffentlichen Rechtes* (public law corporation status) to Muslim associations. Therefore, Muslim associations are not considered legal groups that can levy taxes on their members. Second, even if Muslim groups make claims by introducing court cases they may face difficulties when their claims are met. For example, in the case of the ritual slaughtering of animals, implementation has been restricted, and the slaughterhouses allowed to practice ritual slaughter have been subject to suspicious and violent attacks. A Muslim slaughterhouse that won the right to ritual slaughtering in a court case in Hessen was firebombed on November 27, 2004. Third, even if Muslim groups receive permission from the German courts to practice their religious customs and meet no other resistance from German society Muslim associations may not always be fully equipped to carry out the procedures. They may be handicapped because of their lack of institutionalization or by restrictions in their organizational structure. For example, Burhan Kesici says that the leaders of Islamische Föderation have trouble finding appropriate teachers:

Many well-educated theology teachers came to us, but we did not take them, because their perspectives did not overlap with ours. Or their perspectives were not appropriate for this society. They have to know the psychology of these children. They have to know the social environment of these children. For example, the Islam that is lived in Turkey or the Islam that is lived in Saudi Arabia is different from the Islam that is lived in Berlin.[30]

Mustafa Yoldaş, chair of Schura (Hamburg Council of Islamic Communities), emphasizes the difficulties of finding imams (religious leaders) who can speak sufficient German to express themselves during the Friday religious services (*cuma*) and who are fully acquainted with German norms, values, and social life. Some religious leaders even give anti-German speeches in mosques. An example is the imam's Friday speech (*hutba*) at Mevlana mosque, a well-established mosque in Kreuzberg directed by the Islamische Föderation in Berlin. The imam was filmed by German TV station ZDF during an anti-German speech to Muslim men who had come to the mosque for Friday services. Among other things, the imam said Germans will go to hell, they do not shave their armpits, and they stink. After the broadcast, the imam apologized, but the IFB decided to remove him from his position. As shown in this example, the pro-integration claims of Milli Görüş can be destroyed by lack of organizational structure and insufficient control over community members.

Moreover, Bundesverfassungsschutz reports characterize *Milli Gazete* as the mouthpiece of Milli Görü ş and as a promoter of anti-Western, anti-Semitic, and isolationist ideology. Yeneroğlu, German Milli Görüş's chief legal officer, acknowledges differences of opinion with the editor of the newspaper. Further, *Milli Gazete* is independent; thus, Oğuz Üçüncü, general secretary of Milli Görüş, admits that he is unable to control it. Nevertheless, *Milli Gazete* is widely circulated at Milli Görüş mosques. The discrepancy between the message of Milli Görü ş leadership for integration and the above examples raise concerns as to whether Milli Görü ş has a double agenda (also known as *takiyye*): putting on an acceptable face for outsiders but maintaining a political Islamist rhetoric for insiders. The young leadership is prioritizing the concerns and needs of young Muslims in Europe, but such leaders do not yet have the power to transform the whole organization. Thus, relations between German state authorities and Milli Görüş have been contentious, and while Milli Görüş has been successful to some extent in gaining communal rights, suspicions of its Janus-faced character remain.

Diyanet, the counterpart of Milli Görü¢, has limited relations with the German state authorities. It has not raised any court cases or made any legal claims in Germany. Instead, it acts as a religious representative of the Turkish state in Germany and refrains from making any statements that would offend German–Turkish state relations. As Diyanet has limited relations with German state authorities, and more intensive relations with the Turkish state, it acts as a formal representative of the Turkish state in Germany. As Milli Görü ş is listed in the Bundesverfassungsschutz as an anti-integrative association, Diyanet seems a reliable alternative for many Muslims who refrain from contentious political issues and who seek merely to join religious services at their mosques.

Diyanet's aim is explained by an executive committee member, Ali Gülçek:

> When DITIB [Diyanet] was founded in 1983 there were various religious communities, such as Milli Görü ş or Süleymancılar. The state [authorities] knew that these Milli Görüş or Süleymancılar have political positions. But our community does not have political tendencies like theirs. Then we decided to establish DITIB. It is founded as a private association with the contribution of the *hodjas* [religious leaders] from DITIB in Turkey. This is the first and last aim of the DITIB: to provide a better and conscious religious service for our community.[31]

Gülçek witnessed the foundation of Diyanet and related mosques in Germany; in fact, his father was one of the founders. Although he is an electrical engineer, he has worked actively with mosque members and in the youth associations related to these mosques. He says that Diyanet was founded to provide religious services, such as supplying Turkish state-appointed imams for German mosques, but has since expanded to include other social services; it now has a wide range of sub-associations, including women's organizations, Koran-reciting courses, a funeral fund, and a youth organization.

Although Gülçek insists that Diyanet has no political affiliations, except its alliance with the Turkish state, this is not entirely true, and, in fact, is somewhat of a paradox. Diyanet represents the ideology of a religion that is accepted and regulated by the Turkish state. Therefore, it is difficult to receive in-depth information from

Diyanet officers and executive committee members, as they do not want to make statements that would go against Turkish politics or stir up relations between Turkey and Germany; they watch their words very carefully. Yet the religious attaché and the imams appointed by the Turkish state for five-year terms cannot speak German, deliver their sermons in Turkish, and are not informed about social, political, and cultural events in Germany. These religious leaders refer interviewers, researchers, and journalists to Diyanet executive committee members. In effect, the religious leader appointed by the Turkish state has symbolic power rather than an active role in Diyanet. Almost all religious and social services are conducted by Diyanet members who are permanent residents in Germany.

Although the religious leaders have only symbolic power they bring a sense of stability to Diyanet by representing the Turkish state. For example, an important source of income for Diyanet is the Funeral Fund. This fund has attracted many Turkish immigrants who pay installments to be buried in Turkey. As evidenced in the popularity of this fund, Diyanet has been successful mainly because it has strong and reliable contacts with Turkish state authorities.

The relations between Milli Görüş and Turkish state authorities have not been as successful as Diyanet's. As mentioned above, Milli Görü ş in Germany is the diasporic network of the religious parties banned in Turkey. The first Milli Görü ş party in Turkey, Milli Nizam Partisi (National Order Party) was banned in 1971 for being against the secular system in Turkey. This ban implied that Milli Nizam Partisi had the desire to establish a state based on Islamic law. Basically, Milli Görüş has a political ideology that attempts to save Turkish economy and society from Western imperialism and democracy and seeks to found a just Islamic society. Its emphasis on bringing Islamic religious order to the Turkish political system is considered a threat to the secular Turkish republic. As a result, Milli Görü ş is a contentious issue in transnational political relations between Germany and Turkey.

After the ban of the religiously oriented Fazilet Partisi (Virtue Party) in 2001, the Milli Görüş community was divided into two camps—conservatives and innovators. Conservatives supported Necmettin Erbakan, the spiritual leader of Milli Görü ş. They founded Saadet Partisi (Felicity Party) in 2001. The innovators supported Recep Tayyip Erdoğan, prime minister of Turkey and chair of Adalet ve Kalkınma Partisi (Justice and Development Party, AKP), the current governing party. In the last decade, Milli Görüş has seceded from Erbakan's strict ideology and gained new impetus in Turkey and Germany. The seceding group is comprised of a younger generation called *yenilikçiler* (innovators). With the establishment of two major parties from within the Milli Görü ş community, the question naturally arises as to "the real representative" of Milli Görü ş ideology.[32] Recep Tayyip Erdo ğan, the leader of the innovators, founded the Justice and Development Party, which received 46.6 percent of all votes in the 2007 general elections and was re-elected as the governing party of the Turkish Republic. This is a surprise for Turkey, which had been governed by unstable and contentious coalition parties for many years.

Prime Minister Erdoğan was a follower of Erbakan and an activist in Milli Görüş, specifically in the youth groups. He was first elected municipal chair in Istanbul, then separated from Erbakan and founded his own party. He is specifically recognized by his statement: " *Milli Görüş gömleğini çıkardık"* (we took off the Milli Görüş shirt), which may reflect his break from his Milli Görü ş past. Serdar Sen questions whether the Justice and Development Party can really offer new political perspectives to Turkish society.[33] For some, the Justice and Development Party is just another Milli Görüş party in the evolution of Milli Görü ş ideology; for others, the Justice and Development Party reflects a major change in Milli Görü ş ideology. It seems that generational change in Milli Görü ş in Turkey marks a major shift in this community. However, it should be emphasized that this is a shift in party politics and should not be seen as a break from the Milli Görüş community.

A similar split between conservatives and innovators can be observed in the Milli Görüş community in Germany. Conservatives can be described as the first-generation immigrants who formed a rigid structure around Erbakan, whereas the innovators emphasize the importance of understanding the facts about Germany. They underline that it is necessary to be flexible and to adapt to German realities. In the view of German innovators, Erbakan is not informed about the realities of immigrant lives in Germany or about current political debates. Here, it may be useful to compare the discourse of the former Turkish parliamentary speaker from the Justice and Development Party, Bülent Arınç, to Milli Görüş representatives in Germany:

I mean we are in a closed circle, in a roller coaster. In this tradition, certainly Erbakan has a role. I am a very close person to Erbakan; but I also criticized Erbakan for that. I have said that this is wrong in the national executive meetings and in city representatives meetings. Erbakan listened to me with respect…. After our congress neither the chair nor Erbakan asked us what is to be done. They did not want to learn. They expressed that they are uncomfortable about it.[34]

In fact, the discourses of Arınç and Milli Görü ş representatives in Germany both pay tribute to Erbakan; at the same time, they both express resentment. According to the innovators in Germany:

We cannot be removed [from the Bundesverfassungschutz] before Erbakan dies. I don't know. He was born in 1926, he must be around 78. I mean, I like my *hodja*, and I respect him. But my hodja does not know the facts of [Germany]. Of course, if he would say, 'This is a flag race. I ran for 1000 meters and I will hand in the flag to the next person,' then the problem will be solved smoothly. But instead [he said]: 'These are children, they don't understand anything.' He scared many people. I personally resent the position of my *hodja*. He could have been recorded as a hero in history, but he couldn't make use of it.[35]

The shift from Erbakan and the conservatives to Erdo ğan and the innovators marks a major event in the evolution of Milli Görüş. It is essential to understand that party politics in Turkey are reflected in Milli Görü ş in Germany. Even so, many innovators in the Milli Görü ş community in Germany argue that Germany has a different political atmosphere and has its own social dynamics, independent of Turkish politics. In that sense, they say, discussing the Milli Görü ş fractions in Turkey does not bring anything to Milli Görü ş in Germany; rather, it should be perceived in its own social and political atmosphere.

Conclusion

Diyanet and Milli Görüş have very different experiences of the Turkish state and its politics. Hence, they have very different functions in Germany. Diyanet supports the Turkish state in Germany; perhaps paradoxically, this relationship brings reliability to its activities. Meanwhile, for many decades, Milli Görüş leaders have had contro-versial relations with Turkish state authorities, thus rendering suspect its religious and political activities in both Germany and Turkey. Even though Milli Görü ş is trying to peel off the "bad Muslim" label that accompanies its listing on the German Bundesverfassungsschutz, the current Diyanet services seem sufficient for many Turkish Muslims who, after September 11, only want a secure atmosphere for prayer. Muslim communities in Germany may eventually require a legitimate body to convince the German state authorities to meet Muslim immigrant needs. That body may well be one of the two Turkish Muslim associations discussed here, but only time will tell which is best able to fill that role.

Is Milli Görüş really trying to create a space for Muslims in Germany that is inde-pendent from Turkish politics? Is Diyanet İşleri really campaigning for intercultural dialogue rather than promoting Turkish-Islam as a religious ideology in Germany? Do Muslim associations in general really have a hidden agenda that they will reveal once they receive legal status? Considering the growing Muslim population in Germany and in Europe in general, it is clear that the discussion will only become more intriguing.

Notes

1. Some of this data has been used in Gökçe Yurdakul's monograph *From Guest Workers into Muslims: The Transformation of Turkish Immigrant Associations in Germany* (Newcastle, UK: Cambridge Scholars, 2009) in an earlier version of this article.
2. Islamische Gemeinschaft Milli Görü ş, "Münchener Poliziei tritt den Rechtsstaat mit den Füßen," September 30, 2004, www.igmg.de.
3. "Die Ehre des Kennenlernens," *Der Tagesspiegel* (daily German newspaper), July 23, 2004.
4. Mahmood Mamdani, *Good Muslim, Bad Muslim: America, the Cold War and the Roots of Terror* (New York: Pantheon, 2004).
5. Also see Jonker Gerdien, "What is Other about Other Religions?: The Islamic Communities in Berlin between Integration and Segregation," *Cultural Dynamics*, Vol. 12, No. 3 (2000), pp. 311–29.
6. Werner Schiffauer, "Das recht, anders zu sein", *Die Zeit*, November 18, 2004.
7. Yasemin Karakaşoğlu, "Custom Tailored Islam? Second Generation Female Students of Turko-Muslim Origin and Their Concepts of Religiousness in the Light of Modernity and Education," in

R. Sackmann, B. Peters and T. Feist (eds.), *Identity and Integration: Migrants in Western Europe* (Aldershot: Ashgate, 2003), pp. 107–226.

8. Gökçe Yurdakul, "Secular Versus Islamist: The Headscarf Debate in Germany," in Gerdien Jonker and Valérie Amiraux (eds.), *Strategies of Visibility: Young Muslims in European Public Spaces* (Bielefeld: Transcript Verlag, 2006), pp. 151–168.
9. Gökçe Yurdakul, interview with Hüseyin Mıdık, 2003.
10. Ahmet Yükleyen, interview with Hasan Damar, 2004.
11. Faruk Şen, " 'Euro-Islam' Avrupa'daki Göçmen Müslümanların Yeni İslam Anlayışı," ['Euro-Islam' Immigrant Muslims' New Understanding of Islam in Europe], 6th International Antalya Symposium, Antalya, Turkey. Survey of Stiftung Zentrum fur Turkeistudien, Essen, Germany, 2004, http://www.zft-online.de.
12. Gökçe Yurdakul, interview with Ali Gülçek, 2003.
13. Gökçe Yurdakul, interview with Mustafa Yeneroğlu, 2004.
14. "Das Kopftuch ist nicht so Wichtig," ("The headscarf is not so important") *Die Zeit,* June 3, 2004.
15. Schiffauer, "Das recht, anders zu sein."
16. Michal Bodemann, "Unter Verdacht," ("Under Suspicion") *Süddeutsche Zeitung,* November 30, 2004; Schiffauer, "Das recht, anders zu sein," ("The right to be different").
17. "Das Kopftuch ist nicht so Wichtig."
18. Dagmar Schieck, "Just a Piece of Cloth: German Courts and Employees with Headscarves," *Industrial Law Journal*, Vol. 33, No. 1 (2004), pp. 68–73; Gökçe Yurdakul, interview with Yenero ğlu, 2004.
19. Gökçe Yurdakul, interview with Safter Çınar, 2005.
20. Pressemitteilung Üçüncü, "Generalsekretär Ücüncü warnt vor Ausgrenzung muslimischer Frauen," (Press release, "Secretary General Ücüncü warned against the exclusion of muslim women") July 4, 2002, www.igmg.de.
21. Ibid.
22. Gökçe Yurdakul, interview with Yeneroğlu, 2004.
23. Gökçe Yurdakul, interview with Mustafa Yoldaş, 2004.
24. Gökçe Yurdakul, interview with Mustafa Yoldaş, 2004.
25. Gökçe Yurdakul, interview with Yeneroğlu, 2004.
26. "Milli Görüşe John Deste ği," (John's support for Milli Görüs) *Sabah,* July 10, 1999; Ulf Häußler, "Muslim Dress Codes in German State Schools," *European Journal of Migration and Law* , Vol. 3 (2001), pp. 457–74.
27. Gökçe Yurdakul, interview with Burhan Kesici, 2004.
28. Website for *Die Islamische Föderation in Berlin* 2005 and 2008, at http:// www.islamische-foederation.de.
29. *Islamische Gemeinschaft Milli Görüş,* (Islamic Community Milli Görüs) Islamische Portal, 2005, at www.igmg.de.
30. Gökçe Yurdakul, interview with Burhan Kesici, 2004.
31. Gökçe Yurdakul, interview with Ali Gülçek, 2003.
32. Serdar Şen, *AKP Milli Görüşçü mü?* (Is AKP from Milli Görüs?) (Istanbul: Nokta Kitap, 2004), p. 10.
33. Ibid.
34. Rusen Çakır and F. Çalmuk, *Recept Tayyip Erdoğan: Bir Dönüşüm Öyküsü* (Recep Tayyip Erdogan: The Story of a Transformation) (Istanbul: Metis, 2001).
35. Gökçe Yurdakul, interview with Mustafa Yoldaş, 2004.

"The Light of the Alevi Fire Was Lit in Germany and then Spread to Turkey": A Transnational Debate on the Boundaries of Islam

ESRA ÖZYÜREK

Department of Anthropology, University of California, San Diego, United States

ABSTRACT *Research on the transnational Alevi Muslim community in Berlin, Vienna, and Istanbul suggests that the Muslim identities and political agendas that seek recognition in Europe are largely made in Europe and hence are indigenous to Europe. Thus it is the political, legal, and social context of the post-Cold War European Union and the unique conditions of individual European countries that shape the way Muslim communities define themselves in that sociopolitical geography. These new identities that come into being at the core of Europe transform the debates and definitions of Islam in the Muslim-majority peripheries of Europe rather than vice versa.*

Introduction

More often than not European policymakers and public intellectuals frame the problems Muslim residents of Europe face in terms of their lack of "integration." [1] A wide variety of events ranging from the killing of Theo van Gogh by a Dutch Muslim in the Netherlands to the low success rates of Muslim students in Britain [2] and from the demands of Muslim female students to attend school in their headscarves[3] to the reaction to cartoons of Muhammad are seen as related to fundamental beliefs and practices central to the Islamic religion that prevents Muslims from being part of the new Europe that is in the making. In turn, European Muslims frequently frame their demands as an issue of absence of "recognition" of their difference.[4]

Integration is an increasingly prevalent issue in the redefinition of post-Cold War Europe. When European leaders met at Maastricht in 1991, two years after the fall of the Berlin Wall, they agreed to transform the basis of the European Union from an economic alliance to a political confederation and hence changed the name of their organization from the European Economic Community to the European Union.

They defined culture as one of the central issues of social cohesion that would incorporate the original members with the 12 new countries from the socialist bloc. [5] As Europe stopped being the mediator between the United States and the Soviet Union, Europeans turned inward to look for a common denominator that would define themselves and were therefore faced with the "anxiety of Europeanization."[6]

Post-Cold War European identity is increasingly based on the idea of an "integral Europe," which "recasts European society as a moral framework, analytical construct, and empirical fact."[7] Politicians on both the right and the left make a claim about what defines the basis of integral Europe, or its Spirit, in the Hegelian sense, as something larger than the institutional organization of the European Union.   [8] Right-wing politicians in many European countries increasingly state that there is a fundamental European culture based on a long history and that Christianity is one of its central pillars.[9] Following Vaclav Havel's call to the European Parliament on March 8, 1994, the first draft for a charter of European Identity was prepared by the European Union delegates in 1997. Even though it never became the official charter, it is significant that this first draft attests to an essentialist understanding, as it puts Christianity at its center. It states:

> [b]uilding on its historical roots in classical antiquity and Christianity, Europe further developed these values (i.e. tolerance, humanity, and fraternity) during the course of the Renaissance, the Humanist movement, and the Enlightenment, which led in turn to the development of democracy, the recognition of fundamental and human rights, and the rule of law.[10]

Manifestations of this understanding, which sees certain values as essentially European and directly related to Christianity, are abundant both in relation to the treatment of Muslim communities in Europe and objections raised against the possible integration of Turkey for inclusion in the European Union. Most often Muslim minorities in Europe and Turkey, a Muslim-majority candidate for inclusion in the European Union, are principally defined through their religious affiliation, regardless of the fact that many Muslim Europeans do not practice their religion and that Turkey is a militantly secular country where public expression of religion is strictly limited.[11]

Leftist liberals, on the other hand, argue that what makes Europe special is its commitment to secular, democratic, and humanitarian values. Despite their universalistic approach, which ostensibly decentralizes Christianity, leftists are often the most vociferous in their critique of certain Islamic practices, such as the headscarf, circumcision, and the ritual slaughtering of animals. They believe such practices should be prevented not because they are non-Christian but because they represent a culture that promotes extreme submission to religion and hence does not allow individuals to subscribe to secularist values. Therefore, both the left and the right question the capacity of Muslims to be part of the new, integral Europe.[12]

The assumption underlying the so-called poor prospects for integration is that immigrant Muslims bring with them their alien beliefs, concerns, and practices.

Based on research on the transnational Alevi Muslim community in Berlin, Vienna, and Istanbul, however, it can be suggested that the Muslim identities and political agendas that seek recognition in Europe are largely made in Europe and hence are indigenous to Europe. In other words, it is the political, legal, and social context of the post-Cold War European Union and the unique conditions of individual European countries that shapes the way Muslim communities—and others—define themselves in that sociopolitical geography. [13] These new identities that come into being at the core of Europe, in turn, transform the debates and definitions of Islam in the Muslim-majority peripheries of Europe, such as Turkey, Morocco, and Egypt, rather than the process working the other way around.

On the other hand, Muslim minorities develop parallel discursive strategies to legitimate their demands for recognition. Like their (post-) Christian counterparts, Muslim activists argue that Muslims come to Europe with already defined identities, priorities, and lifestyles that need to be recognized as different and respected. Yet the politics of recognition are themselves a post-Cold War phenomenon, mostly developed in Europe and its European settler colonies such as the United States, Canada, and Australia. [14] As the welfare state is shrinking throughout Europe the politics of recognition are replacing the politics of redistribution. [15] In Europe at the turn of the twenty-first century, official recognition of difference is one way to access material resources as well as legal rights and political power. Thus, the demand for recognition has a particular shape and meaning in the new legal and economic context of an enlarged Europe; when particular demands of recognition originally developed in Europe travel to other contexts they often do not translate well or politically benefit the minority groups in the same way.

One useful way to understand how Muslim immigrants in Europe increasingly make their political demands on the basis of recognition of religious difference—as opposed to class or national origin—is to examine the transformations in the self-understanding of the heterodox Muslim community of Alevis in Europe. European Alevi organization is especially significant because it transformed the conceptualization of Alevi identity in Turkey as well as debates on the issue of Muslim diversity in Turkey. This article discusses the way in which the German government's policy to recognize religious minorities as independent units allowed Alevis to define their religion as a seperate belief system. It is suggested that the politico-legal conditions in Germany and the newly available resources that the European Parliament provides to Europe-wide immigrant groups have encouraged Alevis to define themselves as separate from Sunni Muslims and make demands based on the recognition of this difference. Simultaneously, because Turkey is in the process of integration with the European Union, European Alevis have found themselves in a position to demand specific group rights for Alevis in Turkey. Since in Turkey the politics of redistribution are not based on recognition of difference, Alevi identity politics caused heated debates about the nature of religion and minority status. Some of the positions and demands developed in the German context have proved not easily transferable or always translatable to the Turkish context.

Yet the level of transnational dialogue between Muslims in Germany and Turkey suggests that the very definition of Islam and what is acceptable in it is always under negotiation. In that sense, this article aims to move the understanding of debates in Europe away from the themes of "integration" and "recognition" of already existing and well-defined minority religious systems that are treated as ill-fitting transplants. Instead, it advocates a globally contextualized understanding of religious identity and positioning based on the divergent social, political, and legal contexts in which these identities are continuously made and remade. The research for this article was based on participant observation in *cemevis* (Alevi houses of worship) in Istanbul, Berlin, and Vienna during the summers of 2004 and 2005. The author attended numerous *Cems* (ritual gatherings) in *cemevis*, met and conducted unofficial interviews with about twenty *cemevi* attendants in all three locations, conducted formal interviews with ten individuals in leadership positions, and followed debates about Alevism in Alevi and popular media in Turkey and in Germany.

A Brief History of Alevism

It is difficult to articulate an easy description of Alevism that will be accepted by a majority of Alevi activists, scholars, and believers at a time when dozens of organizations across Turkey and Europe are struggling with it. Many scholars define Alevis as a heterodox Muslim group with roots in Turkey; a few activists identify it as a distinct belief system and lifestyle that is outside Islam. [17] Although practiced differently in various parts of Turkey, Alevi belief is marked by a mystical understanding of religion that emphasizes a deeper spiritual message of the Koran; an internalized sense of God that can be attained through by the Alevi path; an overwhelming love for Ali, Muhammad's cousin and son-in-law who is revered as the keeper of the mystical knowledge; commemoration of the martyrdom of Hasan and Hussein, Ali's sons; and practice of a communal ritual named *cem* in which men and women participate. At first sight Alevism displays similarities with Shi'a Islam. Yet a great majority of Alevis do not see their belief as affiliated with Shiism and feel distant from the Shi'a regime in Iran. Historians of Alevism also argue that although influenced by Shiism, Alevi belief has its distinct features that are formed through syncretistic integration of Central Asian Turkish shamanistic beliefs, mystical Islam, and local religions in Anatolia, including Christianity.[18]

The difficulty of conceptualizing Alevism is related in part to the fact that the word "Alevi" is a recent invention, at most 100 years old. The word Alevi, which literally means "descendants of Ali," is a misnomer. A leading scholar of the community, Irene Melikoff, argues that Alevis today are the descendants of heterodox nomadic Turkish and Kurdish groups living in Anatolia that used to be called Kizilbash and of followers of the Bektashi orders who lived in western Turkey and the Balkans. The Ottomans treated these heterodox groups differently throughout their history. Between the sixteenth and the nineteenth centuries Ottomans embraced their mystic practices and made them central to the organization of the Janissaries, the elite Ottoman infantry. In 1826, however, the Janissaries were slaughtered, the

Bektashi orders were made illegal, and the Kizilbash were massacred. [19] In the late nineteenth century the Ottoman state officials systematically attempted to convert the heterodox groups to Sunni Islam.[20]

Because the groups that constituted Kizilbash were persecuted during the Ottoman period many of them welcomed the foundation in 1923 of the secular Turkish Republic.[21] They hoped to live in peace in the new republic and be considered equal to Sunni citizens; they also hoped that a secular government would not interfere in their religious practices. The republic fulfilled their expectations to some degree but not fully. In the history of the Turkish Republic, Alevis were not systematically persecuted. Granted, hundreds of Alevis were killed by Sunni Muslim and Turkish nationalist fanatics in Sivas (1978 and 1993), Kahramanmara ş (1978), Çorum (1980), and Gazi in Istanbul in 1997.[22] These events were different from the Ottoman massacres in the sense that none were openly organized by the state officials, nor were the killings openly against the Alevis. Early republican officials were sympathetic towards Alevis because they considered them as racially Turkish—despite the fact that some Alevis are Kurdish and some are Arab—and admired their Turkish interpretation of Islam, supposedly uncontaminated by Arab influences.[23] Moreover, because Alevis do not follow the five pillars of Islam and live an ostensibly more secular lifestyle they seemed as ideal citizens for the new Turkish Republic. Though Alevis live a relatively peaceful life in the Turkish Republic, compared to that of the Ottoman Empire, they still are not equal citizens. The Republic's nationalist and secularist ideology has resulted in support of a homogeneously Sunni interpretation of Islam, strictly controlled and monitored by the Turkish state. In this new, strictly uniform interpretation, Alevis found themselves unsupported and unrecognized. When asked, many Alevis say that they began to feel especially threatened in the 1990s, when political Islam became increasingly powerful and Islamist parties became part of the government.[24]

Today, the Department of Religious Affairs, which promotes and serves Sunni Islam, has a larger budget than many other ministries, approximately one billion dollars. In 2005, the department employed 60,000 imams in Turkey and abroad and funded 4,221 Koran schools. [25] Yet Alevis, who constitute somewhere between ten to 30 percent of Turkey's population of 70 million, receive none of these services. Their houses of worship, the *cemevi*, are not recognized, nor are they provided the free water and property tax breaks that mosques, churches, and synagogues receive. Alevism is not taught in textbooks or in the state divinity schools. Alevi prayer leaders, *dedes*, are not trained or funded by state resources.

Alevi Revival: From Germany to Turkey

Despite the fact that they practiced their religion in far from ideal conditions Alevis did not make public demands during the first 70 years of the Turkish Republic. Many observers assumed that Alevis would assimilate as they migrated to the cities and lost their contacts with their local religious leaders. However, the 1990s witnessed an unexpectedly lively Alevi revival. Alevis built hundreds of religious gathering places across Europe and Turkey. They wrote and read hundreds of books defining the history and basic features of Alevism. They also established dozens of Alevi Internet sites and participated in lively debates about Alevism. As David Shankland put it: "A rural, remote, diverse, private, largely oral Islamic society has become urban, public, active, secular, and to a great extent, begun the express process of codification of its previously diverse largely unrecorded culture within the modern city setting."[26] Today, the Alevi revival movement in Turkey comprises a wide spectrum of organizations, from those that see Alevism as a socialist resistance movement (*Pir Sultan Abdal Derneği*) to those that see it as a Turkish interpretation of Islam (*Cem Vakfı*) and others that see it as a Shi'a interpretation (*Ehl-i Beyt Vakfı*).[27]

Alevi activists and intellectuals as well as non-Alevi researchers often list several reasons for the Alevi revival, the most common being the recent urbanization of the Alevi population. Researchers suggest that because Alevis were massacred during Ottoman times many moved to isolated mountain villages. [28] For the same reason, only Alevis who lived in isolated mountain villages were able to protect their belief systems and rituals without being persecuted or assimilated into the Sunni community. They were not connected to each other and were committed to their religious identity through *dede-talib*. Alevi religious leaders (*dedes*) visited their followers (*talibs*) once a year during winter in their villages to resolve disputes and conduct the *cem* ceremony. When Alevis came to the cities they lost their connections with their *dedes*. Moreover, though they migrated to cities in large numbers they were not able to claim any part of these cities as distinctively Alevi. [29] Yet they met other Alevis who shared similar beliefs but followed different practices. The *cemevis*, a uniquely urban phenomenon of the 1990s, became a new way for Alevis to claim their communal identity. In rural settings many Alevis conducted *cem* gatherings in the largest houses of their villages rather than setting aside a separate building for this purpose. Later, *cemevis* started to be built in rural areas as well, thanks to remittances that Alevi immigrants in Western Europe sent home for this purpose. [30] *Cemevis* became places where Alevis would meet and try to codify their religion and make it appropriate for its new urban context.[31]

A more significant factor, which is not as readily expressed by the Alevi activists in Turkey, has been the organization of Alevis in Europe, especially in Germany. [32] The massive migration of Turkish citizens to Germany in the 1960s upon the invitation of the German government so as to overcome labor shortages transformed the economic and political terrain in Turkey.[33] As new generations of Turks and Kurds grew up in Germany they began to organize politically in ways that had not been possible in Turkey, especially in the politically oppressive atmosphere of the post-1980 military coup. [34] These groups also sent ideas and financial sources to their hometowns in Turkey [35] and made it possible for parallel Alevi organizations to flourish. Because Alevis lived in more isolated rural parts of the country they have been more willing than Sunnis to move to Germany and other European countries,[36] and they constitute about 30 percent of immigrants from Turkey. Soon after they settled, Alevis began to gather around political organizations they established, albeit not openly or exclusively Alevi ones. Alevi identity in Germany was quite latent until the late 1980s.

As Rıza Ataç, the chairman of the Alevi *cemevi* in Berlin said in an interview in summer 2005, "the light of the Alevi [revival] fire was lit here and then spread to Turkey." When I asked why this was the case, he responded, "after the early immigrants secured their bread, they became involved in social life and began engaging in politics to make this a better world." The Turkish Worker's Union (Türk Ameleler Birliği) was the first organization in which Alevis in Germany became politically active in the 1960s. The association was soon replaced by the Patriot's Union (Yurtseverler Birli ği), and it was affiliated with the Union Party (Birlik Partisi), an understatedly Alevi political party established in Turkey in 1969. Yet because in the 1970s the great majority of Alevis were influenced by socialist ideals they chose to organize around nonsectarian leftist organizations, and the Alevi movement did not take off in either Germany or Turkey. After the military junta came to power in 1980 Turkey began to prosecute leftist activists. As Germany began to accept immigrants as political refugees, newer and established Alevi activists organized exclusive Alevi organizations. The decision to shift the basis of political organization from socialism to Alevism was influenced in part by a legal change at the European level. In 1986, the European Parliament decided to subsidize associations that promote immigrant cultures and identities across Europe, and Alevis began to organize and coordinate activities at the European level as Alevis.[37] The organization of Alevis in Germany was also facilitated by the fact that the coalition of Socialists and Greens that started in 1989 emphasized anti-racism and multiculturalism and hence encouraged alternative forms of immigrant organization that go beyond ethnic lines.[38]

As Alevis began to organize in Germany they found that the same characteristics of their faith—such as not going to the mosque, not praying five times a day, men and women praying together, women not covering their hair—that are frowned on by the Sunni majority in Turkey were favored by Germans as progressive and tolerant.[39] Many Alevis in Germany, Austria, and Turkey point to these characteristics of their faith as what makes them similar to Christians and thus allows them to integrate easily in Christian Europe.[40] A 60-year old retired Alevi man at the Berlin *cemevi* took pride in the fact that as soon as Alevi women moved to Germany they adapted to its dress and lifestyle. A 33-year old woman who grew up in Germany and works as an assistant at a doctor's office quietly related that as an Alevi she does not even mind eating pork. For similar reasons, the German government considers Alevis as closer to the state and less alien than their Sunni counterparts.[41] One of the most concrete fruits of the Alevi organization that is facilitated by Germany's favorable economic, social, political, and legal conditions was the writing of the Alevi Manifesto in 1989 by mostly Alevi and some Sunni intellectuals in the Hamburg Alevi Association. The manifesto was published in the main left-wing newspaper in Turkey a year later, in 1990. The document defined Alevism as a branch of Islam and aimed to make the demands of Alevis publicly known. It asked for recognition of Alevism as a different faith and culture, asked for equal representation and opportunity in education and in the media, and for proportional assistance in religious services.[42]

In 1994, after the Alevi Manifesto was published, Alevis organized across Europe under the umbrella organization of the European Alevi Unions Federation in Cologne. As of summer 2005 the federation was organized in nine countries and had 184 affiliated organizations. These organizations became spaces for Alevis to come together to discuss and define the nature of Alevi politics, but more significantly they allowed Alevis to define Alevism as a publicly expressed independent religion, an opportunity more readily available to them in Germany than in Turkey. It is important to note that this transformation from a political to a religious federation did not come easily to Alevis. The tensions among Alevis in terms of their organizational strategies were made acutely clear in talking to Mehmet Ali Çankaya, the leader of the Austrian Alevi Association who has a bakery in Vienna. At the beginning of the conversation Çankaya related that he himself is not religious, yet he believes it is important for Alevis to organize as Alevis. He told me that his friends often complain to him about naming their organization as Alevi. Çankaya explained:

> They tell me that we are making ourselves a religious organization by calling it Alevi Association. But I disagree with them. If we gather here as Alevis, we should say so. We are not here for religious purposes only. The struggle we engage here for the recognition of Alevi rights is necessary for democracy and human rights both in Turkey and in Europe. Alevism is not only a matter of belief. It is an integral part of secularism and democracy in Turkey. We promote democracy, dialogue, and social peace. We are not a radical religious organization. Our primary goal is to provide a language to talk about differences and promote democracy in Turkey.

Alevis who organized in Europe financially and ideologically supported their networks in Turkey to organize as Alevis to build *cemevis* and organize as Alevis. When the German government encouraged immigrants to return to their home countries in the 1990s, the return migration had a profound influence in Alevi identity politics in Turkey. The returnees provided both leadership and the monetary resources for the Alevi movement.[43]

Another development that fundamentally transformed debates among Alevis was facilitated by another event that took place in Germany. In 2002, the local government in Berlin recognized Alevism as an official religion and gave the Alevi community the right to teach Alevism. [44] This development followed the 2000 decision to grant to the Islamic Federation in Berlin the right to teach Islam in public schools.[45] Today in Berlin Alevi educators are teaching Alevism on a voluntary basis. Teachers' salaries are partly met by the German government and partly by the Alevi organization. The education program in Berlin faces many problems, especially because not all Alevi parents want their children to learn about Alevism, fearing they will be discriminated for being different from Sunni Turks. In addition, it proved difficult to transport sufficient number of children from different schools located throughout the city for classes. Yet the idea of teaching Alevism as a separate faith other than Islam has been revolutionary in the way the belief system is conceptualized or publicly expressed as an independent religion.

The legal decision of the German officials had two significant consequences. First, because Alevism has been an oral religion based on the esoteric knowledge of the *dedes* who lead their communities, Alevi intellectuals and religious leaders had to come together to create a written and standardized definition of their religion. Moreover, though the variation in Alevi practices in Turkey made writing a textbook difficult, this very process introduced the standardization of Alevi beliefs, rituals, and practices. Second, when the German officials in Berlin gave the Alevi organization the right to teach the Alevi religion, they also opened the possibility for Alevism to be officially recognized as a separate religion from Islam in general. In Germany, at the federal level Islam has yet not received the formal status of an officially recognized religion, despite the fact that Sunnis have been seeking this status for three decades.[46] Gaining this right is important because according to Article 140 of the German Constitution, recognition as a public religion ensures legal autonomy and allows the government to collect taxes from the members of the religious group to be handed to the religious officials.[47] Today, both Sunni Muslims and Alevis are pursuing legal processes to be recognized as an official religion in each state.[48] In Austria, where the same legal category also exists, Islam has been recognized as an official religion since the Austro-Hungarian Empire heavily relied on Muslim Bosnian soldiers.[49] The Alevi association in Austria applied to the Austrian government in 2004 to be recognized as a separate religious community since they did not feel part of the Sunni Muslim community. Çankaya said that the members of his organization believe Alevism is a belief system specific to Anatolia, independent from Islam. He said that

> if Alevism was part of Islam, it would be just like Islam. Since it is not, it is a different belief. That is why we applied to the Austrian state to be recognized as a different religion. Many German and Austrian scholars studied our religion. They also concluded that it is an independent religion.

This kind of an official recognition of Alevism as a separate religion has become possible only because the German and Austrian politico-legal systems allow religious groups to obtain an independent legal status if they fulfill certain criteria.[50] The directors of the Islamic Federation in Berlin complained that the German officials define religion based on their particular understanding of Christianity and that they had a hard time accepting their application because some of the characteristics of Christianity cannot be applied to Islam.[51] The German Constitution requires official religious communities have a church-like organization, which defines the boundaries of the religion, has the capacity to excommunicate members, and trains clergy.[52] In addition, because there is no pope or archbishop in Islam, dozens of groups applied to be considered as the representative of the Muslim community in a given state in Germany. [53] The federation had to seek the authority of experts and explain to the officials that no such power is available to any individual in Islam. Compared to Sunni Islam, Alevism has even fewer formal characteristics. Many of the Alevi sources are oral, and esoteric rituals and some of the basic beliefs show great variation across different communities. This window of opportunity presented to them by the German legal system forces Alevi leaders to face the challenging task of defining their religion in terms of mainly Christian-derived criteria of religion.

Belief or Religion: Defining Alevism in Turkey

When the possibility of the recognition of Alevism as a religion separate from Sunni Islam was introduced in Germany and Austria, it put the nature of Alevism into question in Turkey as well. Yet in a different social, political, and legal context the issue took on a different from. The issue quickly divided the Alevi organizations into difficult-to-cross lines. Tensions surrounding the controversy were so high that in several nationwide television programs where Alevi leaders were asked to debate an issue their discussions concerning whether Alevism is within or outside Islam devolved into fisticuffs.

Regardless of different positions in relation to the issue, the public expression of Alevism brought with it a strong desire to define Alevism. An Alevi who works at a *cemevi* library in Istanbul talked about his frustration with the lack of a clear definition of Alevism by saying: "We need a commonly accepted systematic definition of Alevism." When challenged with the claim that Alevism seems to have survived well for a long time without a rigid definition, he said:

We need to define things better in order to face Sunni Islam. The richness we have in Alevism is good but it also leads to chaos. Diversity of things in relation to Alevism confuses people. It is especially a major problem when we have to defend ourselves against the state or Sunni Muslims. The fights we are having among ourselves are hurting Alevism.

Similarly, Ali Rıza Gülçiçek, a politically active Alevi returnee from Germany and a contemporary MP in the parliament with the opposition secular Republican People's Party related during an interview that one of the most important needs of Alevis today is a meeting of a consultative committee to define Alevism. He said: "The problem is that we do not have a written tradition. We need a committee to gather and define Alevism once and for all of us."

Though the efforts of the Alevi Bektashi Union in Europe have been crucial to public recognition of Alevism as a separate belief system their line of argumentation did not translate well into the Turkish context. The majority of Alevis in Turkey define Alevism within Islam, even though they recognize that it is different from Sunni Islam.[54] Therefore, the Alevi Bektashi Union is not as popular in Turkey as it is in Europe.[55] The leader of the Okmeydanı Cemevi, affiliated with the European federation, said that Alevis in Turkey do not approve of its position that Alevism is outside Islam. The leadership in Okmeydanı believes this disapproval is shaped both by the fear that Alevis will be marginalized and by the new political situation under the government of the Justice and Development Party (Adalet ve Kalkınma Partisi, AKP), led by Islamists. He claimed that Alevis in Turkey are in a double bind.

> If we say we are Muslims, then the government officials will tell us to go to mosques and abolish our *cemevis*. But if we say we are not Muslims, then we will be subjected to discrimination and possibly persecution. Even though I believe that Alevism is independent from Islam, this view is not popular.

He added that for centuries Alevis have been subjected to persecutions on the basis that they are not Muslims, and he thinks it is ironic that most Alevis today claim that Alevism is the true Islam.

The best organized and the most popular Alevi organization in Turkey today is the Cem Foundation, established by İzettin Doğan, a law professor from a *dede* lineage. He argues that Alevism is not a belief independent from Islam; rather it is the Turkish interpretation of Islam and in that sense it is the "essence of Islam" (*İslamın özü*).[56] As opposed to the European Alevi Federation, the Cem Foundation demands that Alevis be recognized as a separate sect within Islam and asks for representation in the Department of Religious Affairs as well as services in proportion to their demographic numbers. Supporters of other organizations find the Cem Foundation conservative and too closely connected to the Turkish government.

An administrator interviewed at the Cem Foundation stated that the difference between Alevism and Sunni Islam lies only in their interpretation:

> We recite the *Fatiha* [the opening chapter of the Koran] in Turkish and they recite it in Arabic. We pray only on Thursday evenings, they pray five times a day. Sunnism is based on fear. Our understanding of God is based on love. We believe in peace and tolerance. We see everyone as our brothers. We accept Islam and its principles at its very foundation. We respect the family of the Prophet. We have extreme love towards them.

According to Ali Rıza U ğurlu, the head of the Alevi Islam Religious Services Department in Cem Foundation established in 2003, "people who say Alevism is not Islam are not aware of the nature of religion." During an interview he said that all religions are the same:

> What people think as separate religions is only different moments in the maturation of the same religion. People who do not know better think that every prophet invented a new religion. The duty of the prophet is just to declare not to invent. We have all been Muslims since creation. As Alevis we believe in the Koran but we do not see it as the words that constitute it. We try to understand the meaning of the Koran in its totality. Otherwise Islam is not only about the daughter getting one share of the inheritance and the son

acquiring two shares of it. These rules are for the ignorant ones. The mature ones understand it at another level.

With this view of religion, the Cem Foundation positions itself against the European Alevi Bektashi Union. The former accuses the latter of making the same argument with the anti-Alevi Sunnis that Alevis are not Muslims. The same administrator in the Cem Foundation headquarters in Istanbul defended their position against the European organizations in following words: "Organizations in Europe say that we are outside Islam. They argue that Alevism comes from Shamanism. Then we ask them, what is your religion, who is your prophet. All religions should have them. Then they cannot give us an answer."

To provide answers to these questions that they pose for themselves, members of Cem Foundation devoted its energies to organizing and codifying Alevism single-handedly. Ali Rıza Uğurlu stated that in order to guide Alevi religious leaders in the best possible way they started *dede* training programs. He claimed:

> For generations *dedes* practiced what they had seen from their fathers. The left-ist political organizations have not been respected *dedes*, so they felt alienated. Alevis merging together from different regions into the cities brought conflicts into Alevism. So we decided that Alevi religious leaders also had to organize and define Alevism.

To attain this goal the foundation established an organization of *dedes* and now have 3,000 *dedes* affiliated with them throughout the world. In this way, the Cem Foundation aims to institutionalize Alevism. The hope is that its extensive *dede* organization will enable Alevis to receive resources from the Department of Religious Affairs in proportion to the Alevi population in Turkey. Yet Turkish officials are not willing to allocate special resources to Alevis. Rather, they promote the view that Alevis are equal citizens because they are not willing to recognize their difference.

Transforming the Minority Paradigm in Turkey

After Turkey became a full candidate for the European Union in 1999 Alevi leaders in Europe worked closely with European political leaders to draw attention to discrimination against Alevis in Turkey. Even though Alevis in Turkey were reluctant to get help from the European Union, efforts of the Alevi lobby resulted in the European Union's *Regular Report on Turkey*, dated October 6, 2004, which pointed to difficulties Alevis face in Turkey and defined them as a "non-Sunni Muslim minority." The phrase generated much critique in the Turkish government and nationalist circles with accusations that European Union officials were undermining Turkey by aiming to divide and weaken the country. More interesting, Alevi leaders in Turkey resented being defined as a minority.

To understand the controversy over the term minority, some background is help-ful. The definition of minorities in Turkey was established in the 1923 Lausanne treaty, which was signed by the newly established Turkish Republic and the Allies after World War I. The treaty recognizes only Armenians, Greeks, and Jews as minorities. It grants these groups equal protection and freedom from discrimination, permits them to establish schools and provide education in their own language, allows them to settle family-related issues in accordance of their own customs, and guarantees the right to religious freedom. [57] These rights are reminiscent of the socio-legal order of the Ottoman Empire, which recognized the legal independence of the non-Muslim groups while giving them a subordinate position.[58]

The Lausanne treaty, which acknowledges only non-Muslim groups numbered in the thousands as minorities, left unrecognized much larger Muslim ethno-linguistic groups whose populations number in the millions, such as the Kurds, the Laz, and the Circessians, and heteredox Muslim groups such as the Alevi. Citizens who propagate the idea that any of these groups are minorities or aim to establish associations to promote their rights are imprisoned for challenging the national unity and harming the country by being divisive. In fact, the Article 216 (formerly 312) of the Turkish Penal Code states that it is a crime to "instigate a part of the people having different social class, race, religion, sect or region to hatred or hostility against another part of the people in a way dangerous for the public security," punishable up to three years; if committed by means of media, punishment is to be increased by one-half.

As Turkey became increasingly more committed to being admitted to the European Union, government officials took the necessary steps to fit the human rights criteria set at Copenhagen in 1993. [59] Between 2001 and 2003 the Turkish parliament adopted 34 constitutional amendments and a set of seven reform packages. [60] Although the parliament took steps to improve its human rights records in order to achieve integration with the European Union, the penal code remained unchanged, and the recognition of Alevis' rights as a Muslim religious minority caused concern in Sunni-dominated political circles. The latter accused Alevi organizations in Europe as serving the interests of the European powers in dividing the country, which put Alevis in Turkey in a vulnerable position.

Government officials, Sunni nationalists, and Alevi activists alike were disturbed by the use of the word "minority" to define the Alevi community. Many Sunni leaders, religious and non-religious, saw this as a dangerous move on the part of Alevis. Soon after the report was released both the president and the prime minister gave powerful messages indicating that they do not recognize Alevis as a minority. Former president Ahmet Necdet Sezer claimed that Alevis are "the elements of the majority," and Prime Minister Recep Tayyip Erdo ğan dismissively stated their claim to be a minority by saying "if Alevism means to love and follow Ali … then I am more Alevi [than the Alevis]." [61] Both statements overlooked Alevi demands to be recognized as different, insisting that they belonged to the majority and hence did not qualify for special rights.

Towards the end of 2007, Reha Çamuro ğlu, an Alevi MP in the AKP, organized an action plan where he demanded that *cemevis* should be recognized as prayer houses and receive the same privileges of being tax exempt and having free access to water and that Alevi *dedes* become state employees, just like imams. His proposal was similar to the one suggested by the Cem Foundation, which actually opened a lawsuit to have access to these rights. On January 11, 2008, MP Çamuro ğlu organized a breaking of the fast dinner during Muharram, which is commemorated by Alevis and not Sunnis in Turkey. Although PM Erdo ğan and many Sunni political leaders from the AKP participated in the event, most Alevis remained suspicious of these efforts and did not take part in the event. It is also significant that rather than participating in a *cem* gathering, which is unique to Alevis and considered unorthodox for Sunnis, AKP officials chose to participate in an event that is commemorated by Shi'a Muslims, a sect that this considered legitimate by Sunnis. Although this gathering was a major step on the government's part towards recognizing Alevis, many Alevis took it as another effort towards assimilating Alevis into Sunni or Shi'a Islam. Ironically, two days later, on January 13, 2008, the Cem Foundation's demands towards recognition of *cemevis* as prayer houses were rejected by the court.

Sunni activist Müfit Yüksel's statements in a right-wing daily in Turkey explained the Sunni nationalist position on the issue:

If the European Union recognizes Alevis as a minority, Alevism will inevitably be recognized as a religion outside Islam. Because in Turkey and in the Muslim world when you say minority, it means non-Muslims. And this society which associates minorities with non-Muslims cannot handle seeing Alevis as non-Muslims. This will lead to divisions and partitions in the country. These partitions may end up being bloody such as the fights among Sunnis and Shi'as in Pakistan.

Yüksel further argued that it is the Alevi organizations in Europe that take an active part in defining Alevis as a minority. In a veiled threat he warned Alevi organizations in Turkey against the dangerously divisive aims of the European Alevis.[62]

With regard to the view of Alevi organizations in Turkey, those not affiliated with the Alevi Bektashi Union were highly critical. In an interview reported in the same article, the chair of the Şahkulu Dergah Association, Mehmet Çamur, accused the Alevi Bektashi organization of attempting to "prioritize the sub-identities, divide the nation-state, and Balkanize Turkey." [63] Many Alevis in Istanbul expressed similar dislike for the term "minority" because they assumed if they accepted this position it would consign them a status lower than that of Sunni Turks. During a conversation with Alevis at the Yenibosna Cemevi in Istanbul, as he was waiting for a *cem* ceremony to begin, Adnan, a 35-year old man who owns an electric supplies store said:

Alevis are not a minority, even if they have been isolated and oppressed. When you say a minority it feels like a group that is totally isolated. Jews, Armenians, or Greeks are minorities. I am not saying this in a negative sense. But if we call Alevis a minority it will be unfair to them.

When asked why he thinks that Alevis are different from these minority groups he mentioned, Adnan answered:

I think being a minority is a bad thing in this country. We are not like Armenians or Jews. There is pressure on us but we also have some freedom. I am afraid that the term 'minority' in the European Union report can be used in a harmful manner. If they see us just like they way they see Armenians, it will be worse for us. You know, they may even see us in oppositional terms with nationalism.

Adnan thus recognizes that the Alevi religious position is already questionable in relation to the Sunni majority and hence what holds the Turkish nation together. He is afraid that if Alevis are recognized as a minority, their allegiance to the Turkish nation will be questioned. Other Alevi friends emphasized that they did not like the fact that the European Union report puts them and Kurds in the same category, minorities.[64] For example, a librarian at the Cem Foundation stated: "There is a difference between having been exposed to injustice and being a minority. [Unlike Kurds] Alevis do not want a separate land or a flag. All they want to do is to be able to practice their worship." In other words, for Sunnis and Alevis alike, the term "minority" and the right to be recognized as a separate group indicate not belonging to the nation and even being in contradictory terms with it.

When confronted with the reaction of their counterparts in Turkey, the European Alevis met with the European officials who wrote the report and asked them to leave the word "minority" out. Turgut Öker, the leader of the Alevi organization in Europe, argued that because people were so focused on the word, other important issues cited in the report, for example the need for Alevis to have prayer houses and elimination of compulsory religious education that promotes Sunnism, have been overlooked.

The European context of the late 1980s and 1990s that allowed Alevis to be recognized as a religious minority separate from Sunnis had profound influences on the way Alevis are conceptualized in Turkey. Yet when translated to the Turkish context the demand to be recognized as a minority meant something totally different and not necessarily something that Alevi activists considered beneficial to their political struggle in Turkey.

Conclusion

This essay has argued against the statement that Muslim residents in Europe have difficulty integrating into European society because of their alien beliefs and practices. Similarly, it has been shown that Alevis' demand for recognition is not a natural extension of their insurmountable difference. The interconnectedness of the Alevi movement in Europe and in Turkey demonstrates that the European context and sociopolitical forces shape the religious identities, beliefs, practices, and political agendas of its Muslim residents. The demand by both Sunni Muslims and Alevis to be defined and recognized as separate groups is shaped and motivated by the present political and legal context of the enlarged Europe. When new political positions and even theological reinterpretations of Islam develop in Europe they are transported into the Muslim-majority peripheries of Europe and lead to quite divergent consequences. Therefore, the interaction among member states of the Christian-majority European Union and its neighboring Muslim-majority countries is more complicated than many European observers acknowledge.

Although here the case of a marginal heterodox Muslim community has been analyzed, the findings show parallels with other mainstream Muslim communities as well and most likely with other religious minorities. Other researchers have demonstrated that the longer Muslims stay in Germany the more religious they feel. In other words, the religiosity of European Muslims, who have been declared not to fit European society, is actually produced in that geography and society. In a parallel vein, today if there is even a conversation about the possibility of a transnational European Muslim identity it is thanks to the sociohistorical conditions that brought different groups of Muslims to Europe and to the structuring of the European Union bureaucracy. For example, because the European Parliament financially supports immigrant organizations that are active across Europe, Muslim organizations find it enticing to organize around Europe and establish links despite the fact that they are divided along ethnic, national, class, and generation lines. [65] The European Union's legal structure allowing local Muslim groups to bring to Brussels grievances that have been unmet in their own countries encourages them to coordinate their needs and demands and this is crucial in the formation of a Euro-Islam. [66] It is because of the particular structure of the social, political, and legal contexts the European Union provides for Muslim communities that major cities in Europe, such as London, Paris, and Berlin, have become home to the most exciting intellectual and theological discussions among Muslim leaders representing different traditions. [67] If a "Euro-Islam" ever comes into being it will owe its existence not only to recent waves of migration from the Muslim-majority colonies of Europe to the core but also to the historical and structural opportunities and limitations that the European Union provides Muslims. What will be more interesting to observe in the coming decades is if Muslim politics in Europe transform the way in which religion and secularism are conceptualized and practiced in Muslim-majority contexts.

Acknowledgements

Earlier versions of this article were presented at the University of Illinois, Urbana-Champaign and the University of California, Irvine. A version of this article will appear in a book published by California University Press in 2009 titled *Transnational Transcendence* edited by Thomas Csordas. The author would like to thank the audiences in two settings: Marc David Baer, Keith McNeal, and Damani Patridge for their critical comments and Gökçe Yurdakul and Şebnem Köşer Akçapar for helping give the article its final shape. Marc David Baer participated in countless *cem* gatherings with the author, and Alev Korun introduced her to Alevi leaders in

Vienna. She is most grateful to Alevis in Berlin, Vienna, and Istanbul who welcomed her to their *cemevis*, generously shared their *lokma*, and patiently explained what it means to be an Alevi.

Notes

1. Norbert Geis, "Integration ist Ohne Alternative: Rede zur Auslander-Integration und Islamismus Bekampfung," [Integration is without an Alternative: Discussion over Foreigner Integration and Islamism Debate] CDU/CSU Fraktion in Deutschen Bundestag, 2004, www.cducsu.de; Angela Merkel, "Merkel verspricht Regierung der Taten," [Merkel Promises of Government Action] Spiegel Online, 2005, www.spiegel.de/politik/deutschland; see also Douglas Klusmeyer, "A Guiding Culture for Immigrants? Integration and Diversity in Germany," *Journal of Ethnic and Migration Studies*, Vol. 27, No. 3 (2001), pp. 519-32.
2. Joel S. Fetzer and J. Christoper Soper, *Muslims and the State in Britain, France, and Germany* (Cambridge: Cambridge University Press, 2005), p. 44; Anna Korteweg, "The Murder of Theo van Gogh: Gender, Religion and the Struggle over Immigrant Integration in the Netherlands," in Michal Bodemann and Gökçe Yurdakul (eds.), *Migration, Citizenship, Ethnos* (New York: Palgrave Macmillan, 2006), pp. 147-66.
3. John Bowen, *Why the French Don't Like the Headscarves: Islam, the State, and Public Space* (Princeton: Princeton University Press, 2007); Christian Joppke, "State Neutrality and Islamic Head-scarf Laws in France and Germany," *Theory and Society*, Vol. 36, No. 4 (2007), pp. 313-42.
4. Charles Taylor, *Multiculturalism: Examining the Politics of Recognition* (Princeton: Princeton University Press, 1994).
5. Esra Özyürek, "The Politics of Cultural Unification, Secularism, and the Place of Islam in the New Europe," *American Ethnologist*, Vol. 32, No. 4 (2005), pp. 509-12.
6. John Borneman, *Subversion of International Order: Studies in Political Anthropology of Culture* (Albany: State University of New York, 1997), p. 488.
7. Douglas R. Holmes, *Integral Europe: Fast-Capitalism, Multiculturalism, Neofascism* (Princeton: Princeton University Press, 2000), p. xi.
8. Borneman, *Subversion of International Order*.
9. John Borneman argues that "Europeanism, tied to values of progress, liberty, and freedom did not extend throughout the continent until the end of the eighteenth century." See Borneman, *Subversion of International Order*, p. 490.
10. Charter of European Identity, 1997. http://www.cise.it/eurit/Eurplace/diba/citta/cartaci.html.
11. Esra Özyürek, *Nostalgia for the Modern: State Secularism and Everyday Politics in Turkey* (Durham: Duke University Press, 2006).
12. Özyürek, *Nostalgia for the Modern*.
13. Levent Soysal, "Europe and the Topography of Migrant Youth Culture in Berlin," in Mabel Berezin and Martin Schain (eds.), *Europe without Borders: Remapping Territory, Citizenship, and Identity in a Transnational Age* (Baltimore: John Hopkins University Press, 2003), pp. 197-215. In his work on migrant youth culture in Berlin, Soysal similarly argues against conceptualization of Turkish youth as lost in an in-between state. He states "their cultural projects are not revivals of an essentialized Turkishness (or Islam) in response to alien formations of modernity. Rather (…) their projects contribute to the remapping, remaking of the new Europe, unsettling the conventional configurations and conceptions of belonging and otherness" (p. 220).
14. Elizabeth Povinelli, *The Cunning of Recognition: Indigenous Alterities and the Making of Australian Multiculturalism* (Durham: Duke University Press, 2002).
15. Taylor, *Multiculturalism*; Nancy Fraser, *Justice Interreptus: Critical Reflections on the "Post-Socialist" Condition* (New York: Routledge, 1997); Seyla Benhabib, *The Claims of Culture: Equality and Diversity in the Global Era* (Princeton: Princeton University Press, 2002).
16. For a discussion of different approaches to citizenship in Europe, see Rogers Brubaker, *Citizenship and Nationhood in France and Germany* (Cambridge, MA: Harvard University Press, 1992) and

Riva Kastoryano, *Negotiating Identities: State and Immigrants in France and Germany* (Princeton: Princeton University Press, 2002).

17. According to survey research conducted by Ali Aktaş among Alevis who visited the main Alevi shrine in Haci Bektash in the 1990s, 43 percent defined Alevism as a sect, 17 percent as a way of life, 16 percent as culture, and ten percent as religion (in Aykan Erdemir, "Incorporating Alevis: The Transformation of Governance and Faith-based Collective Action in Turkey," Ph.D. dissertation. Harvard University, 2004), p. 31.

18. Irene Melikoff, *Hacı Bektaş: Efsaneden Gerçeğe* [Hacı Bektaş: From Myth to Reality] (Istanbul: Cumhuriyet Kitapları, [1998] 2004). However, some scholars such as Gunter Seufert identify Alevis as the Shi'a community in Turkey; see Gunter Seufert, "Between Religion and Ethnicity: A Kurdish-Alevi Tribe in Globalizing Istanbul," in A. Öncü and P. Weyland (eds.), *Space, Culture, and Power* (London: Zed Books, 1997), pp. 157-76.

19. Eric Zürcher, *Turkey: A Modern History* (London: I.B. Tauris, 1998).

20. Selim Deringil, " 'There is No Compulsion in Religion': On Conversion and Apostasy in the Late Ottoman Empire, 1839-1856," *Comparative Studies in Society and History* , Vol. 42, No. 2 (2000), pp. 542-75.

21. Herald Schüller, *Türkiye'de Sosyal Demokrasi: Particilik, Hemşerilik, Alevilik* [Social Democracy in Turkey: Partisanship, Co-locality, Alevism] (Istanbul: İletişim, 1999); Hülya Küçük, *The Role of Bektaşis in Turkey's National Struggle* (Leiden: Brill, 2002).

22. Joost Jongerden, "Violation of Human Rights and the Alevis in Turkey," in Paul J. White and Joost Jongerden (eds.), *Turkey's Alevi Enigma: A Comprehensive Overview* (Leiden: Brill, 2003), pp. 71-89.

23. For an interesting comparison of the fate of the syncretistic Muslim-Jewish group called Dönme and the Alevis after the foundation of the Turkish Republic see Marc Baer, "The Double Bind of Race and Religion: The Conversion of the Dönme to Secular Turkish Nationalism," *Comparative Studies in Society and HiSociety and History* , Vol. 46, No. 4 (2004), pp. 682–708, who argues that because Dönme were ostensibly Muslim, they were left undisturbed under the Islamic Ottoman Empire but suffered discrimination under the nationalist Turkish Republic because they were considered as racially non-Turkish. The heterodox Alevis, however, were at times persecuted by religious cleansing movements under the Ottomans but were embraced by the Turkish Republic since they were considered racially Turkish.

24. The religiously inclined Welfare Party won major electoral victories in the 1994 local elections and became the first party in the 1995 general elections, receiving 21 percent of the votes, but it had to enter into a coalition with the center-right True Path Party. The party resigned following the 1997 recommendations of the Turkish army to the government. In 1998 the Welfare Party was disbanded on the basis of having violated the secularist principle of the Turkish Republic and was replaced by the Virtue Party. This party was then replaced by the Justice and Development Party, which adopted a pro-capitalist and pro-Western policy and came to power in the 2002 elections, receiving 34 percent of the votes.

25. http://www.diyanet.gov.tr/turkish/tanitimistatistik.asp.

26. David Shankland, *The Alevis in Turkey: The Emergence of a Secular Islamic Tradition* (London: Routledge Curzon, 2003), p. 13.

27. For different categorizations of the contemporary Alevi movement see Tahire Erman and Emrah Goker, "Alevi Politics in Contemporary Turkey," *Middle Eastern Studies*, Vol. 36, No. 4 (2000), pp. 99-118; Faruk Bilici, "The Function of Alevi-Bektashi Theology in Modern Turkey," in T. Olsson, E. Ozdalga and C. Raudvere (eds.), *Alevi Identity: Cultural, Religious, and Social Perspectives*, (Istanbul: Swedish Research Institute, 1998), pp. 51-62; and Reha Çamuroğlu, *Değişen Koşullarda Alevilik* [Alevism in Changing Conditions] (Istanbul: Ant Yayınları, 1992).

28. Şehriban Şahin, "The Alevi Movement: Transformation from Secret Oral to Public Written Culture in National and Transnational Spaces," Ph.D. dissertation, New School for Social Research, 2001.

29. Shankland, *The Alevis in Turkey*.

30. Helga Rittersberger-Tiliç, "Development and Reformulation of a Returnee Identity as Alevi," in T. Olsson, E. Ozdalga and C. Raudvere (eds.), *Alevi Identity: Cultural, Religious, and Social Perspectives* (Istanbul: Swedish Research Institute, 1998), pp. 69-87.

31. Some attribute the Alevi revival to the loss of popularity of the socialist ideals to which many Alevis subscribed; see Herald Schüller, *Türkiye'de Sosyal Demokrasi: Particilik, Hem şerilik, Alevilik* [Social Democracy in Turkey: Partisanship, Co-locality, and Alevism] (Istanbul: İletişim, 1999); and Karin Vorhoff, "The Past in the Future: Discourses on the Alevis in Contemporary Turkey," in Paul J. White and Joost Jongerden (eds.), *Turkey's Alevi Enigma: A Comprehensive Overview,* pp. 94-109. Erdermir suggests that it is attributed to neoliberalism, which promoted the shift of power to nongovernmental organizations that encouraged the Alevi organization in Turkey; see Aykan Erdemir, "Incorporating Alevis: The Transformation of Governance and Faith-based Collective Action in Turkey," Ph.D. dissertation, Harvard University, 2004. When one asks Alevis in Turkey and in Europe about the Alevi revival, they immediately mention the 1993 massacre in Sivas of 37 Alevi artists who were staying at a hotel to participate in a conference on Alevism and were murdered by Sunni fanatics. Many Alevis interviewed claimed that when this event happened they realized that they needed to organize and have their voices heard. To this day, at the entrance of many *cemevis* one can see pictures of the victims of the massacre.

32. Leyla Neyzi, "Zazaname: The Alevi Renaissance, Media, and Music in the Nineties," in Paul J. White and Joost Jongerden (eds.), *Turkey's Alevi Enigma: A Comprehensive Overview* pp. 112-24; Isabella Rigoni, "Alevis in Europe: A Narrow Path Towards Visibility," in Paul J. White and Joost Jongerden (eds.), *Turkey's Alevi Enigma: A Comprehensive Overview* , pp. 159-73.

33. Ayse Şimşek Çağlar, "German Turks in Berlin: Migration and Their Quest for Social Mobility," Ph.D. dissertation, McGill University, 1994; Ruth Mandel, "'Fortress Europe' and the Foreigners Within: Germany's Turks," in Victoria A. Goddard, Josep R. Llobera and Cris Shore (eds.)*The Anthropology of Europe: Identity and Boundaries in Conflict* (Oxford: Berg Publishers, 1994), pp. 113-24.

34. Eva Østergaard-Nielsen, *Transnational Politics: Turks and Kurds in Germany* (London: Routledge, 2003).

35. Rittersberger-Tiliç, "Development and Reformulation of a Returnee Identity as Alevi."

36. Şehriban Şahin, "The Rise of Alevism as a Public Religion," *Current Sociology*, Vol. 53, No. 3 (2005), pp. 465-85.

37. See Şahin, "The Rise of Alevism as a Public Religion." There have been attempts among Turkish citizens to organize collectively. Yet, the political, ethnic, and religious cleavages among have made this impossible. See Østergaard-Nielsen, *Transnational Politics*.

38. Ayhan Kaya, "Multicultural Clientelism and Alevi Resurgence in the Turkish Diaspora: Berlin Alevis," *New Perspectives on Turkey*, Vol. 18 (Spring 1998), pp. 23-49.

39. Ruth Mandel, "Ethnicity and Identity among Migrant Guestworkers in West Berlin," in N. Gonzales and C. McCommon (eds.), *Conflict, Migration, and Expression of Ethnicity* (Boulder, CO: Westview Press, 1989), pp. 60-74.

40. Many in Turkey also emphasized similar symbolism between Alevism according to its real sources and Christianity. The topic came up when Alevis assumed that the author's American husband is a Christian and wanted to show him there is not much difference between their beliefs and—what they supposed to be—his beliefs.

41. Kira Kosnick, "Speaking in One's Voice: Representational Strategies of Alevi Turkish Migrants on Open-access Television in Berlin," *Journal of Ethnic and Migration Studies* Vol. 30, No. 5 (2004), pp. 979-94.

42. The Alevi Manifesto can be found in Riza Zelyut, *Öz Kaynaklarina Göre Alevilik* (Istanbul: Anadolu Kültür Yayınları, 1990).

43. Rittersberger-Tılıç, "Development and Reformulation of a Returnee Identity as Alevi."

44. This development followed the fact that the Islamic Federation in Berlin was granted the right to teach Islam in classes in 2000; see Havva Engin, "Avrupa'da Hayatın ve   İnancın Diyaloğu İçin: Alevi-Islam Dersi" [Alevi-Islam Classes: For the Dialogue of Life and Belief in Europe] in Ismail Engin and Havva Engin (eds.), *Alevilik* (Istanbul: Kitap Yayinevi, 2004), pp. 499-504.

45. Ibid.
46. Gerdien Jonker, "What is Other about Other Religions? The Islamic Communities in Berlin between Integration and Segregation," *Cultural Dynamics*, Vol. 12, No. 3 (2000), pp. 311-29.
47. Fetzer and Soper, *Muslims and the State in Britain, France, and Germany*, p. 108
48. Ibid. German law requires religious groups to formally submit an application in their region and to show that they have existed for at least 30 years, that the members of the group constitute at least 1/1000th of the total population in that region, and that the group respects the law.
49. In interviews, Sunni Muslim activists in Austria stated that having this category works to their benefit, especially when there is a need to defend needs and rights of Muslims. Practicing Muslims in Austria and Germany agree that today it is much easier to live as a Muslim in Austria than in Germany.
50. It is likely that one of the reasons why the Alevi movement and organization is not strong in France, despite the fact that France is second to Germany for the number of Turkish-origin residents, is the lack of such a law.
51. Gökçe Yurdakul, "Muslim Political Organization of Turks in Germany," *Council of European Studies Newsletter*, Vol. 35, Nos. 1 & 2 (2005), p. 10.
52. Engin, "Avrupa'da Hayatın ve Inancın Diyalogu   İçin" [For the Dialogue of Life and Belief in Europe]; Jonker, "What is Other about Other Religions."
53. Fetzer and Soper, *Muslims and the State in Britain, France, and Germany*.
54. Cihan Tuğal, "Islamcılığın Dini Co ğunluk Alanındaki Krizi: Alevi AçmazııHakkında Bazı Açılımlar," [The Crisis of Islamism in the Field of Religious Pluralism: Some Thoughts on the Alevi Paradox] in Tanıl Bora and Murat Gültekingil (eds.), *Modern Türkiye'de Siyasi Düşünce: Islamcılık* [*Political Thought in Modern Turkey: Islamism*], Vol. 6, (Istanbul: Birikim Yayınları, 2004), pp. 493-502.
55. For a discussion of different Alevi organizations see Çamuro   ğlu, *Değişen Koşullarda Alevilik* [*Alevism in Changing Conditions*]; Erman and Göker, "Alevi Politics in Contemporary Turkey;" and Şahin, "The Alevi Movement."
56. The Cem Association website states that Sunni Islam is the Arab interpretation of Islam, and Shi'a Islam is the Persian interpretation. www.cemvakfi.org.
57. However, as many international human rights and international human rights watch reports indicate, Turkish governments have been inconsistent and often unwilling to provide these rights granted to non-Muslim minorities. See Dilek Kurban, "Confronting Equality: The Need for Constitutional Protection of Minorities on Turkey's Path to the European Union," *Columbia Human Rights Law Review*, Vol. 35, No. 1 (2003), pp. 151-214.
58. For a critical discussion of the Ottoman administration of religious groups, also called the "millet system," see Bruce Masters, *Christians and Jews in the Ottoman Arab World: The Roots of Sectarianism* (Cambridge: Cambridge University Press, 2001).
59. Meltem Müftüler-Baç, "Turkey's Political Reforms and the Impact of the European Union," *South European Society and Politics*, Vol. 10, No. 1 (2005), pp. 17-31.
60. Many of these changes were of major importance, such as the abolishment of the death penalty and other seemingly small but symbolically substantial changes, such as the granting of rights for broadcasting and education in ethnic languages. According to some observers, the members of the Turkish parliament have been more open to granting these rights since the decade-long war between Kurdish guerillas and the Turkish army seemed to have come to a conclusion with the victory of the latter and the imprisonment of Abdullah Öcalan, leader of the Kurdish guerilla movement. However, though the implementation of the constitutional amendments granting these rights has been hesitant, the restrictions still apply and citizens cannot often practice these rights freely.
61. *Radikal*, October 9, 2004.
62. *Akşam*, May 24, 2005.
63. Ibid.
64. Here it is important to note that many Kurdish activists also were not happy about the Kurds being defined as a minority in the report. Leaders of the Democratic People's Party (DEHAP), representing

the Kurdish voice, also argued that Kurds are one of the foundational elements of the country and are of majority. *Radikal*, October 14, 2004.

65. Sami Zubaida, "Islam in Europe," *Critical Quarterly*, Vol. 45, No. 1, 2 (2003), pp. 88-98.

66. Melissa Anne Parker, "The Europeanization of Islam: The Role of the Multi-Level Structure of the EU," paper presented at the Ninth Biennial International Conference of the European Union Studies Association, Austin, TX, March 31-April 2, 2005.

67. Adam Lebor, *A Heart Turned East* (London: Little Brown and Company, 1997); Peter Mandaville, *Transnational Muslim Politics: Reimagining Umma* (London: Routledge, 2001).

Organizing for Access? The Political Mobilization of Turks in Amsterdam

LAURE MICHON & FLORIS VERMEULEN

Institute for Migration and Ethnic Studies, Department of Political Science, University of Amsterdam, Amsterdam, The Netherlands

ABSTRACT   *This essay addresses the issue of the relationship between political and organizational mobilization of Turkish immigrants in Amsterdam. Data on Turkish councilors in Amsterdam over time and on the boards of local Turkish organizations in Amsterdam between 1970 and 2002 reveals that a majority of the municipal councilors of Turkish origin in Amsterdam have been on the board of a Turkish organization. However, it seems that the political influence of the Turkish organizations is rather limited in the process of recruitment of the local political elite when compared to the role of Dutch political parties. Interviews with Turkish councilors in Amsterdam show that once elected, the councilors seem to develop more nuanced ties with the Turkish community.*

Introduction

The granting of municipal voting rights to resident foreigners in 1985 has been of great importance for the political mobilization of Turks [1] in the Netherlands. Turks, as no other immigrant group before them, have used the opportunity to participate in the local political system. Compared to other immigrant groups in the Netherlands, Turks have displayed the greatest turnout rate in almost every local election since 1985, and the number of politicians of Turkish origin in Dutch municipalities is higher than for any other immigrant group. This essay seeks to explore the role of Turkish organizations in political participation and to what extent they have served as an instrument for Turkish immigrants to gain access to the local political system. In other words, how are political and organizational mobilizations potentially linked to each other?

It is worthwhile to address this matter considering the common assumption that many local politicians of foreign origin are recruited via organizations. More specifically, it is often believed that politicians of foreign origin benefit both from the organizational experience they gain within migrant organizations and from the (potential) mobilization of the migrant organization constituency during elections. Although this connection is logical—particularly given the fact that involvement in organizations and board membership experience is highly valued in the Dutch public and political arenas—there has been little evidence so far to confirm the correlation between political activities and involvement in migrant organizations. This essay endeavors to offer new insight into the matter by analyzing data on Turkish councilors since the mid-1980s in the particular case of Amsterdam, as well as information concerning the boards of local Turkish organizations in Amsterdam between 1970 and 2002. The overall role organizations play in the local political system goes beyond the scope of this article; the objective here is to examine the political recruitment of local politicians of foreign origin. Moreover, the essay focuses on one particular angle of the larger recruitment picture, namely the organizational experience of councilors of Turkish origin and their ties with Turkish organizations. These matters have rarely been dealt with by the literature on (local) elected politicians in Dutch municipalities in general and even less in studies on participation of foreigners in local politics.

The political mobilization of Turks in the Netherlands is especially a salient issue at the local level for two reasons.[2] First, as mentioned above, non-nationals have the right to vote and to stand in an election at the local level. This right was granted in 1985 to all non-nationals legally residing in the Netherlands for at least five years. One of the main reasons the Dutch political elite of the early 1980s sought to enfranchise foreigners was to promote integration, particularly among non-Western immigrants.[3] The contention was that once immigrants had the right to vote they would show greater interest in the national political system, thus encouraging their integration into Dutch society.[4]

The second reason that the political mobilization of Turkish immigrants is primarily salient at the local level is because their population is concentrated within a few large Dutch cities. The presence of Turks in the Netherlands on the whole is just two percent; across only eight cities (Rotterdam, The Hague, Zaanstad, Enschede, Amsterdam, Utrecht, Arnhem, and Dordrecht), however, that statistic rises to between five and eight percent.[5] Although Turks do not constitute a large group of potential voters at the national level they do so at the local level. With a view to incorporating the Turkish community into the local political system, political parties have therefore been keener on recruiting Turkish politicians at the local level. Differences between parties in the recruitment of Turkish politicians will be examined below.

Given that the issue of the mobilization of Turks is essentially a local matter, a focus on Amsterdam was chosen, mainly for reasons related to the data available for this city. Extensive data on the political participation of Turks and on Turkish organizations in the capital city of the Netherlands can be relied on. Moreover, Amsterdam has city district councils, and thus a high number of politicians elected in local councils. As the links between politicians of Turkish descent and Turkish organizations are of interest in this essay, the case of Amsterdam is particularly suited for this study.

As stated above, this article seeks to examine whether Turkish organizations have functioned as a "breeding ground" for local Turkish politicians and to what extent these organizations may have offered them access to Amsterdam's local political system. The essay begins with a brief overview of the literature on political recruitment; this will be followed by a more specific look at how immigrant politicians are recruited by parties. Some statistics on the political participation of Turks in Amsterdam (turnout rates, party choice, and elected Turkish politicians) will be presented. Then the main features of the Turkish organizational field in Amsterdam will be addressed, followed by a discussion of the links between these organizations and local Turkish politicians. Finally, the analysis will conclude with data from interviews detailing what local Turkish politicians themselves have to say about their ties with organizations.

Political Recruitment

The literature on political recruitment, broadly speaking, has two main fields of interest: the profiles of recruited politicians and their processes of recruitment. While the latter focuses on organizational processes and institutional constraints, the former is more concerned with issues of background, socialization, and "political cultures."[6] Much of the existing literature deals with legislative recruitment that takes place on the national level, though a number of studies offer highly relevant perspectives for the present purposes.

Studies concerned with the individual characteristics of political elites (commonly, national elites) all point to a form of homogeneity that seems to exist among political recruits. That is, elected politicians are highly educated males who rarely come from a modest social background in terms of social class and education.[7] One might wonder to what extent immigrant politicians, or other minority politicians (noticeably women), conform to the homogeneity of elites. To the authors' knowledge, only Rupp and his colleagues[8] have explored this issue for the Netherlands. Their study on the background of all municipal councilors elected between 1980 and 1998 in Amsterdam, Rotterdam, Utrecht, and The Hague revealed that foreign and native councilors have equivalent levels of education.

According to Norris,[9] the rules and procedures of political recruitment are both facilitated and constrained by the legal, the electoral, and the party systems. The recruitment process itself has an effect on the "supply" of prospective candidates, as the demands of so-called gatekeepers (voters, party members, financial supporters, and political leaders) are taken into consideration. The "pool of eligibles" and "the costs and benefits of becoming a candidate in different countries" are determined by electoral laws, the number of seats available, and the frequency of elections. More incidental issues such as the payback of political functions (whether in terms of symbolic or material benefits) and the number of parties in competition moreover determine who gets access to politics and how.

In the Netherlands, non-nationals have full voting rights at the local level. [10] The local electoral system is based on proportional representation. Electoral lists compete for votes and, furthermore, preferential voting is possible. There is still a debate among scholars on the exact effect electoral systems have on party systems and on representation, but it appears that relying on proportionality ensures more accurate representation in terms of gender and social background.[11]

Focusing in particular on women and ethnic minorities, Leijenaar and her colleagues[12] took a detailed look at the recruitment processes of candidates in the Netherlands' 1998 municipal elections. The study showed that there is a bias for the traditional recruitment channels favoring prospective candidates who step forward on their own initiative. Women and ethnic minorities appear to be less likely to run for candidacy on their own volition than men and native party members. [13] Another factor affecting the low proportion of both female and foreign political candidates is the small share of women and ethnic minorities who are members of party selection committees,[14] which play a crucial role in the recruitment process.

Dutch political parties have experimented with new recruitment methods such as scouting, organizational networking (most noticeably, of immigrant associations), and announcing specific calls for potential candidates through targeted media campaigns.[15] Leijenaar and her colleagues explain that the extent to which minorities have a chance at candidacy is influenced by how much importance is given to the overall composition of the electoral list (taking into account people's expertise, gender, geographical representation, age, and their status as incumbent versus newcomer). Moreover, it appears that different parties emphasize distinct criteria. [16] Ethnic diversity is deemed essential by left-wing parties from more urban areas but less important by conservative and liberal parties.[17]

Political Participation of Turks in Amsterdam

Turnout

Since 1994,[18] the Institute for Migration and Ethnic Studies (IMES) at the University of Amsterdam has carried out a number of consistently formatted surveys [19] on migrants' use of local voting rights in Amsterdam and several other Dutch cities. Table 1 is a product of this research, showing the turnout of Turkish voters in Amsterdam from 1994 until 2006.

These results show that there have been significant differences in turnout from one election to another. Most striking is the decreased turnout between 1994 and 2002. Of all ethnic groups Turks show the most significantly lowered turnout for that period,[20] as the rate of their participation fell by more than half within these eight years. In 1994, their level of turnout was above the overall migrant turnout, while in 2002 it was far below this level. In 2006, the turnout of Turkish voters increased again, coming up to par with the overall turnout rate.

Turkish immigrants in Amsterdam have always participated in elections more than immigrants of other national origins (the main groups are Moroccan, Surinamese, and Antillean). A similar pattern can be observed in other Dutch cities. Building on Putnam's work, [21] Fennema and Tillie[22] argue that this has to do with

Table 1. Migrant Voter Turnout in Amsterdam, 1994-2006, in Percentages

Voter Turnout	1994	1998	2002	2006
Turks	67%	39%	30%	51%
Overall Migrants	56.8%	45.7%	47.8%	50.8%

Sources: Jean Tillie, *De Etnische Stem, Opkomst en Stemgedrag van Migranten tijdens Gemeenteraadsverkiezingen, 1986-1998* [*The Ethnic Vote, Turnout and Party Choice of Migrants at Municipal Elections, 1986-1998*] (Utrecht: Forum, 2000); Laure Michon and Jean Tillie, *Amsterdamse Polyfonie, Opkomst en Stemgedrag van Allochtone Amsterdammers bij de Gemeenteraads en Deelraadsverkiezingen van 6 Maart 2002* [Polyphony in Amsterdam, Turnout and Party Choice of Immigrants in Amsterdam at the Municipal and District Elections of March 6th, 2002] (Amsterdam: IMES, 2003); Anja van Heelsum, and Jean Tillie, *Opkomst en Partijvoorkeur van Migranten bij de Gemeenteraadsverkiezingen van 7 Maart 2006* [*Turnout and Party Choice of Migrants at the Municipal Elections of March 7th, 2006*] (Amsterdam: IMES, 2006).

the level of social and political trust of the Turkish community, which in turn depends on the mix of vertical (i.e. hierarchical) and horizontal (i.e. reciprocal) social relations within that community. Their hypothesis is that the more organizations an ethnic group has and the more these organizations tend to function as a civic network[23] the more likely the individuals within the group will demonstrate trust in political institutions and participate in elections. In the same vein as Putnam, Fennema and Tillie[24] speak of social capital when there is a large share of trust within a group. They find that once leaders of the ethnic group are integrated within the local political system, social trust gives way to political trust, and that "the more an ethnic group is engaged in the own community's affairs, the more it participates in local politics."[25]

Nevertheless, degree of civic involvement does not elucidate why turnout levels of Turks were lower in 2002 than in 1994 and 2006. The lessened turnout among all Amsterdam's ethnic groups in 2002 was explained by Michon and Tillie in reference to the municipality's change in policy. [26] Their line of reasoning was that diminished support for organizations established for and/or by migrants has had a negative effect on the structure of the migrant organizational field, leading to a decline in trust, civic involvement, and, as a result, political participation. In 2006, a year in which the municipality's policy had not changed, however, the electoral turnout of migrants increased. Van Heelsum[27] has reasoned that migrants in general were probably reacting to the restrictive policies of the Dutch government and therefore participated at high rates. These explanations hold on to the argument that a correlation between civic involvement and political participation exists, though they are complemented by arguments linked to the specific context of a particular election. Still, it is not known why some Turks or, for that matter, other migrants, have stayed home on election day. At this stage, insufficient research on abstention among migrants in general prevents us from more than mere speculation on changes in turnout from one election to the next.[28]

Party Choice

Table 2 shows how Turks favored Amsterdam's five biggest parties in the elections of 1994, 1998, 2002, and 2006. A notable constant in their selections has been the preference for left-wing parties, in particular for the Labour Party (PvdA). The only party that managed to receive more votes than the PvdA was the (conservative) Christian Democratic Appeal (CDA) in 1994.

If Turkish voters' party choices are examined in greater detail, it appears that gender, age, and migration generation do not introduce significant changes in voting patterns.[29] Level of education appears to have a significant impact on party choices by Turkish voters. Both in 2002 and 2006 highly educated voters of Turkish origin voted less for the PvdA than they did for the green party GroenLinks (GL) and the Socialist Party (SP).[30] Highly educated Turks thus tended to spread their votes across left-wing parties more than less educated Turks did.

The strong preference for the PvdA shown in 2006 may be explained by recollecting the greater political context of the Netherlands in recent years. After September 11, new parties with an anti-Islamic discourse were successful in elections, and the right-wing national governments that were in charge between 2002 and 2007 subsequently issued restrictive immigration and integration policies.[31] It seems as though migrant voters decided to vote for parties that opposed the right-wing government and its anti-Islamic spin-off parties and instead favored the left-wing party that was most likely to win the elections, namely the PvdA.

Ideological (and/or politically strategic) choices thus appear to be most important when it comes to explaining voting patterns among migrant voters. This is confirmed by data on party preferences [32] and votes of respondents in previous years,[33] which appear to stay stable over time and reflect ideologically consistent choices.[34] However, when candidate choice of Turkish voters is examined, it can be seen that ethnicity plays a role as well.

The position migrants get on an electoral list is determined, first and foremost, by the political party. However, because the Dutch electoral system allows for

Table 2.   Party Choices of Voters of Turkish Origin in Amsterdam's Municipal Elections, 1994-2006, in Percentages

Year	SP	GL	PvdA	D66	CDA	VVD	Other parties
1994	*	12%	35%	13%	37%	2%	1%
1998	1%	18%	47%	7%	18%	1%	0%
2002	2%	25%	44%	7%	2%	19%	3%
2006	5%	4%	87%	1%	1%	1%	1%

Sources: Tillie (2000); Michon and Tillie (2003); van Heelsum and Tillie (2006).
Party abbreviations: GL: Green Left; PvdA: Labour Party; D66: Democrats 66 (social-liberal); CDA: Christian Democratic Appeal; VVD: People's Party for Freedom and Democracy (right-wing liberal); SP: Socialist Party (radical socialist).
* No data available.

preferential voting these decisions can be overturned on election day. This was illustrated in the 2002 election of a municipal councilor of Turkish origin for the PvdA. Although his party had placed him at a seemingly ineligible position on the list he was elected after receiving numerous preference votes. It appears that migrants tend to take advantage of preferential voting more often than Dutch nationals do.[35] Moreover, it is not uncommon for migrants to vote for a candidate of their own background. Previous research [36] has labeled this pattern "ethnic voting," something that may lead to the election of seemingly ineligible candidates (such as those low on the electoral list) if enough preferential votes are issued. A majority of Turks voters have voted for a candidate of the same origin in 1998 (67 percent), 2002 (75 percent), and 2006 (50 percent), though the extent to which this occurred changed over time.[37]

Voting patterns may thus well be explained by combining lines of argument. Turkish voters tend to cast votes for the party they deem best represents their "cause": in this case, the left-wing, progressive parties. Ideological beliefs appear to inform party choices, while ethnicity influences candidate choices.

Turkish Elected Politicians

In the Netherlands, Turks form an important group among municipal councilors of foreign origin.[38] After the elections of 2006, more than half of the municipal coun-cilors of foreign origin were Turks (157 out of a total of 302). [39] In Amsterdam as well many politicians of foreign origin are Turkish.

For the present research, as many councilors of Turkish origin elected in Amsterdam as possible were identified, mainly on the basis of names. [40] Thirteen councilors of Turkish origin who held office in the municipal council since 1990 were identified, with a maximum of four councillors simultaneously holding a seat (on a total of 45 seats in the city council of Amsterdam). At the city district level, there is comprehensive data for the 2002 and 2006 elections.

There are a few Turkish politicians who were elected first in a city district council and subsequently in the municipal council. It is uncommon for local politicians to reach for the national level, but two municipal councilors of Turkish origin (both women) have held a seat in the national parliament.

As Table 3 shows, most Turkish councilors in Amsterdam were elected from left-wing parties (11 out of 13), and a large majority were men. Four councilors stayed in office for less than the four years of their mandate, while one stayed in office for two mandates (a total of eight years).

The data concerning the city district councils is less complete, as there is only comprehensive information on the outcomes of the 2002 and 2006 elections. Because for the prior years, systematically collected data is lacking, the researchers have also relied on information gathered in 1990 for a study on migrant municipal councilors and city district councilors. [41] In total, 48 district councilors were included in the study. It appears that most of the Turkish district councilors were

Table 3. Turkish Municipal Councilors in Amsterdam since 1990

Mandate	Gender	Party	Year in	Year out	Time in office
1990-94	F	GL	1990	1993	3 years
	M	GL	1994	1994	1.5 months
1994-98	M	GL	1994	1996	2 years
	M	PvdA	1994	*	(see below)
	M	D66	1997	∧	(see below)
1998-2002	M	PvdA	(1994)	*2002	8 years
	M	D66	(1997)	∧2002	5 years
	F	GL	1998	~	(see below)
	M	CDA	1998	2002	4 years
2002-06	F	GL	(1998)	~2004	6 years
	M	D66	2002	2006	4 years
	M	PvdA	2002	2006	4 years
	M	VVD	2002	2006	4 years
2006-present	F	SP	2006	2006	5 months
	F	PvdA	2006	still in office	?
	M	PvdA	2006	still in office	?

How to read the signs: The male councilor elected for the PvdA in 1994 (indicated with *) was reelected in 1998 and stayed in the council until 2002.
The male councilor who entered the municipal council for the D66 in 1997 (indicated with ∧) was reelected in 1998 and stayed in the council until 2002.
The female councilor elected for the GL in 1998 (indicated with ~) was reelected in 2002 and stayed in the council until 2004.

elected for left-wing parties (39 out of a total of 48) and that, when compared to their representation in the Turkish population's otherwise proportionate male-female ratio, women are largely underrepresented within this elected elite (12 out of a total of 48). After the elections of 2006, the number of Turkish councilors increased slightly (16 elected in 2002, 21 in 2006), thus representing 6.5 percent of the total number of district councilors in Amsterdam. It is interesting to recall here that five percent of Amsterdam's population is of Turkish origin: with this in mind, the group does not suffer under-representation in local politics.

Left-wing parties thus seem the most conducive to electing Turkish candidates. The converse could just as well prove true: that Turkish people with political ambitions choose left-wing parties. The role of political parties is crucial in deciding who gets elected, most notably as electoral lists are compiled. So far, there have been no successful party initiatives by ethnic, migrant, or religious groups. However, voters still do play an important role in determining who is elected, as discussed above.

Turkish Organizations in Amsterdam

The overview of the mobilization of Turks in Amsterdam is continued with a brief presentation of the features of their organizational field in the city. The Turkish organizing process in Amsterdam is deeply enmeshed in the prior status of Turkish immigrants as guestworkers in the Netherlands. The earliest Turkish organizations were mainly involved in protecting the interests of Turkish workers and promoting activities suitable for this male-dominant immigrant group, such as social-cultural events, religious associations, and sporting facilities. The initial phase of the Turkish organizing process in Amsterdam was largely shaped by the unstable political situation in Turkey. Its left–right polarization was transplanted to Western Europe and proved highly influential in determining the establishment of the first Turkish organizations and their ensuing activities. Developments in Turkey have remained important for Turkish groups abroad throughout their organizing processes. One of the most prominent features of the Turkish organizing process in Amsterdam was the strength of Turkey's transnational political influence, which resulted in a highly polarized Turkish organizational population. [42] The major oppositions during the period of 1965 to 2000 were the radical left versus the radical right, Turkish versus Kurdish, state Islamic organizations versus oppositional Islamic movements, and religious groups versus secular groups.

Direct influences from the country of origin notwithstanding, the Turkish organizing process in Amsterdam is predominantly a religious affair. The first Turkish Islamic organizations in Amsterdam were established in the 1970s, though after 1980 Turkish organizers became actively engaged in establishing an entire Islamic organizational structure in the city. This tendency is typical across Europe for the Turkish immigrant guestworker organizing process. The size of the Turkish community in Amsterdam flourished thanks to the process of family reunification, and the population's stay became increasingly more established as the second generation emerged. These elements produced a new, increasingly religious demand among Turkish immigrants and, as a result, a high number of Turkish Islamic organizations were established in Amsterdam after 1980. [43] Other groups that came to color the city panorama were organizations established for interests in left-wing politics, non-political social-cultural activities, arts and culture, and sports (mainly soccer clubs). As of 2008, there were an estimated 200 local Turkish organizations in Amsterdam, which is about the same number that existed five years earlier, yet somewhat fewer than in the 1990s, when the most Turkish organizations were founded in Amsterdam. [44]

Most studies on immigrant organizations in the Netherlands ascribe a low political relevance to Turkish organizations and to immigrant organizations in general. [45] Various explanations are given for the lack of political influence that Turkish organizations have in Europe overall. One reason may be the decentralized structure that is characteristic of Turkish Islamic immigrant organizations, a factor providing ample opportunity for a small faction of the population to undermine a broad-based immigrant collective action. [46] Preoccupation with homeland politics is another cited cause, as are other associational priorities. There also seems to be a strong proclivity for a narrow interest articulation at the local level. At the national level the political relevance Turkish organizations have is therefore even lower. Most interactions between host state authorities and Turkish organizations, particularly those of a religious nature, concern practical issues such as finding accommodation or securing a permit to conduct various activities.[47]

Turkish organizations in Amsterdam have long complained about their lack of influence on the process of policymaking. [48] The main opportunity for Turkish organizations to influence policymaking was located in the Turkish advisory council, which was established in 1986. Requesting a say on policy topics related to immigrants and integration, the council worked to enhance the sociopolitical legitimacy of Turkish organizations that were part of this advisory board to Amsterdam authorities. The advisory council played a political role that was small, yet far greater than any role an individual Turkish organization could expect.[49] Still, the council's relevance and performance were often questioned in policy reports compiled by local authorities as well as by Turkish organizations themselves.[50] The city council ended the activities of the Turkish advisory council in 2003.

Although the impact Turkish organizations had as actors in the local political system may have been limited, their function as a "breeding ground" for local Turkish politicians is a separate issue. The authors argue that the more Turkish politicians serve as board members for such organizations the more political relevance these organizations gain.

Links between Local Politicians and Turkish Organizations

To study the links between Turkish organizations and Turkish councilors in Amsterdam, a database containing 198 formal Turkish organizations that were established in the period of 1965 to 2002 was used. The database allows an empirical investigation for the first time of the presumed correlation between political activities of Turkish migrants and their involvement in Turkish organizations, as the database includes all the active members (1695 persons) who were board members of one or more of the organizations between 1965 and 2002.

It should be noted that despite the richness of the data and methods, some biases do exist. First, information on the board members of Turkish organizations for the period of 2002 to 2006 is lacking. This gap was partially filled by using newspaper archives and Internet searches to locate past or present board memberships (most of 2006's Turkish councilors mention such data on their personal websites). The second challenge was having to restrict the focus on board membership to Turkish organizations. The literature identifies organizations related to Turkish affairs as the most likely place to find associational activity, but this presupposition could not be confirmed because of the lack of a historical database of board membership in non-Turkish organizations. Only for one year (2002) was data available to check individuals' possible non-ethnic civic engagements.[51]

Table 4. Number and Percentage of Amsterdam Councilors of Turkish Origin who Have Been a Board Member of a Turkish Organization

		Number of Turkish Councilors	Number of Turkish Councilors Who Have Been Turkish Organization Board Members	%
Elected before 2006	City Council	10	7	70
	City District Council	33	18	55
	Total	43	25	58
Elected in 2006	City Council	3	2	67
	City District Council	15	4	27
	Total	18	6	33

The research focuses on the number of local Turkish politicians who have been board members of a Turkish organization; the different parties that have recruited Turkish politicians with links to Turkish organizations; and the types of Turkish organizations whereby Turkish politicians have served as board members.

Table 4 presents the number and percentage of Turkish politicians who were on the board of a Turkish organization before they were elected. A distinction is made between municipal councilors and city district councilors, and the period until the local elections of 2006 is separated from the period after the elections of 2006. The table shows that among Turkish municipal councilors a large majority were active in a local Turkish organization (70 percent for the period until 2006 and 67 percent after 2006). The number of Turkish city district councilors who had gained civic experience in one of Amsterdam's Turkish organizations was less significant than at the municipal level; however, for the period until 2006, the majority had still been board members (55 percent). Among the currently elected city district councilors of Turkish origin there is a significant decrease in the number of associational leaders who were elected (only four in 2006).[52]

Table 5 displays the number and percentages of Turkish politicians across the different parties and their pre-election experience on the boards of Turkish organizations. This table shows that among the liberals (People's Party for Freedom and Democracy [VVD] 83 percent, Democrats [D66] 75 percent) and the CDA (67 percent), a majority of Turkish councilors have served as board members of Turkish organizations in Amsterdam. By contrast, among the left-wing parties (PvdA 44 percent, GL 38 percent) a minority of Turkish politicians have been active in a local Turkish organization.

Both at the city council and at the city district council levels Turkish left-wing and right-wing organizations tend to have the most board members who go on to be elected. The main difference observed between the city and the city district levels is the importance cultural organizations have for the former: 36 percent of Turkish organizations with a Turkish councilor on their boards are organizations that promote Turkish arts and culture. Secondly, no municipal councilor has ever served

Table 5. Number and Percentage of Amsterdam Councilors of Turkish Origin Who Have Been a Board Member of a Turkish Organization, According to Political Party

	Number of Turkish Councilors	Number of Turkish Councilors Who Have Been Turkish Organization Board Members	%
PvdA	32	14	44
GL	13	5	38
VVD	6	5	83
D66	4	3	75
CDA	3	2	67
Total	58	29	50

as a board member for a social-cultural or religious Turkish organization, despite the fact that these types of Turkish organizations are the two most commonly found in Amsterdam. However, a number of Turkish councilors for the city districts have sat on the boards of non-political and religious Turkish organizations. The (non-religious) PvdA is almost solely responsible for recruiting politicians from these two types of Turkish organizations.

Furthermore, the recruitment by parties of councilors who were active within Turkish organizations is consistent with parties' ideological backgrounds. The right-wing party VVD and the Christian democratic CDA almost exclusively scout Turkish candidates who have been on the boards of right-wing and/or extreme right-wing Turkish organizations, whereas the Green GL (and, for that matter, the social-liberal D66) mostly recruit those who were board members of left-wing Turkish organizations. The PvdA is the only political party showing a more diversi-fied distribution of the types of Turkish organizations with which their Turkish councilors have ties, present or past. Aside from right-wing groups and Turkish sports associations—of which no politician from the party has been a board member—the PvdA has had Turkish politicians linked to cultural, left-wing, reli-gious, and non-political Turkish organizations. It is interesting to see that Turkish PvdA councilors frequently foster ties with non-political Turkish organizations. Here "non-political" mainly refers to an organization that lacks a clear-cut ideology or persuasion (such as left-wing, right-wing, or religious). Non-political Turkish organizations may include all kinds of foundations and associations (such as youth clubs and social-cultural organizations).[53]

A majority of the councilors have sat on the board of a Turkish organization, but this does not say much about the actual strength of ties between a councilor and an organization. For example, what if a councilor was only briefly active? Or, what if a councilor's period of greatest activity took place more than a decade before he or she got elected? In such cases, Turkish organizations would not so much have functioned as a recruiting ground—or even as a pertinent source for local Turkish politicians to garner civic and administrative experience. The average duration of activity on the boards of Turkish organizations and the average period between the moment people left the board and the moment they were elected were therefore calculated. The average period of organizational activity was more or less six years, which demonstrates significant engagement within an organization. The average period between board membership in a Turkish organization and the political position in the city or city district councils was three and a half years. A majority of the Turkish councilors (almost 60 percent) were still board members at the time they were elected, which illustrates the link between organizational and political activities.

Table 6 provides information on membership in non-Turkish organizations based on data provided for 2002. Here it is seen that relatively few Turkish politicians were active in a non-Turkish organization before being elected. Turkish city council politicians proved to be most active in these organizations (around 30 percent). Meanwhile, city district councilors were even less likely to be members of a non-Turkish organization. Amsterdam's incumbent councilors (elected in 2006) notably appear to have kept away from the realm of non-Turkish organizations. In 2002's complete database of the Chamber of Commerce Amsterdam only two city district councilors can be traced back as having served on the board of a non-Turkish organization, four years prior to being elected.

To summarize, a large majority of Turkish councilors had been active on the boards of local Turkish organizations before they were elected. It appears, there-fore, that Turkish organizations did function as recruitment areas for all political parties, though especially for the right-wing VVD. The hypothesis is that this party, because it did not have a large Turkish constituency, probably did not know many other pools from which it could scout Turkish politicians—and, moreover, increase their Turkish constituency. The data also shows that it is unlikely that non-Turkish organizations function as recruitment areas for any political party in Amsterdam.

Table 6. Number and Percentage of Amsterdam Councilors of Turkish Origin who Were Board Members of Non-Turkish Organizations in 2002

		Number of Turkish Councilors	Number of Turkish Councilors Who Were Board Members of Non-Turkish Organizations in 2002	%
Elected before 2006	City Council	10	3	30
	City District Council	33	7	21
	Total	43	10	23
Elected in 2006				%
	City Council	3	1	33
	City District Council	15	2	0.1
	Total	18	3	17

Reflections by Turkish Politicians on Their Membership in Organizations

Fully exploring the spectrum of ties between elected Turkish politicians and Turkish organizations in Amsterdam, interview data that gives some voice to Turkish politicians themselves is now presented. This information gives an indication of how Turkish politicians feel about links with their organization(s) and their ethnic community, and more broadly, what role their ethnicity may play in politics.

In a recent study, Michon re-interviewed a number of ethnic minority councilors elected and interviewed in the early 1990s. [54] Nine Turkish respondents had been interviewed in 1990: two were women and seven were men; four were GL members; two PvdA members; and two CDA members. One respondent had been elected for the PvdA in 1990, switched to the D66 in 1994, and finally joined the GL in 1998. The average age was 32, the youngest respondent being 24 and the eldest 39. All were first-generation immigrants. Two respondents came to the Netherlands as children, in the frame of family reunification; the other respondents came to the Netherlands as young adults to study, to work, and/or because their family lived there. Five respondents mentioned belonging to minority groups: two are Kurdish, two are Syrian-Orthodox, and one is Alevi. The respondents were highly educated, either having completed higher vocational education (five respondents) or having pursued an academic education (four respondents). Except for one woman who studied in Turkey, all interviewees have pursued higher education in the Netherlands.

One respondent was elected to a city district for the first time in 1987, while the eight other respondents were elected for the first time in 1990. One respondent had obtained refugee status in the Netherlands but still held Turkish nationality. The eight other Turkish respondents had already obtained Dutch nationality by the time they were first interviewed, three of them having renounced their Turkish nationality in the process. Looking at the year of naturalization, it appears that all but one respondent acquired Dutch nationality after 1985. The state's decision to   enfranchise foreigners in 1985 therefore had direct consequences for these politicians, enabling them to participate in local elections before they acquired Dutch nationality.

The databases detailing organization boards show that seven of the nine Turkish respondents were board members during a period that ranged some time between 1982 and 2002, and a majority of them were on the board of a Turkish organization. Two respondents were particularly active in the Turkish organizational field. One man, who had been elected to the city district council and to the municipal council for the CDA party, sat on the board of three Turkish organizations (mainly entrepreneurs' organizations) that could be classified as right-wing. The other notably active respondent was a woman who was very involved in left-wing and cultural organizations. Conversely, two other respondents were board members of non-Turkish organizations.

Looking at what councilors said when they had just been elected in 1990 regarding their associational activities, the information is rather disparate. Five respondents said that they were not members of Turkish associations, and four others said that they had ties with Turkish organizations. Two of them said that they were involved in a Turkish association, though stressing the fact that these were neighborhood youngsters associations. One interviewee was very explicit about the role Turkish organizations played in his candidacy. It was clearly important to him that his community backed him as he entered the local political arena:

> I could not have said, 'I am a candidate for the Turkish community,' without taking the pulse of the community. I consulted Turkish organizations and Turkish inhabitants of the neighborhood. They approved of my candidacy. They said that it was good to have one of us, a Turkish man, in the council. They know me in the Turkish community—I have a lot of support among the Muslim community (man, 29, PvdA, June 12, 1990).

Two respondents spoke explicitly of their numerous activities in the Turkish associational field. One of them was a municipal councilor who underscored her role in the progressive Turkish community:

> I have been a member of Turkish organizations for a very long time... the [name of left-wing organization omitted for anonymity's sake] and the [name of another left-wing organization omitted for anonymity's sake], and a few other small organizations. I am a member of almost all left-wing Turkish organizations! I was very active in these organizations—only Turkish organizations—but I am less active now. I have never been involved in a Dutch organization. (woman, 39, GL, December 7, 1990)

This respondent said that the GL (which she joined shortly before the 1990 elections) knew her as a Turkish left-wing activist within the Turkish community. A second respondent who also talked about his numerous activities within the Turkish community (partly within the Syrian-Orthodox community) was a social democrat elected to a city district council. His involvement, however, was reflected in less detail in the database.

With the exception of the three respondents who spoke openly about their ties with Turkish organizational activities, in general the respondents did not talk much about that. The impression given is that these councilors wanted to avoid implications that they were representatives of solely that group or that they served Turkish interests only. They did not want fellow Turks to have such an impression of them, nor did they want parties to see them as biased. One woman elected in a city district explained her attitude towards the Turkish community in such a way:

> I think that Turkish people here in this district believe that I represent them, I fight for their interests, and that I will arrange everything for them. They probably think this way. However, my point of view is that I represent everyone. I do call attention to the problems of migrants, but I don't see myself as being there for migrants only. I do not want to take care of their sole interests. (woman, 32, GL, June 21, 1990)

Eight of the nine respondents said that they represented the whole population or, for that matter, all the voters who chose their party. One respondent specified that most people who vote for her are of Turkish origin or, more generally, are migrants, and that these are the people she represented. However, even if they said that as councilors they were representing a whole population, three respondents explained that they also had a special interest in issues that concern migrants and/or their own community.

Three respondents mentioned yet a very different role that Turkish organizations played, namely the function of putting councilors of Turkish origin in contact with different political affiliations. This was spelled out by a city district councilor: "As councilor, you get in touch with various organizations, you meet at different occasions, social-cultural events or political happenings. That is how I met some Turkish politicians of other parties" (man, 29, PvdA, May 24, 1990).

It is not only the community, however, that emphasizes its perceived common identity with councilors of Turkish origin. Political parties themselves hone in on Turkish identity and show an invested interest in fortifying relations with a Turkish constituency. This becomes especially visible during electoral campaigns. In fact, parties have traditionally composed diversified electoral lists that appear to favor ethnic minorities. The 1990 elections show that some amount of latent positive discrimination [55] may have favored candidates belonging to Amsterdam's most significant ethnic minorities (Turks, Moroccans, and Surinamese). Some respondents expressed their fear that in this process personal qualifications were not fully recognized.

In general, the respondents revealed a sense of self-awareness, acknowledging that origins played a role in their access to local politics. None of them, however, believed that this was the only criterion taken into account in their election.

These interview excerpts thus show that the ties Turkish politicians had—or did not have—with Turkish organizations specifically and with the Turkish community at large is part of the wider ranging question about how origins play into politics. Coming from both the Turkish electorate and their own party certain presuppositions based on a rather imposed identity as a Turk fell on councilors of Turkish origin. Because they did not want to be considered token representatives of Turks the politicians tended to present their ties with Turkish organizations in a more nuanced scheme.

Michon's series of interviews conducted in 2007 focused on how these councilors' political careers developed. Seven of the nine original respondents of Turkish origin were re-interviewed, and four of them said they were not members of Turkish organizations. Only one respondent said that he was still very active within the Turkish organizational field. It seems as if after their experience in politics the interviewees distance themselves more from Turkish organizations than they had before.

Conclusion

The first—and maybe most important—remark to be made about the political mobilization of Turks in Amsterdam is that this group has significant opportunities to participate in the local political arena. Very often they seize these opportunities. The turnout rates and numbers of politicians of Turkish origin show that the Turkish community is an important local political actor.

The focus of this study has been on the link between local politics and the Turkish organizational field. One of the compelling yet puzzling facts that is highlighted here is a mismatch between the dominant pattern of the political behavior of Turks and the most important feature of the Turkish organizational field in Amsterdam. The political participation of Turks in Amsterdam is clearly oriented towards left-wing political parties—most of the votes of the Turkish electorate go to these parties, and a large majority of the Turkish councilors are affiliated with them. Yet the structure of Turkish organizations taken as a whole reveals a different picture: the organizational field is characterized by high rates of polarization along several cleavages that are predominated by religious organizations. The inconsistency is also made apparent by the fact that only very few Turkish elected politicians have served on the boards of religious organizations.

As the organizational affiliation of voters or the political choices of those who engage in organizational activities are not known (nor is it even known which orga-nizations have the most members), it is still difficult to adequately address this mismatch between features of the political and the organizational mobilizations of Turks in Amsterdam. The contradiction does, however, point to an already visible phenomenon: religious organizations, which form the cluster comprising the most Turkish organizations, have limited—that is, if any—ties with the local political arena through Turkish politicians. Religious organizations, therefore, do not serve as recruitment areas where political parties find future councilors.

Still, one of the indisputable findings of this study is that a majority (58 percent) of Turkish councilors who were elected in Amsterdam have served on the boards of Turkish organizations. In this sense, organizations do play an important role. More-over, there is strong reason to believe that some parties have recruited politicians via Turkish organizations. On a different level, others researchers have argued that a well-organized community has a positive influence on political participation. [56] As pools of recruitment, as places where people have gained relevant experience, and as carriers of necessary social and political trust, Turkish organizations have there-fore played a role in politics that should not be overlooked.

It cannot be concluded from the data presented on Turkish politicians and Turkish organizations in Amsterdam that organizations have a direct bearing on the politics of Amsterdam or that they influence the recruitment process within parties. Parties are the key actors when it comes to the matter of who gets assigned what position on an electoral list. Parties are free to choose how and where they recruit such individu-als. The fact that a majority of Turkish councilors of the PvdA and the GL have no ties with Turkish organizations—and that those who do have links to myriad organi-zations—underscores the sovereign strategies that political parties enjoy. Right-wing, liberal, and conservative parties have more often recruited Turkish politicians with ties to Turkish organizations. Turkish organizations have acted as obvious pools of recruitment for these parties, providing candidates with organizational experience and a potential electorate. In contrast, left-wing parties probably have multiple points of access to the Turkish community, and Turkish organizations are just one of the different paths of access to politics.

Once elected Turkish councilors seem to distance themselves from Turkish organizations and the Turkish community. They most probably do this in order to retain some independence as representatives but also because political parties are wary of overtly expressed strong ethnic ties. Once a blessing—a symbol of skills put to good use and felicitous relations with the electorate—affiliation with a Turkish organization can become difficult for elected politicians to bear. Based on the interview data presented here (from 1990, 2000, and 2007), the political role of Turkish organizations would in fact be even further weakened.

In other words, Turkish organizations are an important political actor, but they are certainly not the most crucial actor in processes of political recruitment. Mobilization via involvement in an organization is probably not the most successful strategy to gain access to the local political arena, though neither is it a senseless undertaking. The influence organizations have on the access of Turks to local politics is a matter of perspective: is the glass half full or half empty?

Notes

1. "Turks" (or "of Turkish origin") refers to first- and second-generation immigrants of Turkish origin, regardless of their nationality. This terminology follows that of the Dutch administrative definition (see website of Statistics Bureau (CBS) www.cbs.nl).
2. At the national level, since the elections of 2006 there has been one secretary of state (Justice) of Turkish origin and three members of parliament (*Tweede Kamer*), out of a total of 150 MPs. In the Senate (*Eerste Kamer*), there are no elected politicians of Turkish descent. If they hold Turkish nationality only, Turks are not entitled to vote at the national level. Approximately two thirds of the Turkish population has dual citizenship. See staline.cbs.nl.
3. Dirk Jacobs, *Nieuwkomers in De Politiek. Het Parlementair Debat omtrent Kiesrecht voor Vreemdelingen in Nederland en België (1970-1997)* [Newcomers in Politics. The Parliamentary Debate on the Enfranchisement of Foreigners in the Netherlands and in Belgium (1970–1997)] (Gent: Academia Press, 1998), p.114–17.
4. Jean Tillie, *De Etnische Stem, Opkomst en Stemgedrag van Migranten tijdens Gemeenteraadsverkiezingen, 1986–1998* [The Ethnic Vote, Turnout and Party Choice of Migrants at Municipal Elections, 1986–1998] (Utrecht: Forum, 2000), p.12.
5. In 2006. See CBS Statline, http://statline.cbs.nl.
6. Samuel J. Eldersveld, Lars Strömberg and Wim Derksen, *Local Elites in Western Democracies, a Comparative Analysis of Urban Political Leaders in the U.S., Sweden and the Netherlands* (Boulder: Westview Press, 1995), p.3.
7. Robert D. Putnam, *The Comparative Study of Political Elites* (Englewood-Cliffs: Prentice-Hall, 1976), pp.22–23; Jacques Lagroye, Bastien François and Frédéric Sawicki, *Sociologie Politique* [Political Sociology], 4th edition (Paris: Presses de Sciences Po/Dalloz, 2002), p.468.
8. Jan C. C. Rupp, John Schuster and Huibert Schijf, "Toetreding en Terugdringing: de Opkomst van een Lokale Politieke Elite," [Getting in and Pushing Back: The Emergence of a Local Political Elite] in Meindert Fennema and Huibert Schijf (eds.)*Nederlandse Elites in de Twintigste Eeuw*[Dutch Elites in the Twentieth Century] (Amsterdam: Amsterdam University Press, 2003).
9. Pippa Norris, "Introduction: Theories of Recruitment" in Pippa Norris (ed.), *Passages to Power, Legislative Recruitment in Advanced Democracies* (Cambridge: Cambridge University Press, 1997), pp.1–14.

10. This is also the case in a majority of EU countries. See Rainer Bauböck, "Migration und poli-tische Beteiligung: Wahlrechte jenseits von Staatsgebiet und Staatsangehörigkeit," (Migration and political interest. Voting rights from the side of national territory and nationality) in Manfred Oberlechner (ed.), *Die missglückte Integration? Wege und Irrwege in Europa* (The failed integra-tion? Paths and wrong paths in Europe), (Wien: Braumüller, 2006), pp.115–29.

11. David M. Farrell, *Electoral systems, a Comparative Introduction* (Basingstoke: Palgrave, 2001), pp.165–66.

12. Monique Leijenaar, Kees Niemöller and Astrid van der Kooij, " *Kandidaten Gezocht," Politieke Partijen en het Streven naar Grotere Diversiteit onder Gemeenteraden* [Candidates in Demand, Political Parties and the Strive for Greater Diversity in Municipal Councils] (Amsterdam: Instituut voor Publiek en Politiek, 1999).

13. Ibid., p.41.

14. Ibid., p.105.

15. Ibid., pp. 46, 105.

16. Ibid., pp. 66–74.

17. Below, it is shown that this is reflected in the number of Turkish politicians affiliated with these different parties.

18. There are studies that predate 1994: Paul Pennings, *Migrantenkiesrecht in Amsterdam. Een Onderzoek naar de Participatie en Mobilisatie van Etnische Groepen bij de Gemeenteraads-verkiezingen van 19 Maart 1986* [Migrant Enfranchisement in Amsterdam. A Study of the Participation and Mobilisation of Ethnic Groups at the Municipal Elections of March 19th, 1986] (Amsterdam: Gemeente Amsterdam, Bestuursinformatie, Afd. Onderzoek en Statistiek & Universiteit van Amsterdam, vakgroep Politicologie, 1987); Jan Rath, *Kenterend Tij. Migranten en de Gemeenteraadsverkiezingen van 21 Maart 1990 te Rotterdam* [Turning Tide, Migrants and the Rotterdam Municipal Elections of March 21st, 1990] (Utrecht: RUU, Vakgroep Culturele Anthropologie, 1990). However, the research methods that were used are very differ-ent and results are therefore difficult to compare with the findings of 1994, 1998, 2002, and 2006.

19. The surveys held for each election since 1994 followed the same procedure. On the very day the municipal elections were held, voters coming out of pre-selected polling stations were asked to fill in a questionnaire about their party choice and, more generally, their party preferences, as well as some personal characteristics (e.g., gender, age, birthplace, education level, and ethnicity). An important element at stake was the definition of ethnicity, which is identically defined by all Dutch municipali-ties on the basis of the respondent's country of birth as well as his or her parents' birthplaces. All voters, even those who did not complete the questionnaire, were counted to assess turnout rates over-all. Turnout was measured by comparing the number of all people leaving a chosen polling station with the number of registered voters for each ethnic group in the same polling station (the latter number was provided in advance by the municipality).

20. Laure Michon and Jean Tillie, *Amsterdamse Polyfonie, Opkomst en Stemgedrag van Allochtone Amsterdammers bij de Gemeenteraads- en Deelraadsverkiezingen van 6 Maart 2002* [Polyphony in Amsterdam, Turnout and Party Choice of Immigrants in Amsterdam at the Municipal and District Elections of March 6th, 2002] (Amsterdam: IMES, 2003), p.8.

21. Robert D. Putnam, *Making Democracy Work, Civic Traditions in Modern Italy* (Princeton N.J.: Princeton University Press, 1993).

22. Meindert Fennema and Jean Tillie, "Political Participation and Political Trust in Amsterdam: Civic Communities and Ethnic Networks," *Journal of Ethnic and Migration Studies*, Vol.25, No. 4 (1999), pp.703–26.

23. Fennema and Tillie use the number of interlocking directorates that exists across organizational boards, which measure the density of the network, as an indicator of civicness. See Fennema and Tillie, "Political Participation and Political Trust in Amsterdam."

24. Ibid., "Political Participation and Political Trust in Amsterdam." See also Meindert Fennema, Jean Tillie, Anja van Heelsum, Maria Berger and Rick Wolff, *Sociaal Kapitaal en Politieke Participatie*

van Etnische Minderheden [Social Capital and Political Participation of Ethnic Minorities] (Amsterdam: IMES, 2000), p.19.

25. Fennema and Tillie, "Political Participation and Political Trust in Amsterdam," p.721.

26. Michon and Tillie, *Amsterdamse Polyfonie*, p.44.

27. Anja van Heelsum, "Turnout and Party Choice in the Local Elections in the Netherlands," paper presented at the Metropolis Conference, Lisbon, October 2–6, 2006, p.10.

28. An exception is the study of Boelhouwer, who suggests that structural abstention is mostly observed among people with low income and/or a low level of education, youngsters, and the unemployed. See Jeroen Boelhouwer, "Achtergronden van Niet-Stemmers," [Background of Non-Voters] in Paul Dekker (ed.), *Niet-Stemmers, Een Onderzoek naar Achtergronden en Motieven in Enquêtes, Interviews en Focusgroepen,* [Non-Voters. A Study of Background and Motives in Surveys, Interviews and Focus Groups] (Den Haag: SCP, 2002), p. 21–42.

29. Michon and Tillie, *Amsterdamse Polyfonie*, p.15; Anja van Heelsum and Jean Tillie, *Opkomst en Partijvoorkeur van Migranten bij de Gemeenteraadsverkiezingen van 7 Maart 2006* (Amsterdam: IMES, 2006), p.12–14. However, in 2002, second-generation Turks voted relatively more for the social-liberal party Democrats 66 (D66), and relatively less for the Green Left party (GL) than did first-generation Turks.

30. Michon and Tillie, *Amsterdamse Polyfonie*, p.17; van Heelsum and Tillie, *Opkomst en Partijvoorkeur van Migranten*, p.16.

31. Christian Joppke, "Transformation of Immigrant Integration, Civic Integration and Antidiscrimination in the Netherlands, France, and Germany," *World Politics*, Vol.59 (2007), pp.243–73.

32. Party preferences were measured by people's response to the question: "Do you think you will ever vote for this party in the future?" See Tillie, *De Etnische Stem*.

33. Voters surveyed in the IMES studies of 1994, 1998, 2002, and 2006 were asked about the parties they had voted for in previous elections.

34. Tillie, *De Etnische Stem*, p.78; Michon and Tillie, *Amsterdamse Polyfonie*, p.39.

35. Michon and Tillie, *Amsterdamse Polyfonie*, p.32.

36. See Tillie, *De Etnische Stem*.

37. Tillie, *De Etnische Stem* ; Michon and Tillie, *Amsterdamse Polyfonie*; van Heelsum and Tillie, *Opkomst en Partijvoorkeur van Migranten*.

38. Matthijs Rooduijn and Lisette Dekker, *Politieke Participatie van Migranten in Utrecht* [Political Participation of Migrants in Utrecht] (Amsterdam: Instituut voor Publiek en Politiek, 2004), p.15; Instituut voor Publiek en Politiek (IPP), *Nieuwsbrief Zomer 2006* [Newsletter Summer 2006] (Amsterdam: IPP, 2006), p.8.

39. It is important to note, however, that only three percent of all municipal councilors in the Netherlands have a foreign background (Amsterdam, IPP, 2006), p.8.

40. This method of identification based on the ethnic origins that names evoke is reliable to a certain extent. Martiniello discusses the advantages and shortcomings of this method in Marco Martiniello, "Les Elus d'Origine Etrangère à Bruxelles: Une Nouvelle Etape de la Participation Politique des Populations d'Origine Immigrée," [Representatives of Foreign Origin in Brussels: A New Step in the Political Participation of the Population of Immigrant Background] *Revue Européenne des Migrations Internationales* [European Journal of International Migrations], Vol.14, No. 2 (1998), pp.123–47. See p.134. Whenever possible, the origins of councilors were cross-checked using newspaper archives, Internet searches, and information supplied by political parties.

41. See Brieuc-Yves Cadat and Meindert Fennema, "Les Hommes Politiques Issus de l'Immigration à Amsterdam: Image de Soi, Image des Autres" [Politicians of Immigrant Background in Amsterdam: Self- and Other-Images,] *Revue Européenne des Migrations Internationales* [European Journal of International Migrations], Vol.14, no. 2 (1998), pp.97–121.

42. Floris Vermeulen, *The Immigrant Organising Process. Turkish Organisations in Amsterdam and Berlin and Surinamese Organisations in Amsterdam, 1960–2000* (Amsterdam: Amsterdam University Press, 2006).

43. In the 1980s these religious organizations were mainly the DITIB, Suleymanci, and Milli Görüş organizations. Affluent Islamic organizations in this period were Hollanda Diyanet Vakfi Fatih Amsterdam, Sociale Culturele Vereniging Milli Görüş, and Stichting Islamitisch Centrum Amsterdam.

44. Vermeulen, *The Immigrant Organising Process*.

45. Marlou Schrover and Floris Vermeulen, "Immigrant Organizations," *Journal of Ethnic and Migration Studies*, Vol. 31 (2005), pp. 823–32; Floris Vermeulen and Maria Berger, "Civic Networks and Political Behavior: Turks in Amsterdam and Berlin," in S. Karthick Ramakrishnan and Irene Bloemraad (eds.), *Civic Hopes and Political Realities: Immigrants, Community Organizations and Political Engagement* (New York: Russel Sage Foundation, 2008), pp.160–92.

46. Steven Pfaff and Anthony J. Gill, "Will a Million Muslims March? Muslim Interest Organizations and Political Integration in Europe," *Comparative Political Studies*, Vol. 39 (2006), pp.803–28.

47. Anja van Heelsum, *Migrantenorganisaties in Nederland Deel 1 Aantal en soort organisaties en ontwikkelingen* [Migrant Organisations in the Netherlands Part I Number, Kind of Organisations and Developments] (Utrecht: FORUM, 2004).

48. Floris Vermeulen, "Organizational Patterns: Surinamese and Turkish Associations in Amsterdam, 1960-1990," *Journal of Ethnic and Migration Studies*, Vol. 31 (2005), pp. 951–73.

49. Vermeulen, *The Immigrant Organising Process*.

50. Ibid.; Vermeulen, "Organizational Patterns: Surinamese and Turkish Associations in Amsterdam."

51. For 2002, a database containing all of Amsterdam's registered non-profit organizations and their active board members was used.

52. This could be an indication that active board membership and political positions are now less often linked with each other, but it also could be a consequence of the limitations of our database.

53. The most common non-political Turkish organizations in which these councilors have served are Turks Platform Bos en Lommer en De Baarsjes, Amsterdams Turkse Jongeren Vereniging, and Stichting Turks Volkshuis Osdorp. These organizations have also functioned as bridge-builders between different ideological camps of the polarized Turkish organizational field in Amsterdam. Turkish organizational leaders of the different movements have met in these neutral organizations incorporating all different parties from the Turkish community (Vermeulen and Berger, "Civic Networks and Political Behaviour (cited in endnote 45)).

54. See Cadat and Fennema, "Les Hommes Politiques Issus de l'Immigration à Amsterdam."

55. Positive discrimination here refers to what may, in a non-European context, be more commonly called "affirmative action."

56. Fennema and Tillie, "Political Participation and Political Trust in Amsterdam"; Fennema *et al.*, *Sociaal Kapitaal en Politieke Participatie van Etnische Minderheden*.

Towards a Success Story? Turkish Immigrant Organizations in Norway

JON ROGSTAD

Department of Sociology and Human Geography, University of Oslo and Institute for Social
Research, Norway

ABSTRACT *This article looks at the organizing processes of residents of Norway who have
Turkish origins. It describes the distribution of Turkish organizations in Norway and
discusses the different organizing processes of ethnic Turks and ethnics Kurds. It pays particular attention to the Turkish Youth Association, which has become politically relevant in
Norwegian society.*

Introduction

The aim of this article is to study the significance of civil society on the Turkish
minority in Norway. It highlights the role of immigrant organizations in the
voluntary sector as platforms of political engagement and participation. Ideally,
civil society can accommodate and foster collective identities while promoting
intergroup dialogue. In such an ideal situation voluntary organizations offer vital
training and teach valuable social skills, thereby stimulating political engagement
and participation.

In Norway, the Turkish community is particularly interesting insofar as Turks
were part of the first wave of what is termed modern immigration, which began in
the late 1960s. At first, most immigrants were looking for work. This peaked in
1975, after which family reunion became the main reason for migration from
Turkey to Norway. Given the relatively long history of the Turkish community in
Norway, this article sets out to explore whether this minority community is involved
in the political landscape. To do so, it focuses on the organizing process and the
distribution and role of immigrant organizations.

Norway's case is a particularly interesting one. The country is located
geographically at the margins of Europe, and its migration history is relatively
short. Moreover, Norway is a robust welfare state and has a particularly high rate of
citizen involvement in voluntary organizations. [1] A deep vein of anti-establishment
sentiment in parts of the Norwegian population has spawned numerous organizations.

In this way, Norwegian civil society constitutes a corrective to mainstream political processes and is an important mechanism of political empowerment.

The next section of this article provides some general background information, including contextual variables related to the organizing process and political engagement, such as employment, voting behavior, and engagement in civil society by the immigrant groups. Then, the role of civil society in the Norwegian democratic regime is briefly noted, paying particular attention to immigrant organizations. The main part of the article draws attention to Turkish organizations. After a description of the organizations, the differences in the organizing processes of ethnic Turks and ethnic Kurds are highlighted. Finally, the importance of generation is noted, and the Turkish Youth Association, which has become politically relevant in Norwegian society, is discussed.

The data is derived from a comprehensive survey of political engagement among respondents of Turkish, Bosnian, Pakistani, and Norwegian descent. Three hundred respondents were interviewed in each group, for a total of 1200 respondents. In addition, 12 qualitative interviews were conducted in different organizations aimed at engaging persons of Turkish origin. Information on the number and distribution of immigrant organizations was taken from the Directorate of Integration and Diversity (IMDI), which distributes funding to immigrant organizations in Norway. Finally, available statistics from Statistics Norway were used.

Turks in Norway: An Overall Picture

Since the late 1960s the relative number of immigrants and their descendants in Norway has multiplied several times over. By early 2008, Norway's population included 460,000 immigrants, or 9.7 percent of the total population. Non-Western immigrants constituted about 7.5 percent. The highest ratios were in the cities. In Oslo, one in five residents was of non-Western origin, and the percentage of non-Western children and adolescents was even higher.

Individuals of Turkish descent have been in Norway longer than most other ethnic minorities.[2] The first wave came as economic migrants in the late 1960s; since then, family reunification has ensured a steady influx of new inhabitants of Turkish origin. According to Statistics Norway there were almost 16,000 people with at least one parent of Turkish origin (not including persons from Turkmenistan) living in Norway in 2006.[3] Approximately 3000 (20 percent) had Kurdish origins. Furthermore, 34 percent were second generation—children of immigrants—who were born and raised in Norway. Statistics Norway also shows that 74 percent of the population with Turkish origins held Norwegian citizenship in 2006. This group is characterized by having little formal education and low employment rates compared with other non-Western immigrant communities.

The following section presents background material relevant to the organizational patterns discussed later in the article. In this section employment, voting behavior, and engagement in civil society are considered.

Employment

Table 1 compares the employment rates of various immigrant groups in Norway. At an employment rate of 52.5 percent in 2006, Turkish ethnic minorities lagged behind the average for first generation immigrants in the labor market (60.1 percent). That said, more than half the adult population of Turkish origin is involved in the labor market, which is higher than the rate for the population of African origin (45.2 percent), though this is still almost 20 percent less than the employment rate of the total immigrant population (70 percent). The data also shows that women's employment figures are lower than that of men.

Labor market participation is interesting because studies have found a positive correlation between economic and political integration. [4] In other words, people involved in one area of society are likely to be involved in others as well. One might initially expect the opposite: people whose experience of discrimination in the labor and housing market exacerbates their sense of alienation may review their political allegiances and work to reform the system. Political democracy theory says that those affected by political decision-making should have a chance to state their case and influence decisions,[5] but this is not what is observed in Norway.

Voting

Table 2 shows voter turnout for the general election in 2005. Only statistics of non-Western immigrants are included, in a bid to compare people of Turkish descent to others with non-Western backgrounds. One must be a Norwegian citizen to vote in national elections. Results corroborate those found in labor market participation. That is to say, turnout in the Turkish community during the 2005 elections was slightly lower than the average for non-Western groups. The difference is not large: 43 percent of the Turkish group voted as compared to the 49 percent rate of all non-Western immigrant groups. Increasing age and period of residence in Norway increased voting likelihood in all instances.

Table 1.　Employment Rates in Percent of Residents Aged 16-74, by Country of Origin and Sex. (First Generation Only), Fourth Quarter 2006

	Total	Male	Female
Population in General	70.0	73.3	66.6
First Gen. Immigrants Overall	60.1	65.7	54.5
Western Countries	70.9	76.3	63.6
African Origin	45.2	51.3	37.5
Asian Origin (including Turks)	53.3	60.4	46.8
Turkish Origin	52.5	62.2	39.7

Source: Statistics Norway, http://www.ssb.no/emner/06/01/innvregsys/tab-2007-06-20-01.html.

Table 2. Voter Turnout Rates by Sex, Age, Length of Residence and Year, Parliamentary Elections 2005

	Non-Western immigrants	Asia	Turkey
In all	49	50	43
Male	48	51	42
Female	50	50	44
Age			
18-25	38	38	34
26-39	47	50	47
40-59	54	57	51
60+	55	52	-
Residence in years			
0-9	44	42	43
10-19	47	50	47
20-29	50	52	41
30+	65	64	-
Turnout 1997	58	57	49
Turnout 2001	45	45	44
N	103,283	54,471	6,380
Male	52,436	27,916	3,480
Female	50,847	26,555	2,900

Source: http://www.ssb.no/emner/02/rapp_200729/rapp_200729.pdf, p. 118.

To put this into a larger context, 77 percent of the overall population voted in the 2005 election, 34 percent more than the Turkish community. The divide, it appears, is widening, using a comparison of recent turnout figures for elections spanning the years 1997 to 2005. Between 1997 and 2005 the Turkish community's turnout rates fell by nine percentage points while remaining relatively unchanged for the general population. If voter turnout is taken as an indicator of political integration, far from increasing it seems to be falling off.

Engagement in Civil Society

There are some isolated studies of immigrant communities' activity patterns in civil society. One is a study undertaken by Jon Horgen Friberg (2005). [6] It addresses the situation in the capital, where a large contingent of Norway's immigrant population lives and, thus, it is particularly enlightening. At the same time, however, groups in Oslo may differ substantially from similar groups elsewhere in the country.

Horgen Friberg's 2005 study is based on interviews with 2998 adolescents, most of whom were 16 at the time. He finds noticeable differences between the majority population and non-Western immigrants. While 72 percent of ethnic Norwegians

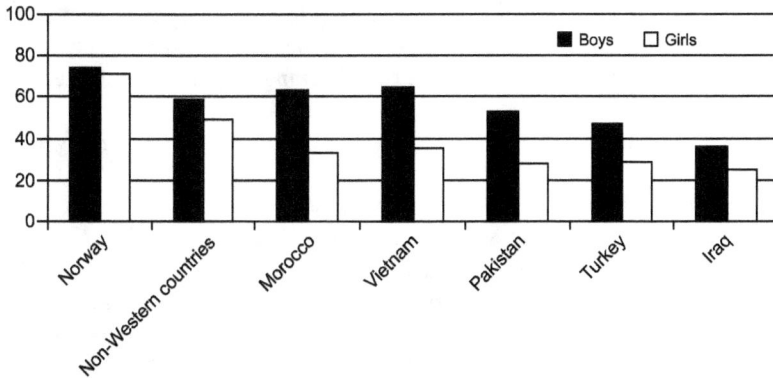

Figure 1. Organization membership by gender and country affiliation in percent. (N = 2,998).[8,6]

reported membership in at least one organization (Fig. 1), only 51 percent of non-Western respondents did so.[7] Further, he found a wide difference based on gender regarding the activity variable. While boys and girls generally are more or less equally active, this is not the case for adolescents from non-Western ethnic communities. Nearly six in ten boys are members of an organization, as compared to only four to five girls (59 and 44 percent respectively). Girls of Moroccan, Vietnamese, Pakistani, Turkish, and Iraqi descent stand out as having a very low membership rate. Nevertheless, the number of respondents in each group is very low if the sample is divided by country affiliation, and the likelihood of error is particularly high. However, the tendency is clear, especially if all non-Western immigrants are grouped together, bringing the sample to 799.

As Friberg's work shows, the percentage of ethnic Turks involved in organized activities is exceptionally low. About six in ten boys of the wider non-Western population are members of an organization, as compared to fewer than five in ten boys of Turkish descent. The relative difference is about the same for the girls. This means that membership rates are about ten percent lower for girls of Turkish descent than for minority ethnic girls as a whole.

It is important to note that immigrant organizations are included in the data but seem unable to attract a large membership. That does not necessarily entail a positive correlation between membership size and commitment of members or organization. Some non-Western immigrants may not want to join an organization mainly involved in homeland politics. Furthermore, political refugees might be skeptical of joining an organization because it could put them in jeopardy, and not wishing to appear on membership lists is perfectly understandable.

Sports organizations are unique in having both large memberships and high activity rates. This is also the case among non-Western immigrants, but many more boys than girls are active, and less is done to promote membership of sports organizations among girls. Sociologist Åse Strandbu questions whether sports do in fact promote integration.[9] Low participation by minority girls, she explains, has to do with certain features of Norwegian sports culture. As she is at pains to stress, a young person's involvement in sports relies heavily on strong backing at home, something which may be lacking in parents from non-Western cultures. Strandbu also mentions the impact of ingrained, embodied motivation in terms of minority girls' gender identity.

Apart from sports clubs, youngsters from minority ethnic groups are likely to join youth clubs, special interest organizations, and religious communities. As this study goes on to point out, organizations with a political agenda have a particularly low score on non-ethnic majority membership. However, these organizations have a voice in places where important decisions are made, and their demographically biased recruitment practices are easily observed.

The Norwegian Regime and Civil Society

There is a significant corporative dimension to a voluntary organization, aligning it with the country's established power structure. This corporative element has a *substantive* side, helping maintain high person/year yields in civil society, and an *ideological* side, in that the voluntary organization is considered to be of value in and of itself. In other words, it is a meaningful, proper way of activating people and integrating them with the wider community. Emblematic of the tertiary sector in Norway is its "that's how we do things round here" mentality, described by Charles Taylor.[10] Its most tangible expression is in the criteria and guidelines organizations are obliged to meet to qualify for government support. The majority are therefore stewards of a highly institutionalized concentration of power in the form of grant procedures.

At the same time, organizations enjoy a high degree of autonomy. Indeed, historically, civil society has played a unique role as an engine of social progress in Norway. Voluntary organizations give members and their interests a "voice and a vote," a pursuit with considerable democratic significance. Furthermore, organizations offer a way of getting concerns and demands across to the government. By advancing the political views of their members, organizations act as a political corrective by virtue of their capacity to mobilize and articulate anti-establishment opinion.

It is by engaging with and influencing policy-making that organizations fulfill their key social function. Organizations coordinate and promote the interests of different sectors and groups, providing political input and helping to legitimize deliberative democracy. This latter form of participation is particularly vital for multicultural societies because of differences in the right to act politically. In more academic language, institutionalized rights are often referred to as a political opportunity structure.[11] Immigrant organizations help meet the needs of politically concerned but non-enfranchised people. This includes immigrants who have not lived in the country long enough to acquire Norwegian citizenship (seven years), which is necessary for voting in national elections. It also includes minors (age of majority in Norway is 18). As one respondent, representing a Turkish organization put it:

> Our aim is to grasp the situation among the young people living in Norway with a Turkish background. You know, the young ones they don't have the right to vote in regular elections, and to put it frankly, I think that we [the association] are doing a better job than the political parties. The parties are boring, while we have all the fun.

Organizations help solve another democratic problem, that of promoting trust and introducing new citizens to the workings of democracy. By engaging with the individual, voluntary organizations act as "schools in democracy." Robert Putnam says that organizations provide a platform for face-to-face exchange, something which is essential to the development of mutual trust. [12] It is necessary for democratic involvement, he adds, as trust is an offshoot of organizational activity that promotes loyalty to and confidence in collective arrangements. Voluntary organizations are also important for dialogue, identity formation, and the maintenance of the cultural idiosyncrasies of different groups. A dynamic, vigorous, and heterogeneous civil society is a cornerstone of a government's strategy for promoting tolerance and discouraging racism and discrimination.

However, identities can and do cross national borders. Words like transnationalism and diaspora denote people living in one place but whose identities, at least partly, are with another country, a form of political affiliation described in Benedict Anderson's apt phrase "long-distance nationalism." [13] However, ethnic and cultural minorities resident in different countries can have overlapping identities. [14] Such identity components—political viewpoints and commitments, for instance—may derive from the country of origin or country of residence, as in anti-racism work or shared perceptions as outsiders. In other words, transnationalism comprises at least two elements, one of which refers to practice—that is, regular contact across national borders.[15] The second element of transnationalism is the role of collective identities in promoting a sense of community among individuals who see themselves as inhabiting an intermediate world somewhere between the place of origin and the place of residence.

Immigrant Organizations

The political (corporative) system relies on organizations playing the role of stakeholder in the democratic system. Members are socialized as good citizens, and the apparatus of government connects with organizations via consultations, direct contact, or negotiations. Participation is the keyword with regard to elections and other forms of political activity.

It does not necessarily follow that an active civil society will promote political involvement, empowerment, or affiliation. Powerful groups can use civil society to consolidate their dominance by setting the terms of debate, by amassing cultural expertise, and by attracting new participants. On the one hand, then, civil society may reproduce the conditions under which a "we–them" mentality thrives; on the other hand, however, it provides an opportunity for immigrants to become participants, to shape society by words and deeds.

In Norway, the state subsidizes voluntary organizations, including immigrant organizations. When this system was instituted in the early 1980s, the government only subsidized one organization per nationality; eventually, help was forthcoming to all organizations whose membership exceeded a certain figure. Norway is a world leader in organizational involvement, but active membership in an organization is characterized basically by two things: higher education and higher income. [16] Involvement in one sector of society tends to predict involvement in others.

It would be reasonable to posit these factors as an explanation for the recruitment bias affecting minority and majority populations. As noted above, systematic differences separate majority and minority groups in terms of labor market involvement, among other things. Unequal access to resources violates fundamental democratic rights. To the extent that participation in different spheres is mutually reinforcing it is important to ask what sort of strategy the organizations need to adopt to increase ethnic minority membership.

Another cause of concern relates to changes within the voluntary sector. The role civil society gives immigrant organizations today must be examined, and, in light of ideals of the importance of organizations to democracy and engagement, so too must the role allotted to civil society by the immigrant organizations be studied. How robust is democracy within immigrant organizations, and how robust should it be? Internal democracy is not particularly important to democracy *per se*, according to Meindert Fennama and Jean Tillie. [17] However, it is better for democracy to have undemocratic organizations than no organizations at all, they contend.

Floris Vermeulen explains two important factors involved in participation in immigrant organizations among Turks in Amsterdam. [18] On the one hand, he notes group-related factors in the *immigration process*, such as the character of the immigrant population and organizational influence from the country of origin. On the other hand, he points to the importance of *receiving society-related factors* and political opportunity structures.

In Norway there is a strong link between the level at which an organization operates and its democratic credentials. Whether an organization is national or local is more important than whether it pursues political or other aims. National and political organizations are not necessarily more democratic than local organizations. Quite the contrary, in fact: the local organizations that promote culture, traditions, and identity are obliged to have general assemblies to receive funding, while the national organizations that take part in the larger political struggles have no such requirements.

Because this point is crucial to an understanding of the Norwegian associational regime it is necessary to understand the differences between national and local immigrant organizations. A national organization is one that operates across the country or addresses issues of a national character. It should promote the interests of immigrants in Norway across nationalities and ethnic affiliations. It must substantiate its claim to national status by satisfactorily answering at least two of the following five points: where inquiries to the organization originate; where activity initiated by the organization takes place; what types of issues are addressed by the organization—whether local or national; what the partnerships and connections of the organization are; and what characterizes the organization's structure—local branches, centralized, or regional offices?

Nine organizations fit the classification in 2006. They share one particular feature: none are democratic in the sense of having a membership. With the exception of one organization they resemble centers of expertise with employed leaders who justify themselves by force of argument rather than support from the ranks. The national organizations can be divided into three groups. [19] The first comprises the *equality* organizations that operate as lobbyists, using the media to shape public opinion and political decision-making on matters concerning minorities. The second is the *aid* organization, which gives practical help to immigrants and asylum seekers. The third group contains the *bridge builders*, with facilities where local organizations and people interested in topics such as racism can get together and exchange views.

It is questionable whether such a small number of national organizations could be said to be representative in any democratic sense, as they should be classed as issue-oriented political bodies whose executive management represents and justifies itself by virtue of its expertise in a given area. [20] They can be said to spearhead the deliberative turn of which they are part. This is not limited to immigrant organizations. Several leading organizations involved in matters as different as climate change, distributive justice, and stewardship of the natural environment are organized according to the same undemocratic template. However, are these organizations necessarily undemocratic? Coming from a conventional reading of democracy the answer is yes. Yet if a more deliberative approach is permitted, where representation is not sought in the distribution of members but in the diversity of arguments made and interests pursued, they can possibly be seen as democratic.

It is difficult to obtain a satisfactory overall picture of the local immigrant organizations because a large number of immigrant organizations working at the local level are not eligible for government grants. Jørgen Melve has estimated the number of organizations to be somewhere between 350 and 1000. [21] He arrives at the lower figure by narrowing the criteria to include only government-funded organizations. Of these, there are two types, he suggests. [22] The first seeks to promote solidarity among like-minded individuals, the second to harness communities behind actions. The first, he concludes, is becoming increasingly important. Coalitions of identity are probably even more numerous if non-government funded organizations are included in the estimate.

Local organizations must satisfy two criteria to qualify for government funding. They must first be open to all, irrespective of ethnic background. They also must be run according to democratic principles. In other words, members should elect an executive board at a general assembly. On this latter point the local organizations differ markedly from the national.

As organizations must adopt an open membership policy to access government funds their operations have to be managed according to type of activity, not according to the ethnic affiliations of the membership. The government's line has had a marked effect on the national organizations, which divide activities into sectors or issue areas, such as anti-racism, refugee politics, and women's issues. For the local immigrant organizations the situation is different. There is a gap between political ideals about access to all and procedures on the ground which, in effect, is a form of ethnic filtering. Many adopt names to indicate their target constituency, such as the Turkish Youth Association, the Pakistani Student Association, or the Bosnian Group in Norway. How the organizations can do this and still receive government money is a good question. The answer is that despite the name, they are officially open to all comers. The bottom line, however, is that while the statutes legislate openness, in reality, the organizations recruit members of a similar background.

Organizations for Turks

In 2007, 15 government-funded organizations were operated by and for the Turkish community, including the Turkish Youth Association, the Turkish Children and Youth Organization, the Turkish Organization for Family and Culture, the Turkish Organization for Help and Support, and the Turkish Woman Association. [23] The obvious question here is whether 15 is a big or a small number of organizations. This number can be compared to the number of Kurdish organizations. Turkish Kurds make up only 20 percent of the Turkish community in Norway, but there are 30 Kurdish organizations with government funding, including the Kurdish Association, the Kurdish Association for Culture, the Kurdish Woman Association, the Kurdish Democratic Association, Kurdish Group SOS-Racism, Kurdish Radio, and the Kurdish Theatre Group. [24] While these organizations include members with Kurdish relations in countries other than Turkey, a large proportion is Turkish in origin. Thus, they have clearly identified themselves as Kurdish, not Turkish. The number of Turkish associations, therefore, seems rather small.

According to Nødland, the government-funded community organizations are primarily bridge builders, with some occasional use as aid organizations. [25] The political reason for giving public support to local organizations is to promote engagement, diversity, and dialogue among different origin groups. Funding is meant to cover the day-to-day work of the organization as well as its more ad hoc activities. There is no clear delineation of the kind of activity permitted, but it must be related to cultural dialogue between groups, identity, and activities within the local community. In 2008, the official year of diversity in Norway, Deichmann (the public library) cooperated with eight Turkish organizations (the Turkish Woman's Association, Norwegian-Turkish Friends in Cooperation, the Turkish Islam Union, the Turkish Organization for Children and Youth, the Islam Culture-Centrum, the

Turkish Organization for Help and Support, the Turkish Family Association, and the Turkish Organizations National Association in Norway)[26] to produce a program that included lectures on Turkish history, books, and movies, as well as Turkish food and Turkish theatre and dance performances.

The Kurds have twice as many organizations but account for only a fifth of the population. While this is an interesting finding in and of itself, it prompts a discussion of the Norwegian system and its highly differential treatment of migrant groups, especially refugee (more often Kurds) and economic (more often Turks) migrant groups. While the first group is taken under the wing of the welfare state, economic immigrants are largely left to their own devices. In short, refugees come to a system ready to spring into action on their behalf; they learn how the system works and are helped by key figures. They are introduced to a network with information on, among other things, how to set up an organization and apply for government funding. The situation for the economic immigrants and their families is quite different. Respondents reported numerous failed attempts to organize the Turkish community. The lack of success, they say, comes from a lack of awareness of the help available. Active associations are mainly concerned with family reunification and, as such, are only partly eligible for support. In practice, many elect to leave the grant system alone because they do not see what they will get in return for joining the established corporative system and because they do not believe that subsidies will be forthcoming. These organizations, then, operate outside the orbit of the majority and are in that sense invisible to the authorities and general public—which is not to say they are insignificant.

The previous section on the "role of the civil society" referred to the corporative element of both the substantive and the ideological arenas of associations. While the substantive aspect is often obvious the ideological aims of an organization may be more problematic. Arguably, voluntary organization is of value in and of itself. From a public point of view it is meaningful to activate people and integrate them into society, but there is a problem if economic immigrants and their children are less integrated than others. Moreover, while organizations may play a role as "schools in democracy," to be important politically they need to attract a sufficient number of people. The statistics on voting behavior and the relatively small number of active Turks in organizational life show there is a long way to go.

A Success Story? The Turkish Youth Association

The Turkish Youth Association (Tyrkisk Ungdomsforening) has attracted attention in recent years, partly because a few determined leaders with well-developed entrepreneurial skills have demonstrated their ability to mobilize members across a range of causes. The organization is a well-recognized, highly active player in several arenas.

One key initiative of the leaders has been to ensure that the organization dovetails with the mainstream system of organizations run by the majority population. To this end, the organization became a full member of the Norwegian Children and Youth

Council (Landsrådet for barne- og ungdomsorganisasjoner, LNU) in 2004 and joined the Council of Children and Youth in Oslo (Landsstyret for Ungdomsorgan-isasjoner) in 2005. It is relevant to note that by adopting the majority's management philosophy the organization raised public awareness, received funding, and activated many adolescents with Turkish affiliations.

The Turkish Youth Association can also be used to illustrate two sets of logic operating in the Norwegian system. Under one set of logic, funding is given on the basis of the organization's membership numbers; in other instances, funding is based on the organization's purpose. The Norwegian system has tended to give priority to membership. The Turkish Youth Association reacted vehemently to this practice, not least because many active members were disinclined to have their names appear on a membership list. As one member told me: "We were afraid their parents wouldn't like what we were doing. They're apprehensive about all types of organized work."

Fear of parental reaction is not a concern for majority organizations in Norway, so it is particularly interesting to see the changes brought about by the Turkish Youth Association, which paradoxically embraced many of the principles of the majority organization system by addressing this exclusionary issue. A public commission, whose members included the leader of the Turkish Youth Association, recommended overhauling the funding criteria and putting more emphasis on activity.[27] In sum, the Turkish Youth Association of Norway is an example of an organization with the ability to challenge and change established practices. An important factor is its decision to work within the establishment, albeit on its own terms.

The next question concerns how members work within the organization. Improving qualifications seems to be a key concern. A member said: "We had attended training and competence building courses to help youngsters learn how to run their own organizations and how organizations work generally in Norway." In other words, it is essential to learn about the various funding oppor-tunities, to set up mechanisms in collaboration with majority youth organizations, and to raise awareness of the latter among the organization's active participants. In many respects the Turkish Youth Organization underlines the importance of face-to-face contact while serving as an arena for democratic socialization. In fact, raising the organization's profile has led several members of the Turkish Youth Association to work in organizations such as European Youth, the Council of Children and Youth in Oslo (BURO), and the Norwegian Children and Youth Council (LNU).

From the profile of the Turkish Youth Association as it appears on its website it appears to have accepted the government's strictures against ethnic discrimination:

NTGD STUDENT is an organization with no allegiance to any of the political parties or religions. It is an organization mainly for students at university level but also for students in further education with an interest in Turkey and Turkish culture.

Yet they also say they are interested in Turkey and Turkish culture. How many, if any, are not of Turkish origin remains to be seen. Nor do profiles designed for government consumption necessarily tell the whole story. Much can be gleaned from a profile posted on Facebook by an association with almost identical ambitions. Its self-description targets members with Turkish credentials:

Turkish Student Association of Norway has been established! The intention for the organization is to unify Turkish students in Norway. We try to reach out to as many students as possible, from all around the country.

This is a group for all students who [are] interested in getting to know other students, and then create a network. Opportunities related to higher education and work after studying, trainee, exchange and last but not least social events will come.

We have to work together if we want to realize these goals! All of our students are highly recommended to involve themselves. (Source: Facebook.com, TSF - Norges Tyrkiske Student Forening.)

As has been shown, the Turkish Youth Association has changed the basic architecture of the system to which it belongs. However, to do so it had to move into the majority's court. Some might see this as a strategy to gain leverage. Others might say the organization has alienated itself from the task of consolidating identities and preserving culture. The question is whether one should judge immigrant organizations in terms of their social power. One can approach this question by considering how political and organizational commitments interact.

Social Capital: Organizations and Democratic Commitment

Social capital is frequently invoked in analyses of civil society's place in modern society. A much-cited theoretician in this area is Robert Putnam, whose books deal with the social preconditions of healthy democracy. [28] According to Putnam, active citizenry depends on the health of the civic community. In *Bowling Alone*, he notes that people are connected via networks. [29] These networks foster a form of mutual trust or solidarity that extends beyond the interpersonal, face-to-face encounters of the network. Networks and trust, he says, are the cornerstones of civic and democratic involvement. The definition of social capital used here draws upon a design created by Wollebæk and Selle. [30] In their design, they assign three dimensions to social capital: *trust* (in people and institutions), *networks* (via organizations or informal but regular meetings of friends and acquaintances), and *civic involvement* (an active interest in local politics). In the following, how people from the Turkish community in Norway fare on a social capital score when compared with the majority and other non-Western minorities and how social capital inequalities affect political involvement is considered.

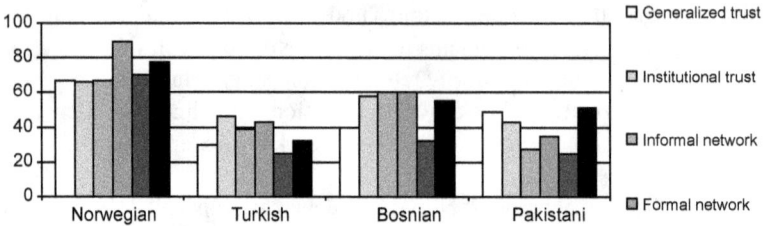

Figure 2. Distribution of respondents attesting to any of the following: reads Norwegian newspapers/listens to Norwegian news bulletins every day; very or quite interested in local politics; member of a formal network (organization); member of an informal network that meets regularly; high generalized trust; high institutional trust. By country of origin, in percent.[4]

The group-by-group distribution of social capital is depicted in Figure 2. One is immediately struck by the gap between the majority and the three minorities (Turkish, Bosnian, and Pakistani). Essentially, Pakistanis tend to trust other people, even though a relatively small number are involved in networks or express political involvement. The Bosnian group, in contrast, scores well on all dimensions except trust. At the other end of the scale are the Turkish respondents, with low scores on several dimensions. Two exceptions are informal networks, where the Turkish group does better than the Pakistani one, and interest in local politics, with similar scores for both groups.

Taking as a starting point the three social capital dimensions, the scores can be used to indicate degree of social integration. One crucial question is why the group of Turkish-affiliated citizens systematically emerges with a lower score than other minorities. If they are compared to the majority population the gap is even more glaring, especially as many of the respondents in the Turkish group have lived in Norway for quite some time: about 50 percent of the group has lived in the country for 20 years or more. In terms of legal ties to the country—that is, nationality—the Turkish community also stands out: three in four individuals of Turkish descent are Norwegian nationals.

A number of studies have examined minorities, social capital, and political involvement.[31] The positive correlation between political activity, such as turn-out at elections, and other variables, such as contact with politicians, wearing political buttons, signing petitions, boycotting certain brands, donating money to a political organization/group, having pieces published in the press, or being featured in the media has been confirmed. [32] Of particular bearing here are the networks (i.e., organizations), but more informal arrangements should also be considered.

While variations in social capital are useful for explaining variations in political commitment the central question is why the Turkish group has so little social capital. What can be done to amend the situation and lay the ground for wider political involvement?

Organizations: A School for Democracy?

As noted above, immigrant organizations are understood to play an important role in the democratic system; they promote dialogue, facilitate empowerment, and socialize members in democracy. Two problems, also addressed above, are the democratic deficit of the nationwide organizations in Norway and the lack of organizations that speak to the Turkish community.

Is it possible that integration ideals are incompatible with the desire to encourage active immigrant organizations? By funding immigrant organizations, can the government really achieve its goal of an integrated and heterogeneous society? In reality, a dilemma inherent to integration policy is that it is impossible for organizations with a homogeneous membership not to reinforce stereotypes of a social split between "us" and "them." Furthermore, as mentioned above, special interest organizations are in the ascendancy in Norway; members are increasingly organized on the basis of a common activity, whether sports, youth associations, political interests, or anti-racism issues. The subject has been reviewed in a public commission report that discusses the government's support of organizations for children and adolescents. [33] The commission spells out three reasons why organizations of and for minorities contribute to a healthier democracy. First, the report notes the social and cultural benefits that accrue from membership in an organization; it makes reference to research on the human need to join communities of like-minded individuals. Second, it says that minorities are underrepresented in key positions in society—in the labor market, in politics, and in the social elite more generally. Finally, it points out that certain segments of minority communities have their own particular concerns; their organizations may be aimed at maintaining contact with the home country or arranging cultural events.

A consideration of like-mindedness and a concern for the underrepresentation of the immigrant population in key areas of society are included in the government's integration policy. However, there must be a balance between catering to the needs of particular groups and attempting to create common interests that cut across ethnic and other divides. Finally, organizations can have an impact far in excess of their mission. Danish political scientist Jørgen Goul Andersen accentuates the positive effect of organizational involvement on democratic culture and the individual citizen.[34] He argues that citizens approach democracy from the bottom up via organizational solidarity. This socialization into a democratic culture does not rely on the organization having a political agenda.

Conclusion

The issue raised at the start of this article is the low level of political activity in the Turkish community in Norway. Simply stated, the community is not well-represented in political decision-making and there is relatively little interest in Norwegian politics generally. This is in addition to the Turkish community's lack of interest in international politics and even domestic politics within Turkey itself.[35]

Vermeulen's distinction between group-related factors and receiving society-related factors can help explain the low level of political participation in Norway. [36] The group-related category comprises three sub-factors: the immigration process; the character of immigrant population; and the organizational influence of the country of origin. This latter factor is another name for political opportunity structure in the host society.[37]

Concerning the immigration process, the question is what the immigrant organizing processes do to the group. A large proportion of the Turkish community entered Norway as economic migrants. Because they came individually on personal labor contracts, the development of a collective Turkish-Norwegian identity may have been slowed. The explanation gains cogency by comparison with the Kurdish community, most of whose members came to Norway as refugees.

Another important factor is the character of the immigrant population. Despite their long period of residence in Norway, a large proportion of Turks have low academic achievements. Furthermore, given the time many have lived there, the relationship between low rates of employment and lack of political participation is striking.

The last of the group-related factors consider influences from the country of origin. As the educational qualifications of most of the early Turkish immigrants were particularly poor there is little reason to assume high involvement in organizational activity while they were still in Turkey. This could help explain the low level of involvement in Norway. As has been suggested, there is a transnational element consisting of informal networks and connections with sister organizations in other countries. However, many of the Turkish youth organizations are very active, and in interviews respondents from these organizations said they mostly thought of themselves as Norwegians. With few exceptions, their parents are not very active politically and much of the activism among the youth is part of the process of becoming Norwegian citizens. An important dimension is the feeling of being a marginalized outsider—of course, this is not limited to those of Turkish origin, but it is certainly a factor in Turkish youth organizations.

As for receiving society-related factors, the acquisition of political rights is clearly relevant but cannot explain the Turkish group's relatively inactive position, especially as three quarters have taken Norwegian nationality. Another point to consider is noted above, namely the disparity in procedures and measures for refugees and economic migrants. While refugees are introduced to civil society, economic migrants have to learn the system on their own. This could help explain the low scores on political commitment by the Turkish community.

The Turkish Youth Association is an important organization in Norway, which has shown a capacity to seek and to gain power on the establishment's terms. From this, it can be hypothesized that new generations of immigrants will engage with society in a different manner than their immigrant forbears. There is a potential for new citizens to group together in organizations, to organize, and to become involved in democratic processes in new and different ways.

Notes

1. Karl Henrik Sivesind, "The Nordic Nonprofit Sector in Comparative Perspective—Is There a Nordic Model of Civil Society?" Paper presented at the CINEFOGO Conference on The Role and Organisation of European Civil Society—Its Relationship to State and Business and Its Importance for Welfare Provision and Social Cohesion, Roskilde, November 15-17, 2006, ISF paper 2006:012, p.1.
2. Pakistani immigrants also arrived early.
3. http://www.ssb.no/emner/02/rapp_200729/rapp_200729.pdf.
4. Jon Rogstad, *Demokratisk fellesskap. Politisk inkludering og etnisk mobilisering* [*Democratic Communities. Political Inclusion and Etnic Mobilization*] (Oslo: Universitetsforlaget, 2007), p. 159.
5. Iris Marion Young, *Inclusion and Democracy* (Oxford: Oxford University Press, 2000), p. 17.
6. Jon Horgen Friberg, *Ungdom, fritid og deltakelse i det flerkulturelle* (Youth, Free time and Participation in the Multicultural Oslo) (Oslo: Fafo-notat, 2005).
7. Ibid., p.16.
8. The study undertaken is the largest study of engagement and membership in voluntary sector among people living in Norway with a non-Western background.
9. Åse Strandbu, *Idrett, kjønn, kropp og kultur. Minoritetsjenters møte med norsk idrett* [*Sports, Gender, Body and Culture. Minority Girls' Meeting with Norwegian Sports*] (NOVA Rapport 10/06, Oslo, 2006).
10. Charles Taylor, "The Politics of Recognition," in Amy Gutman (ed.), *Multiculturalism* (New Jersey: Princeton University Press, 1994), p. 21.
11. Ruud Koopmans and Paul Statham, "Migration and Ethnic Relations as Field of Political Contention: An Oppurtunity Structure Approach", in Ruud Koopmans and Paul Statham (eds.), *Challenging Immigration and Ethnic Relations Politics* (Oxford: Oxford University Press, 2000), p. 32.
12. Robert D. Putnam, *Making Democracy Work: Civic Traditions in Modern Italy* (New Jersey: Princeton University Press, 1993); Robert D. Putnam, *Bowling Alone: The Collapse and Revival of American Community* (New York: Simon & Schuster, 2000), p. 19.
13. Benedict Anderson, *Imagined Communities: Reflections on the Origin and Spread of Nationalism* (London and New York: Verso, 1981).
14. Nina Glick-Schiller, Linda Basch and Christina Szanton-Blanc, *Towards a Transnational Perspective on Migration: Race, Class, Ethnicity and Nationalism Reconsidered* (New York: New York Academy of Sciences, 1992).
15. Alejandro Portes, Luis E. Guarnizo and Patricia Landolt, "The Study of Transnationalism: Pitfalls and Promise of an Emergent Research Field," *Ethnic and Racial Studies,* Vol. 22, No. 2 (1999), pp. 217-37.
16. Sivesind, "The Nordic Nonprofit Sector in Comparative Perspective," p. 12.
17. Meindert Fennema and Jean Tillie, "Political Participation and Political Trust in Amsterdam: Civic Communities and Ethnic Networks," *Journal of Ethnic and Migration Studies* , Vol. 25, No. 4 (1999), pp. 703-26.
18. Floris Freek Vermeulen, *The Immigrant Organising Process: The Emergence and Persistence of Turkish Immigrant Organisations in Amsterdam and Berlin and Surinamese Organisations in Amsterdam, 1960-2000* (Amsterdam, University of Amsterdam, 2005).
19. Svein Ingve Nødland, "Vedlegg," [Attachment] in *Fritid med mening. Statlig støttepolitikk for frivillige barne og ungdomsorganisasjoner* [*Free Time with Meaning. Government Funding Policies for Voluntarily Children's and Youth Organizations*] (NOU 2006), p. 13. Oslo: Kultur og kirkedepartementet
20. Rogstad, *Demokratisk fellesskap* [*Democratic Communities*].
21. Jørgen Melve, "Innvandrerorganisasjoner i Norge" [*Immigrant Associations in Norway*], in *Invandrerorganisationer i Norden Tema Nord* [*Immigrant Associations in The Nordic Countries*] (København: Nordisk ministerråd, 2003), p. 21.
22. Ibid.
23. Translation from Norwegian by the author.
24. See previous note.

25. Nødland, *Fritid med mening* [*Free Time with Meaning*].
26. Translated from Norwegian (*Tykisk Kvinneforening Norsk-tyrkisk Vennskapssamband Den Tyrkisk Islamske Union Tyrkisk barne- og ungdomsorganisasjon Islamsk kultursentrum i Oslo Tyrkisk Hjelpe- og støtteforening Bærum Tyrkisk Familie Forening Tyrkiske Organisasjoners Landsorganisasjon i Norge*).
27. NOU, *Fritid med mening. Statlig støttepolitikk for frivillige barne og ungdomsorganisasjoner* (Free Time With Meaning. Government Funding Policies for Voluntary Children's and Youth Organizations) (NOU, 2006), p.13. Oslo: Kultur og kirkedepartementet
28. See Putnam, *Making Democracy Work*; Putnam, *Bowling Alone*.
29. See Putnam, *Bowling Alone*, p. 19.
30. Dag Wollebæk and Per Selle, "Where Does Social Capital Come From? Socialization and Institutionalization Approaches Compared," Paper Association for Research on Non-Profit Organizations and Voluntary Action (ARNOVA), Washington, 2005.
31. See *Journal of Ethnic and Migration Studies*, Vol 30, 3 (2004).
32. Rogstad, *Demokratisk fellesskap*, p. 147.
33. NOU, *Fritid med mening. Statlig støttepolitikk for frivillige barne og ungdomsorganisasjoner.* [*Free Time with Meaning. Government Funding Policies for Voluntarily Children's and Youth Organizations*].
34. Jørgen Goul Andersen, *Et ganske levende demokrati* (Århus: Aarhus universitetsforlag, 2004).
35. Rogstad, *Demokratisk fellesskap* [*Democratic Communities*].
36. Vermeulen, *The Immigrant Organising Process*.
37. Ibid, p. 31.

The Gülen Movement in Ireland: Civil Society Engagements of a Turkish Religio-cultural Movement

JONATHAN LACEY

Department of Sociology, Trinity College, Dublin, Ireland

ABSTRACT   *In recent years there has been a growing interest among sociologists regarding the transnational engagements of migrant communities and organizations. This paper contributes to this body of knowledge by focusing on a Turkish religio-cultural society in Ireland, namely the Turkish Irish Educational and Cultural Society (TIECS). This society is affiliated with the Turkey-based transnational Gülen movement. Drawing on ethnography and qualitative interviews conducted with members of TIECS, the study examines their contribution to the discourse on Islam and integration in Ireland and shows how they exploit global opportunity spaces in order to expand the Gülen movement's presence in Europe.*

Introduction

Transnationalism in its many guises appears across many academic disciplines and refers to an infinite amount of cross border flows, including trade, finance and capital, people, technology, culture, and ideas. [1] Increases in telecommunications means that people can connect with others across borders with great ease, while in the aviation industry technological advancements have led to low airfares and extensive flight destinations. These factors have led to a dramatic increase in international migration and the emergence of transnational social movements over the last three decades. Though most academic attention has been drawn to cross-border flows of capital and technology, more recently attention has been given to the transnational flows and networks of migrants who engage in activities in both their country of origin and their country of settlement. [2] Though religious movements have been among the oldest transnational actors they have attracted little academic attention.[3]

This paper exploits this gap in the research by focusing on the transnational religio-cultural Gülen movement founded by the controversial Turkish Islamic scholar Fethullah Gülen.[4] The movement's activities have been well-documented in Turkey[5] and Central Asia,[6] yet there has been little research into the movement's activities among diaspora members in the European context. This article focuses on the Gülen movement's presence in Ireland by discussing the role of its representative body, namely the Turkish Irish Educational and Cultural Society (TIECS). This was established by Turkish migrants living in Ireland who already belonged to the Gülen movement. This essay explores how the Gülen movement's TIECS contributes to the debate on Islam and integration in Ireland and illustrates how its members exploit the opportunity spaces created by global conditions to expand the movement's presence in Europe.

Though this paper is principally based on data collected from the eight qualitative interviews conducted with members of TIECS, at times it was useful to draw on interviews conducted with members of the Northern Ireland Turkish Educational and Cultural Association (NI-TECA), TIECS's sister organization in Belfast. The data used in this paper was gathered between November 2005 and November 2007. All of the participants interviewed were male. There are two major reasons for this. Firstly, the most prominent members of the Gülen movement in Ireland (and indeed around the world) are male, and the intention was to interview those involved at the deepest level. Secondly, as several theorists have pointed out, due to the gender segregation among conservative Muslims it is difficult for men to gain access to female interviewees in Muslim populations. [7] Heeding this potential obstacle and fully aware of the conservative nature of the Gülen movement, the author decided to interview only male followers of Gülen.

Ireland provides an interesting site for this study because unlike Holland, France, Britain, and Germany, inward migration is a relatively new phenomenon for this country and likewise, debates on multiculturalism and integration.[8] Piaras MacEinri and Paddy Walley[9] argue that Ireland can now be understood "as a microcosm of the realities of globalisation" and Fintan O'Toole[10] insists that the "Republic of Ireland is the most globalised country on earth." Trade and finance pass fluently in and out of the territorial boundaries of Ireland. As of 1993, Ireland received 25 percent of all new US investment into Europe, employing 94,000 people in 2002.[11][12] This inward investment since the early 1990s, along with EU contributions over the last two decades, has resulted in Ireland's economy flourishing, making it one of the strongest economies in the world. [13] This effervescent economy is necessarily coupled with inward migration to Ireland. Since 1996, Ireland, for so long suffering from an emigration hemorrhage, became an immigration destination. [14] Immigrants were courted by Irish companies and the government to fill job shortages. Consequentially, there have been unprecedented levels of immigration in Ireland and likewise an unprecedented mixture of cultures and religions. Irish culture has moved from one defined by Catholicism, nationalism, and economic isolationism to one oriented towards economic and cultural liberalism. Ireland has moved from a nation that largely perceived itself as homogenous to one that is renegotiating its identity on the recognition of heterogeneity.

Irish culture has been steeped in the Catholic tradition for centuries, and though there has been a decline in the number of practicing Catholics in Ireland, [15] over 3.6 million of the total population of nearly 4.2 million in Ireland still claim to be

Catholic.[16] However, Islam is now the fastest growing religion in Ireland, with over 31,000 adherents,[17] and has become part of the national conversation vis-à-vis Irish identity. Yet the activities of Muslims living there have attracted little academic attention.[18] From the few studies conducted, the most striking revelation is the multiplicity of Islamic expressions based on ethnic, ideological, and theological differences. All of these are involved in a growing competitive market over the "true" expression of Islam. This essay contributes to this debate by looking at the Gülen movement's presence in Ireland and analyzes how it represents Islam in this context.

The paper begins by briefly relating the recent immigration trends in Ireland. This is followed by a description of the origins, objectives, and transnational endeavors of the Gülen movement. This section also attempts to explain the growing presence of the movement in Europe. Subsequent to this is a description of its presence in Ireland through TIECS. Following this is an illustration of the strategic approach by diaspora members of the Gülen movement to court members of the Turkish diaspora and its attempt to influence elites in mainstream Irish society. It then looks at TIECS's attitudes to integration in Ireland. Following this is a description of one of the main annual events TIECS holds in Ireland, namely a conference focusing on the commonalities between the Abrahamic religions. The conduciveness of this series of conferences to interfaith and intercultural dialogue in Ireland is assessed. This paper not only shows the transnational reach of the Gülen movement but also illustrates how a migrant community actively participates in Irish society instead of being subjected by the cultural hegemony of a different environment.

Immigration Trends in Ireland

Ireland has become a country of net immigration since 1996. [19] There are currently three million Irish citizens living outside of Ireland, and though the number of Irish return migrants has increased nearly every year since 1987 their overall share in the total number of immigrants has fallen from 65 percent in the 1980s [20] to 27 percent in 2005.[21] This still represents a significant proportion of overall migrants, but it is non-Irish migrants that have been the driving force in immigration intensification in Ireland in recent years.[22] The 2006 Census indicates that foreign nationals represent ten percent of the population, an increase from 5.8 percent in 2002.[23]

The overwhelming majority of migrants in Ireland are gainfully employed. In the fourth quarter of 2007, foreign nationals represented nearly 16 percent of all persons 15 years and over in employment in the state. [24] Migrants are employed across all sectors of the economy but the hotels and restaurants sector is particularly reliant on migrants, with 37 percent of workers in this area being non-Irish. Over 17 percent of production industries, wholesale and retail trade, and construction industries were staffed by foreign nationals living in Ireland.[25]

International migrants are categorized into two different groups on their entry into Ireland, namely European Economic Area (EEA) [26] nationals and non-EEA nationals. Those with citizenship in countries within the EEA have unrestricted access to the Irish labor market as long as they can verify that they are self-sufficient. Estimates from the last quarter of the 2007 Irish *Quarterly National Household Survey* (QNHS)[27] illustrate that EEA nationals represent the majority of inward migration to Ireland. Poles (63,090), Lithuanians (24,808) and Latvians (13,999) are among the largest recent immigrant groups in Ireland.[28]

Non-EEA nationals living in Ireland come from all over the world, including Africa (42,764), Asia (55,624), and the Americas (38,301). [29] There are a range of legal entry channels, including work permits, work visas, student visas, asylum, and family reunification.[30] Other migrants enter illegally, though there are no reliable estimates to inform how many.

Turkish migrants are, of course, currently non-EEA nationals. According to the 2006 Census, there are only 766 Turkish migrants living in Ireland. However, this is contested by Turkish migrants themselves who suggest it is closer to 3000. Some migrants may have decided not to register with the census due to the negative reception of Turks in other European countries, such as Germany, Holland, and France.[31] Another reason may relate to the negative attention the Turkish construction company GAMA received vis-à-vis the alleged underpaying of Turkish workers in Ireland.[32] Coupled with ever-increasing racism in Ireland, [33] some migrants may have chosen not to declare their nationality in the census. This is rather speculative, but what is certainly apparent is that there are only a small number of Turks living in Ireland. This makes the presence of the Gülen movement in Ireland even more interesting. One expects a presence of the Gülen movement in countries with a large number of Turkish migrants, such as Germany, Holland, France, or England. It is rather less expected in a country with a low density of Turks. As well as outlining the scope of the Gülen movement, the next section of this paper attempts to explain why the Gülen movement has penetrated Ireland.

The Gülen Movement as a Transnational Religio-cultural Movement

As previously mentioned, the Gülen movement is named after Fethullah Gülen, a Turkish Islamic scholar who has a following of up to six million supporters in Turkey and among the Turkish diaspora around the world. Gülen has attracted the attention of a large proportion of the wealthy "Anatolian bourgeoisie,"[34] whose members have developed a vast financial infrastructure to support the activities of the movement. These initiatives include support for hundreds of private schools and universities, predominantly in Central Asia and the Balkans. These schools are also becoming increasingly popular in Europe and the United States. The movement also boasts a media empire, which includes TV stations, a publishing house, radio stations, and one of Turkey's biggest selling newspapers, *Zaman*. Its products are produced in Turkish, English, and several other languages. They have also established a number of interfaith and intercultural dialogue platforms around the globe.

The Gülen movement emerged out of the Nur movement, led by the Turkish Islamic theologian Said Nursi, who was engaged in promoting a new kind of Islamic consciousness that focused on reconciling science and Islam and thereby on creating a modern Turkish society, which has Islam at its core. [35] Nursi had millions of followers, but after his death the movement split into several different factions. The Gülen movement became the largest of these factions, and Gülen uses Nursi's "conceptual framework"[36] to direct his own activities. Though there is no solid evidence linking Gülen to an attempt to create a theocratic state, like Nursi he does intend to bring Islam back into the center of state institutions and everyday life just as it was in the Ottoman Empire. He hopes for the rising of a devout and tolerant Turkish Muslim populace with an influential state. The Ottoman Empire serves as a model for such a project. However, Mücahit Bilici[37] importantly notes that Gülen is fully cognizant that he lives in modern times, and he therefore utilizes modern tools to rouse his followers. Bilici draws particular attention to the emergence of the Journalists and Writers Foundation (JWF), of which Gülen is honorary president. This group organizes a range of high profile activities, including interfaith and inter-cultural symposiums and National Tolerance awards, to name a few (see JWF website[38] for a longer list). These activities are replicated by affiliates of the Gülen movement all over the world.

According to Bilici:

Gülen's public identity is constructed within the amorphous sphere between Islam and nationalism…. Due to his in-betweenness, Gülen has successfully disabled the Turkish state's exclusionary policies by manipulating the very categories used against him.[39]

In Turkey, the only way to gain legitimacy for religion is to dowse it in national-istic rhetoric, thus framing it as an attribute of Turkish national identity rather than as an independent feature.[40] This has been mastered by Gülen and his followers by designating their expression of Islam as Turkish Islam. [41] Turkish sociologist Nur Vergin points out that Turkish Muslims have created a "territorialized version of Islam."[42] Yavuz contends that this can be traced back to the reign of the founding father of the Turkish republic, Mustafa Kemal Atatürk. Yavuz argues that "When Islam was suppressed and forced out of the public sphere during the first three decades of [the] Kemalist secularization program, nationalism became the only habitat where many Muslim intellectuals could take refuge." [43] This left an indelible mark on Islamic thought in Turkey. It became intertwined with nationalism and thus leads many commentators to refer to the dominant Islamic practice in Turkey as Turkish Islam.

Ünal Bilir[44] attributes the popularization of the concept of Turkish Islam to Fethullah Gülen. Narrating the history of Islam in Turkey, Gülen of course recog-nizes that Islam emerged from Mecca and Medina but goes on to insist that Islam did not come directly from these areas but was routed through Central Asia. [45] The Turkic people of Central Asia adapted Islam to their own culture before exporting it through migration to the Anatolian region. A key point, according to Gülen, is the fact that Islam was not forced on the Anatolians but that they embraced it freely and wholeheartedly in great numbers.[46] The corollary of this, he maintains, is that Islam in Turkey has remained "tolerant, open, and un-dogmatic." [47] Gülen calls himself a Muslim Turk because he sees the two as inseparable, noting that "the Turkish nation put its true values on a solid foundation after becoming Muslim." [48] Gülen understands the practice of Islam in the Middle East as quite different from Turkish Islam. Indeed, he holds particular contempt for the practice of Islam in Iran, claiming that Iran is "a sick part of the body of Islam." [49] His disapproval of the Iranian regime avowedly stems from his condemnation of theocratic states. This type of rhetoric is consistent with Gülen's image as a committed Turkish nationalist and secularist, believing that religion and politics should be separate.

Furthermore, Gülen is adamant that one must express one's spirituality through engagement with the world. He motivates his followers to mobilize by insisting that the mere aversion of transgressions is not sufficient for being a "good Muslim." One must also become active in order to improve the conditions in the world. Islam, according to Gülen's articulation, is action-oriented. A defining feature, then, of Gülen's worldview is revealed in the term *hizmet* (service). In Gülen's interpretation, this refers to service to God by serving humanity, and it is a central key to understanding this religio-cultural movement.[50] Indeed, members often refer to their movement as the *hizmet*. In Gülen's notion, one must live one's life for the sake of God. He describes this by saying:

> ... the worldly life should be used in order to earn the afterlife and to please the One who has bestowed it. The way to do so is to seek to please Allah and, as an inseparable dimension of it, to serve immediate family members, society, country and all of humanity accordingly. This service is our right, and sharing it with others is our duty.[51]

In short, Gülen believes that Muslims must serve God by serving other people in order to benefit them in the next life. This has stimulated Gülen's members to donate human and economic capital to fund his activities. Gulay [52] argues that it is this feature of Gülen's movement that distinguishes it from Nurcu's and the Naqshabendi in Turkey. Though these latter two groups do not reject action-oriented Islam, like most Sufi-inspired groups they do not adopt it as a fundamental principle in the same way that followers of Gülen do.

This ethos inspired many of Gülen's disciples to establish a strong presence in Central Asia. With the fall of the Soviet regime new opportunity structures opened up in the newly independent states of Central Asia. The early 1990s saw the Gülen movement invest heavily in this region, setting up schools and universities, propagating what Park [53] refers to as "educational Islamism." This involves the diffusion of Islamic principles in schools rather than overt proselytizing. [54] Religion is not taught in these schools, but students are encouraged to "remember" their Islamic identity, which had been suppressed by the Soviet Empire. This is an extension of Gülen's policy in Turkey, where he attempts to make Islam central to Turkic people's everyday lives. The schools that the Gülen movement operates are fee-paying private schools. This is a concerted effort to attract elites in the host country in which they operate. Once educated in the Gülen schools, it is expected that these scholars will become influential and thus raise the profile of the Gülen movement and encourage their brand of Turkish Islam to diffuse outside of Turkey. Park claims that "through the internalized spiritual transformation of individuals will come a wider social transformation."[55] This social transformation is expected to have Gülen's understanding of Islam at its core.

Gülen's transnational activities are not peculiar to the Turkic and former Ottoman territories. After the soft coup of 1997 the Gülen movement, like most Islamic movements in Turkey, came under increasing pressure from the Turkish secular elites, through the military. As a result, Gülen went into exile in the United States, and according to Bilici, the movement restructured its orientation away from the Turkish state, drawing "more and more upon the global discourse of 'human rights,' 'multiculturalism' and 'democracy.'"[56] Using the language of intercultural and interfaith dialogue the Gülen movement attempts to gain legitimacy and influence around the world, and more particularly in the West. Despite Gülen's friction with the Turkish state he remains a committed Turko-Ottoman nationalist. His mission is to create a greater role for Turkey in international affairs, not just in the surrounding region but in Europe and the United States as well, thus not just restoring the influence of the Ottoman era for Turks but going beyond it.

In his attempt to gain influence in the West, Gülen encourages his followers to migrate in order to become ambassadors for the Turkish state. [57] As a result, many members of the Gülen movement have dispersed around the world. In recent years, the movement has become more visible in Europe and the United States, setting up a range of Turkish cultural centers and dialogue platforms attempting to promote a positive image of Islam and Turkey. Members of the Gülen movement help set up organizations where members of the Turkish diaspora have already established a base. Active members of the movement periodically travel to Gülen-inspired organizations and advise its members on the best way to implement the objectives of the movement.

In 2004, the Gülen movement made its institutional presence felt in Ireland by establishing the Turkish Irish Educational and Cultural Society (TIECS) in Dublin. This organization arranges a number of activities directed by the wider Gülen movement. They include the same repertoire of activities as other sister associations around the world, such as interfaith dialogue conferences, interfaith Ramadan dinners, performances by the Whirling Dervishes, subsidized guided trips to Turkey for indigenous people of the host country, Turkish lessons, and a range of other cultural events. Ireland has become an important European center for business and culture, and the initiation of the Gülen-inspired TIECS may be seen as a strategic move in order to make an impact in Europe. There appears to be a concerted attempt to gain influence in Europe by the Gülen movement in recent years with the initiation of other Gülen associations in Belfast (NI-TECA), Edinburgh (Dialogue Society for Scotland), and across England (Fellowship Dialgoue Scoiety), [58] which all opened in 2004-2005. The Dialogue Society in London preceded these and was established in 1999. One cannot fail to notice that the mushrooming of these organizations run concurrent with the opening up of talks between Turkey and the European Union (EU) regarding Turkey's possible accession into the EU, a position Fethullah Gülen has fully supported in recent years. [59] He maintains that Islamic identity and European identity are not necessarily incongruous but can be complimentary. Given Gülen's support for European integration of Turkey it is plausible to view the emergence of Gülen-inspired organizations as a concerted attempt to promote a positive image of Turkey in an attempt to gain support for European accession.

Another important reason for the growth of the Gülen movement in Europe is due to the opportunity spaces that have opened up. Twenty-first century Europe has witnessed a series of high profile violent incidents set in motion by Islamist groups. These include the bombing of a train in Madrid (March 11, 2004), explosions in London (July 7, 2005), and the murder of the Dutch filmmaker Theo van Gogh (2004). These incidents have exacerbated suspicion in Europe towards Muslims. There has, however, also been a growing acknowledgement among public representatives that engagement with, and understanding of, Muslims is vital in order to curb Islamic fundamentalism. Amid the growing public discourse depicting Islam as inherently violent the Gülen movement actively promotes Islam as tolerant and claims it is consistent with Western values. In this way it attempts to promote itself as an antidote to Islamic radicalism. [60] The next section of this paper focuses on the Gülen movement's presence in Ireland through TIECS before describing how it represents Islam in Ireland.

TIECS: The Gülen Movement in Ireland

TIECS, along with its sister organization NI-TECA in Belfast, was established in 2004 by Turkish migrants who have lived in Ireland for several years. These founding members are businessmen, academics, and professionals who claim to have moved to Ireland for pragmatic reasons, such as improving their standard of living. Given Gülen's encouragement for his followers to migrate in order to spread his ideas, it is likely that this had some part to play in their decision to migrate. The Gülen movement in Ireland has two main target groups, the Turkish diaspora and elites within mainstream society. Those Gülen followers who would later help establish TIECS were eager to court support for the movement among the small Turkish population living in Ireland. The precursor to TIECS involved gatherings of Turkish migrants congregating in order to deal with common bureaucratic issues such as visa problems and issues relating to raising their children in a foreign environment. With Turkey being a non-EAA country, Gülen movement members filled a gap by offering Turkish Muslims help with these practical issues.

Having consolidated some support from Turkish Muslims living in Ireland, members of the Gülen movement established TIECS, which now serves as a tentacle of the global network of the Gülen movement. TIECS firstly offers Turks living in Ireland a chance to reconnect with their Turkish heritage. This typically involves Turkish language and religion. TIECS encourages Turks to teach their children to speak the Turkish language and to re-familiarize themselves with Turkish cultural traits. TIECS offers weekend classes for these children where they learn the Turkish language and how to be respectful, particularly to older people. At the heart of the organization, however, is an attempt to ignite a passion for Islam among Turks living in Ireland. Many Turks living there had stopped practicing their religion. By holding textual gatherings on the works of Said Nursi and Fethullah Gülen and celebrating Islamic festivals such as *Kurban Bayramı* (Festival of Sacrifice)[61] TIECS leaders infused Islam back into members of the Turkish diaspora. It could be said that the Gülen movement has a mission to proselytize Islam to Turks living in Ireland, but there is no evidence that they attempt to proselytize to others. On the contrary, Gülen followers see it as more beneficial to their aims to have Christian sympathizers rather than Christians converting to Islam. They promote their movement as one that is aimed at interfaith dialogue rather than as a missionary movement. Members of TIECS support its activities with economic and human capital, though at times electing to draw on resources from the wider network of Gülen's movement.

Though TIECS was established by members of the Turkish diaspora living in Ireland its composition has changed, and it now includes temporary migrants from Turkey and Turkmenistan.[62] These members come and stay for a few years only. They are typically young, unmarried men, aged between 20 and 30 years. Most of them have attended one of Gülen's schools in Turkey or Central Asia. These men come to Ireland, they claim, to disseminate the teachings of Fethullah Gülen, which are avowedly for tolerance and dialogue. Periodically, older and more established members of the Gülen movement come to Ireland and work for its cause full-time. Due to family reunification difficulties, these older members sometimes do not even last one year. They are, however, quickly replaced by other eager followers of Gülen.

Echoing Gülen's policy of *hizmet*, one member, who had previously taught in schools in Central Asia, states his position: "…if you are doing any job, you must do it for the sake of God, not for yourself. You must live for…other human beings. You must not live for yourself. You must live for other people" (Emre,[63] 32 years, 2006).

Members like this represent what Gülen calls *aksiyon insane,* or man of action.[64] By donating his time to disseminating Gülen's theology this member of TIECS believes he is serving God and will benefit on "Judgment Day." This ethos of *hizmet* underpins all the Gülen movement's activities and accounts for the massive amounts of human and financial resources that are needed to promote its activities. Members insist that though prayer, pilgrimage, and asceticism are core components of Islam, so is engaging in social endeavors to make the world a more peaceful place. This corresponds with Gülen's action-oriented Islam, which members argue is grounded in social engagement with other faith and cultural groups.

Inspired by this principle, members of TIECS engage with the Irish public under the banner of interfaith and intercultural activities. Following Gülen's lead, this engagement is purposive, aimed predominantly at elite groups in society, such as clerics, academics, and politicians. Bilici argues that it is precisely this focus on elites that differentiates Gülen's movement from other nationalist Islamic groups: "The Gülen movement has a vision of reviving a faithful and tolerant Turkish-Islamic tradition as exemplified in the Ottoman Empire. Although most nationalist Islamic groups harbor such a dream, the Gülen community is distinguished in its elitism."[65]

In the Turkish context Gülen has crafted close friendships with leading Turkish politicians and other state authorities, as well as famous Turkish musicians and footballers. This type of activity helps legitimize the Gülen movement among the general public in Turkey. [66] Outside of Turkey Gülen followers pursue the same strategy, and its effectiveness has yielded successful results, with Gülen becoming more and more recognized around the world as a symbol for peaceful coexistence. Gülen's financial adviser claims: "If we had transferred the power we have abroad to Turkey we (as a movement) would have become a political giant." [67] In courting academics, politicians, and civil society actors the *Fethullahci* (followers of Fethullahçı Gülen) attempt to influence leaders within mainstream society. They attempt to promote Gülen's interpretation of Islam and impress upon elites that Turkey is a progressive and moderate country that should be accepted into the European Union. The Gülen movement only institutionalized its presence in Ireland in recent years and is patiently attempting to gain more influence with elites, already managing to get some state funding for some of its activities. With the support from its global network of affiliated organizations around the world it can afford to be patient, as it has access to massive amounts of human and financial resources.

The Gülen Movement and Attitudes to Integration in Ireland

Members of TIECS claim that one of their main goals is to help integrate Turks into Irish society and to contribute to the overall integration of migrants into Ireland, leading to an inclusive society. They are adamant that they do not want to assimilate into Irish society but rather intend to simultaneously integrate while preserving their own culture and traditions and passing these down to their children. Integration, according to these early members, is the key to successful settlement. This is echoed in their mission statement, which emphasizes values such as "tolerance, respect, and compassion."[68]

Members of TIECS insisted that they had learned from the mistakes of other Turkish migrants abroad who made little attempt to integrate in the early years, which led to subsequent generations of Turks feeling displaced and isolated from mainstream society. Several participants pointed to Germany as the principal site where Turkish migrants were caught in an "in between" or "liminal" [69] space. The majority of these Turks are a legacy of the "guestworker" system established in the 1960s.

One member of TIECS claims that:

…what happened to the Turkish people in Germany? They didn't start to do volunteering work or social work 30 years ago and now they have big problems with the young generation because they have a kind of dual identification, actually not dual identification, no identity. They don't feel they belong to any society. They don't describe themselves as German. It is not easy to say 'I am Turkish.' So they are kind of in the middle somewhere. And this is not integration, not assimilation even, just standing in the middle of somewhere and you don't know where you are, who you are. And we want to stop this because we were lucky here, our generation, our children are very small at the moment, so if we start now we can provide them with a healthy environment. (Turgut, 35 years, 2006).

The complex nature of the Turkish diaspora in Germany has been well-documented, with a number of authors pointing out that the German government must take a large proportion of the responsibility regarding the lack of integration of Turkish migrants there.[70] Turgut (the TIECS member mentioned above) is dismayed that Turks in Germany are caught in a liminal space, arguing that they are neither here nor there. They are unsure if they are Turks or Germans. They are neither integrated nor assimilated. In the words of the above respondent they have "no identity"; "they are kind of in the middle somewhere"; "just standing in the middle somewhere, and you don't know where you are, who you are." This articulation of the position of Turkish migrants in Germany has been acknowledged. [71] However, what is less discussed is the important contribution Turkish associations in Germany make to immigration reform and integration through political engagement in Germany.

Gökçe Yurdakul[72] analyzed the role of two Turkish associations, the Berlin-Brandenburg Turkish Federation (TBB) and the Berlin Turkish Community (the Cemaat), in Berlin. Acknowledging the difficulties faced by Turkish migrants in Germany, she shattered the racialized view of the Turkish diaspora in Germany as a single homogenous group by illustrating the diversity in attitudes and actions of its various members. Her principle focus is to show that some Turkish associations in Germany are actively promoting integration and reform through political engagement. She notes that "many German political authorities refer to the TBB and the Cemaat as the supporters and guardians of immigrant integration." [73] Yurdakul's study is important as it shows not all Turkish migrants are caught in a liminal space, but many have adapted to the German context while often preserving their own culture.

Though Turgut referred to Turks in Germany in a stereotypical fashion his main point is that members of TIECS want to avoid the problems of integration that did indeed face many Turkish migrants in Germany. Later in the interview he said: "And also, we are part of this culture. We are not here just here for doing this work. We are living here and we are contributing as part of society" (Turgut, 35 years, 2006).

This is an interesting example of the promotion of integration of the Turkish community in Ireland. The interviewee insists that they are not just there as representatives of Turkey but that they are now also part of Irish society and are keen to contribute. They are part of the broader Irish society and not just part of the diaspora community. However, they claim to have no intention of assimilating but instead intend to integrate while simultaneously showing their culture and learning the culture of others. Though these members are currently resident in Ireland they are always anchored in Turkey, connected to Gülen's global network. Many of these migrants access the movement's TV station and have copies of its newspapers delivered by post as well as access Gülen's ideas on his website, which involves hundreds of articles written by him and like-minded followers. All of these media forums can be accessed around the world as long as one has access to the Internet. This media tie connects the whole Gülen movement around the world in a single circuit. This indeed creates a sense of community belonging as ideas and discussions flow from node to node. It gives community members the feeling that they are, in Levitt's words, "...part of a broad, powerful supranational movement." [74] This helps create solidarity, bypassing territorial boundaries.

The next section of this paper looks at how favorable TIECS' events are in promoting interculturalism in the Irish context, examining whether its avowed commitment to integration is substantiated in practice.

Representing Islam in Ireland

Though Gülen's TIECS organizes a range of cultural activities, the essay focuses on how the group represents Islam in Ireland and considers how conducive its interfaith engagements are to integration in Ireland. These symposiums typically take the form of celebrating commonalities within the Abrahamic religions. They have taken place annually since 2004 and are held in prominent Dublin universities. Though the events are open to the public this platform attempts to attract elite groups in society. Members in the audience are typically academics, clerics, students, and local politicians. Members of the Gülen movement personally contact and visit many of these elite groups, inviting them to these symposiums, framing the event in terms of promoting tolerance among religions. Much human and economic capital goes into designing posters and invitations for these symposiums.

TIECS members ask indigenous prominent academics and clerics to speak at these events. In the past these have included Sean Freyne and Johnston McMasters, two renowned Irish based theologians who represented the Christian perspective on nominated themes such as "trustworthiness and truthfulness" among the Abrahamic religions. Local Jewish speakers also represented the Jewish faith. When it came to representing Islam it was always Turkish speakers who took to the stage. They were invariably members of the Gülen movement. These have included Kerim Balcı, a journalist with the Gülen-inspired *Zaman* newspaper, and Özcan Kelesh, a barrister, academic, and member of the Gülen movement's Dialogue Society in London. The courting of these followers of Gülen to speak at the conference is an illustration of the transnational connections between different associations within the Gülen movement. Furthermore, the themes of the conferences are replicated from others taking place in Turkey, inspired by the thought of Fethullah Gülen. This is a further illustration of the transnational connections and flow of ideas among this globalized movement.

TIECS stages these events so that it can control the discourse and portray itself as the moderate face of Islam that is consistent with Western values and therefore the antidote to so-called Islamic fundamentalism. It sets the topics, which emphasize the compatibility of the Abrahamic religions and which always finish with the representation of Islam by a member of the Gülen movement. It always emphasizes the universality of its message, regarding it as having no particularist idiosyncrasies.

In response to the question as to why TIECS organized these conferences, a member replied:

> The conferences are so important to introduce...the correct Islamic views to the society, because nowadays Islam is one of the main religions, which is... [misunderstood] by the people, especially in the Western world. There are many reasons and also because of the mistakes of some Muslims....Also because of bias[es] and prejudices by some of the intellectuals in the Western world. So as a Muslim, we believe we have some responsibility to introduce our belief to the society...some people have forced it to be recognized as a kind of religion for violence. And it was not easy for us to accept this without doing anything. The conference series is one of the projects which we would like to tackle this misunderstanding problem...(Turgut, 35 years, 2006).

This excerpt shows that the main aim of the interfaith conferences organized by TIECS is to "introduce the correct Islamic view." It seems that interfaith dialogue, which it claims is its primary objective, is of secondary importance to these Gülen members, while promoting their interpretation of Islam takes precedence. This interpretation is, they insist, based on tolerance and peace. They recognize that in the West there is a strong representation of Islam as atavistic and violent. They attempt to counter this depiction of Islam as a threat to the values of the West, thus illustrating that despite the apparent fixity of this representation it can be contested. They do not intend to create their own monopoly on Islam but certainly aim to have their representation considered among the main interpretations.

It is noteworthy that except for Turkish Muslims there are very few other Muslims at these events and there are never any non-Turkish speakers representing Islam. Furthermore, TIECS is not engaged in any intra-Muslim conferences. It appears only interested in promoting Turkish Islam to Turks and elites in mainstream society. These conferences are an attempt to construct one type of Islam while excluding other expressions of Islam at their venues. In the Turkish context, Yavuz[75] notes that Gülen regularly supported intolerant military crackdowns on other Islamic groups. Though TIECS has not made any statements to this effect their lack of engagement with other Islamic groups is consistent with Gülen's apparent exclusivism.

More than challenging the pejorative representations of Islam, the Gülen movement attempts to introduce Gülen's articulation of Turkish Islam. A prominent member of TIECS's sister organization, NI-TECA, is insistent on the separation of the Gülen movements understanding of Islam from that of the Arab culture. He claims that: "First of all we are not Arabs, we are Turkish and we have a Turkish understanding of Islam…. We learn from the thoughts of Fethullah Gülen" (Ayden, 45 years, 2007). The attitude among Gülen members that they have a different understanding of Islam to other cultures is prevalent and indeed replicates that of Gülen himself, who is keen to distance Turkish Islam from the Arab world. [76] In an interview with *Religioscope* in 2004 Yavuz noted that the Gülen movement has little activity in the Arab world. This is partly because the movement is treated with suspicion, and in some Arab countries it is believed to be working for the United States. However, the movement appears to have little interest in the Arab world and, according to Yavuz, Gülen and his followers believe " it does not understand Islam properly…. The movement believes that the best Islam is the Islam of Turkey, the Islam that is defended and promoted by Gülen, who is in favor of dialogue and moderation."[77]

Yavuz further noted that he has yet to see a positive representation of Islamic movements in Arab countries by the Gülen movement in their media empire. He noted that "they are either critical or silent on the subject." [78] Returning to the Irish context, a former secretary of TIECS explains the essential difference, as he sees it, between Turkish Islam and some other expressions of Islam. He tells the story of how a Muslim boy (from Pakistan, Afghanistan, or Arab lands) is sharing a flat with a non-Muslim boy in Ireland. The non-Muslim wants to bring a dog into the accommodation, but the Muslim will not allow it because he cannot pray if a dog has touched his clothes. As a consequence, the non-Muslim leaves the flat. The above respondent says if he were in this position, following the teachings of Fethullah Gülen he would allow the boy to bring the dog into the house, and before praying he would change his trousers. In this way Turkish Islam differs from other expressions of Islam, he claims.

According to this follower of Gülen, this story serves as a microcosm of the differences between Turkish Islam and Islam as practiced by many other Muslims, with the former being flexible and sensible and the latter being dogmatic and uncompromising. It is noteworthy that given the Gülen movement's challenge to the homogenous description of Islam by many people in the West this member appears to describe Islam as practiced in other lands as largely homogenous.

It seems that Gülen's followers appear to have genuinely learned from the negative integration experience of many migrants in Germany and have actively embraced the policy of integration in Ireland. They deserve credit for setting up a platform that attempts to bring together different faith groups while delivering a strong challenge to the hyperbolic pejorative representation of Islam by many Western commentators. However, their failure to fully engage with other Muslim groups in Ireland may stunt their growth and effectiveness in the future.

Discussion and Conclusion

The presence of Gülen's movement in Ireland is a testament to its exploitation of the opportunity spaces made available through the process of globalization. Targeting the Turkish diaspora in the West, the Gülen movement attempts to gain influence over elites and promote its particularist interpretation of Islam. The movement represents itself differently in different contexts. In the Turkish case, its main emphasis was on the nationalization of Islam in an attempt to bring Islam back to the center of Turkish life. In Central Asia, its Islamic identity was rather more covert, while its Turkish identity was promoted as its most distinguishing feature. In this way it appealed to the ancient ethnic affinity between the Turks of Anatolia and the Turks of Central Asia. Though its aims are the same (to promote a positive image of Islam and gain influence for the Turkish state), the movement takes a different strategy in the Western context. Due to the strong tradition of respect for freedom of expression in the West, Gülen organizations like TIECS are typically open about their Turkish and Islamic identity. However, members of Gülen organizations in the West do not advertise their relationship to the Gülen movement,[79] electing instead to reveal the true identity of their organizations only to trusted sympathizers. They construct their image as a group of concerned Turkish immigrants who want to promote integration among different ethnic and faith groups in their host society, preferring not to disclose that they are connected to a global network. This is understandable given the negative attention attached to Gülen in some quarters. This lack of disclosure also helps members to ground their experiences in their host country and improves their chances of accessing state funding, gaining legitimacy for their organization.

It has been argued elsewhere that the Gülen movement can be understood as a transnational community and members of TIECS as transnational actors.[80] However, even though diaspora migrants established the Gülen movement's presence in Ireland, it receives periodic guidance from above by those in higher positions in the movement. As TIECS is connected to the larger movement, it has access to the global resources of the movement, both human and financial. Though most of TIECS's running costs are paid for by donations by Turkish businessmen living in Ireland, this branch of the Gülen movement is predominantly staffed by temporary migrants from Turkey and Central Asia who spend only a few years in Ireland before returning to their country of origin. It has also been claimed elsewhere[81] that Gülen's presence in Ireland is based on a bottom-up strategy, yet the assistance it receives from the wider movement compromises this position somewhat. However, it is not a top-down organization, as it still has a large degree of autonomy from the larger movement. It is perhaps more accurate to refer to it as a meso level organization, which incorporates both the bottom-up strategy of diaspora members and the top-down assistance from the wider movement.

Despite this assistance from the wider Gülen movement, members of TIECS portray themselves solely as a group of concerned migrants who endeavor to become active members of Irish society and promote integration between different ethnic and religious groups. However, as illustrated in the previous section, TIECS has an agenda to promote its version of Islam, guided by the scholarship of Fethullah Gülen. There is certainly a strong attempt to counter the dominant representation of Islam as aggressive and replace it with an image of Islam as peaceful and moderate. Yet there is a strong element of cultural pride among the Gülen movement, and its articulation of Islam is fused with a nationalist element. In the Turkish context this was unproblematic. Indeed Bilici[82] and Yavuz[83] argue that it is necessary in Turkey to articulate Islam as part of the national identity in order to gain legitimacy by the state. However, in European diaspora spaces, there are many different nationalities and many different expressions of Islam, and a strong emphasis on national culture may prove a hindrance to interfaith activities.[84] It has not yet caused a problem for TIECS, as it is predominantly interested in courting the support of elites from the mainstream population, such as politicians, clerics, and academics and appears to have little or no interest in intra-Muslim dialogue. TIECS has not organized any intra-Muslim conferences; as mentioned in the previous section, there are few non-Turkish Muslims at its events; and only Gülen followers represent the Islamic view on the topic chosen by TIECS at its symposiums. The hope is that the audience leaves thinking that Islam as practiced by these Turkish Muslims is moderate and consistent with values in the West.

In its conferences, TIECS draws on commonalities of the Abrahamic religions, arguing that themes such as "truthfulness" and "trustworthiness" are universals to Judaism, Christianity, and Islam. In this way it shares strategies with other religious movements, such as the Baha'i faith,[85] the Unification Church (popularly known as the Moonies),[86] and Soka Gakkai International (SGI),[87] all of which stress the universality of their message and the universals apparent in major religions. However, Robertson[88] and Beckford[89] have pointed out that these "universal values" are usually understood by their promoters in particularist terms. This is evident in the case of TIECS, which always relates its description of "universals" in particularist terms, adhering to the teachings of Fethullah Gülen.

The presence of Gülen's movement in Ireland is only a recent phenomenon, and it is important not to make conclusive remarks, as they are still very much in their development stage. Looking across the water to London it can be seen that the Gülen movement has had a good deal of success in courting elite sympathizers to their cause. Most notably, the Gülen movement's Dialogue Society[90] teamed up with several notable universities, in particular Leeds Metropolitan University, to organize an academic conference dedicated to discussing the "contribution" of the Gülen movement (October 2007). Leeds Metropolitan University Press published all the papers presented. This conference was the result of much patient work by the Gülen movement in the UK, whereby members unwearyingly diffused Gülen's ideas among their elite target group of politicians, academics, and clerics (the same strategy used by TIECS). The conference was called "Muslim World in Transition: Contributions of the Gülen Movement." The very title of this conference indicates an attempt to control the representation of Gülen and his movement. It is interested in the "contributions" of the movement and not in an open critique of its activities.

The conference title suggests that the Muslim world is having major difficulties and that the Gülen movement's worldview is the antidote to these troubles. This was indeed reflected in the conference, which was essentially an attempt to enhance a positive image of the Gülen movement. Each panelist was awarded €500 and all expenses paid (including flights and hotels) for presenting a paper at the conference. This financial reward is unusual in academia and is likely to cause some suspicion. In the American context, Thomas Robbins [91] notes that churches, sects, and cults often court and sponsor academics to research their group in order to gain publicity and possible legitimacy. This has led to academics being accused of a lack of objectivity in their work due to their sympathies with their sponsors. Through these conferences the Gülen movement has cleverly controlled what academics produce and has flooded the market with an array of pro-Gülen academic articles. A similar conference was repeated in Holland in November 2007 with similar results.

By targeting elites it can be seen that TIECS uses the same strategies as its sister organizations, and looking at their activities gives an indication of TIECS aspirations. For such a small organization TIECS has attracted a good deal of attention and developed a strong network of elite sympathizers (academics, clerics, students, local politicians, and local authority workers) in Ireland. Like the Gülen movement elsewhere, they have exploited opportunity spaces made available by European governments and other civil society actors willingness to engage with "moderate" Islamic groups. Members of TIECS are spurred on by their commitment to *hizmet*, which lends itself to a practical manifestation of their faith. However, their lack of engagement with other Islamic groups in Ireland could prove a problem in the future. In the long term, as Islam becomes a more established part of Ireland, Gülen's cultural Islam could clash with other articulations of Islam. To prevent this, Gülen members must make stronger efforts to engage with these alternative views.

All things considered, the presence of the Gülen movement's TIECS in Ireland illustrates the global reach of the movement and contributes to debates on transnational religious movements, migration, and Islam in Europe. It provides further evidence of the growing visibility of Muslims and Islamic movements in public spheres in European countries. Far from isolating themselves, the study of TIECS illustrates that some Islamic movements do not just work with authorities but actively court their support and arrange events on their own terms. In this way they become active participants in the public sphere rather than passive recipients of the dominant cultural hegemony. Indeed, as well as these groups being shaped by their host country, they also contribute to its shape.

Notes

1. Steven Vertovec, "Conceiving and Researching Transnationalism," *Ethnic & Racial Studies*, Vol. 22, No. 2 (1999), pp.447-62; Stephen Castles and Mark J. Miller, *The Age of Migration: International Population Movements in the Modern World* (New York: Palgrave Macmillan, 2003).
2. See Alejandro Portes, Luis E. Guarnizo and Patricia Landolt, "The Study of Transnationalism: Pitfalls and Promise of an Emergent Research Field," *Ethnic and Racial Studies*, Vol. 22, No. 2 (1999), pp. 217-37.

3. Talip Küçükcan, "The Making of Turkish-Muslim Diaspora in Britain: Religious Collective Identity in a Multicultural Public Sphere," *Journal of Muslim Minority Affairs*, Vol. 24, No. 2 (2004), pp. 243-58; Susanne H. Rudolph, "Introduction: Religion, States, and Transnational Civil Society," in Susanne H. Rudolph and James Piscatori (eds.), *Transnational Religion and Fading States* (Boulder, CO: Westview Press, 1997).

4. Fethullah Gülen was voted among the world's "Top 100 Public Intellectuals" by the Washington-based Carnegie Endowment for International Peace *Foreign Policy Magazine* (May/June 2008) (see www.foreignpolicy.com). From this list, over half a million people voted in a poll to select the top public intellectual. To much surprise Fethullah Gülen topped the poll. The Gülen-inspired newspaper, *Zaman,* ran a feature article alerting the public to Gulen's name on the list. This intervention is seen as the key to Gülen's success in the poll. See Tom Nuttal, "How Gülen Triumphed," *Prospect Magazine*, No. 148 (July 2008).

5. See M. Hakan Yavuz, *Islamic Political Identity in Turkey* (New York: Oxford University Press, 2003); M. Hakan Yavuz "Islam in the Public Sphere: The Case of the Nur Movement," in M. Hakan Yavuz and John L. Esposito (eds.), *Turkish Islam and the Secular State: The Gülen Movement* (New York: Syracuse University, 2003), pp. 1-18; M. Hakan Yavuz, "The Gülen Movement: The Turkish Puritans," in Yavuz and Esposito (eds.), *Turkish Islam and the Secular State: The Gülen Movement*, pp. 19-47; Mucahit Bilici, "The Fethullah Gülen Movement and its Politics of Representation in Turkey," *The Muslim World*, Vol. 96 (2006), pp. 1-20.

6. See Berna Turam, "National Loyalties and International Undertakings: The Case of the Gülen Community in Kazakhstan," in Yavuz and Esposito (eds.), *Turkish Islam and the Secular State: The Gülen Movement*, pp. 184-207; Bayram Balci, "Fethullah Gülen's Missionary Schools in Central Asia and their Role in the Spreading of Turkism and Islam," *Religion, State & Society*, Vo. 31, No. 2 (2003), pp. 151-77.

7. See Muhammad Anwar, *Pakistanis in Britain: A Sociological Study* (London: New Century, 1985); Küçükcan, "The Making of Turkish-Muslim Diaspora in Britain."

8. See Ronit Lentin and Robbie McVeigh (eds.),*Racism & Anti-Racism in Ireland* (Belfast: Beyond the Pale, 2002); Ronit Lentin and Robbie McVeigh, *After Optimism? Ireland, Racism and Globalisation* (Dublin: Metro Eireann Publications, 2006); Bryan Fanning, *Racism and Social Change in the Republic of Ireland* (Manchester: Manchester University Press, 2002).

9. Piaras MacEinri and Paddy Walley, *Labour Migration into Ireland: Study and Recommendations on Employment Permits, Working Conditions, Family Reunification and the Integration of Migrant Workers in Ireland* (Dublin: Immigrant Council of Ireland, 2003), p. 18.

10. Fintan O'Toole, *After the Ball* (Dublin: New Island, 2003) p. 4.

11. Ibid, p. 6.

12. However, a recent decline in the house building sector coupled with problems in the global financial markets means that in the short term Ireland is likely to experience recession for the first time since 1983. See Alan Barrett, Ide Kearney and Martin O'Brien, *Quarterly Economic Commentary,* available at the Economic and Social Research Institute (ESRI) website, www.esri.ie, Summer Edition 2008.

13. O'Toole, *After the Ball.*

14. Lentin and McVeigh, *Racism & Anti-Racism in Ireland* ; Martin Ruhs, *Managing the Immigration and Employment of Non-EU Nationals in Ireland* (Dublin: The Policy Institute, Trinity College, 2005).

15. See Tom Inglis, *Moral Monopoly: The Rise and Fall of the Catholic Church in Modern Ireland* (Dublin: Gill and Macmillan, 1998); Hilary Tovey and Perry Share, *A Sociology of Ireland* (Dublin: Gill and Macmillan, 2003).

16. Central Statistics Office (CSO), 2007, www.cso.ie.

17. Over two thirds of Muslims in Ireland are non-Irish nationals, CSO, 2007.

18. Exceptions include Kieran Flynn, "Understanding Islam in Ireland," *Islam and Christian-Muslim Relations.* Vol. 17, No. 2 (2006), pp. 223–38; Tuula Sakaranaho, *Religious Freedom, Multicultur-alism, Islam: Cross-reading Finland and Ireland* (Boston: Brill, 2006); National Consultative

Committee on Racism and Interculturalism (NCCRI), *The Muslim Community in Ireland: Challenging some of Myths and Information* (available at www.nccri.ie, 2007); Jonathan Lacey, "Exploring the Transnational Engagements of a Turkic Religio-cultural Community in Ireland," in *Translocations: The Irish Migration, Race and Social Transformation Review*, Vol. 2 (available at www.imrstr.dcu.ie/firstissue/, 2007); Jonathan Lacey, "Reflecting on the Gülen Movement's Interfaith Dialogue Work through the Activities of NI-TECA, a Gülen-inspired Society Based in Northern Ireland," in Ihsan Yilmaz *et al.* (eds.), pp. 608–19, *Muslim World in Transition: Contributions of the Gülen Movement* (London: Leeds Metropolitan University Press, 2007); Jonathan Lacey, "Investigating the Contribution of Fethullah Gülen through the Activities of a Gülen-inspired Religio-cultural Society Based in Ireland," in Ihsan Yilmaz *et al.* (eds.), pp. 313–28; *Peaceful Coexistence: Fethullah Gülen's Initiatives in the Contemporary World* (London: Leeds Metropolitan University Press, 2007).

19. Ireland witnessed positive net immigration in the 1970s for the first time. See Ruhs, *Managing the Immigration and Employment of Non-EU Nationals in Ireland*, p. 7.

20. Ibid, p. 9.

21. National Economic Social Council (NESC) *Migration Policy* (Dublin; NESC, 2006) p. 7.

22. Ruhs, *Managing the Immigration and Employment of Non-EU Nationals in Ireland*, p. 9.

23. Central Statistics Office (CSO), 2002, www.cso.ie.

24. Quarterly National Household Survey (QNHS), Quarter 4, www.cso.ie (2007), p. 4.

25. Ibid, p. 4.

26. The EEA is made up of the European Union and Iceland, Lichtenstein, and Norway. Switzerland is not part of the EEA but its citizens have the same access rights as EEA members. See NESC footnote (2006), p.10.

27. Quarterly National Household Survey (QNHS), Quarter 4, www.cso.ie (2007).

28. Central Statistics Office (CSO), 2007, www.cso.ie.

29. Ibid.

30. See Ruhs, *Managing the Immigration and Employment of Non-EU Nationals in Ireland*, pp. 7-29; NESC, pp.10-20 for detailed descriptions of these different routes.

31. Castles and Miller, *The Age of Migration*; Gundus Atalik and Brian Beeley, "What Mass Migration has Meant for Turkey," in Russell King (ed.), *Mass Migration in Europe: The Legacy and Future* (New York: John Wiley & Sons, 1993).

32. Mick Barry, *We Are Workers Not Slaves: The Story of the GAMA Struggle* (Dublin: The Socialist Party, 2006).

33. Lentin and McVeigh, *Racism & Anti-Racism in Ireland*; Steve Garner, *Racism in the Irish Experience* (London: Pluto Press, 2004).

34. Yavuz, *Islamic Political Identity in Turkey*, p. 184.

35. Ibid.

36. Yavuz, "Islam in the Public Sphere," p. 3.

37. Bilici, "The Fethullah Gülen Movement and its Politics of Representation in Turkey."

38. www.gyv.org.tr/

39. Bilici, "The Fethullah Gülen Movement and its Politics of Representation in Turkey," p. 8.

40. Yavuz, "Islam in the Public Sphere," p. 16.

41. For a more comprehensive discussion on the origins of the concept of Turkish Islam, see Etga Uğur, "Intellectual Roots of 'Turkish Islam' and Approaches to the 'Turkish Model,'" *Journal of Minority Affairs*, Vol. 24, No. 2 (2004), pp. 327-45; Ünal Bilir, "'Turkey-Islam': Recipe for Success or Hindrance to the Integration of the Turkish Diaspora Community in Germany?" *Journal of Muslim Minority Affairs*, Vol. 24, No. 2 (2004), pp. 259-83; Küçükcan, "The Making of Turkish-Muslim Diaspora in Britain."

42. Cited in M. Hakan Yavuz, "Is There a Turkish Islam? The Emergence of Convergence and Consensus," *Journal of Muslim Minority Affairs*, Vol. 24, No. 2 (2004), p. 218.

43. Ibid, p. 222.

44. Bilir, "'Turkey-Islam.'"

45. Cited in Ali Ünal and Alphonse Williams, *Advocate of Dialogue: Fethullah Gülen* (Virginia: The Fountain, 2000).
46. This point is supported by the historian Bernard Lewis, *The Emergence of Modern Turkey* (London: Oxford University Press, 1961), p.11.
47. Bilir, "'Turkey-Islam,'" p. 267.
48. Cited in Ünal and Williams, *Advocate of Dialogue*, p. 56.
49. Cited in Hasan Kösebalaban, "The Making of Enemy & Friend: Fethullah Gülen's National Security Identity," in Yavuz and Esposito (eds.), *Turkish Islam and the Secular State: The Gülen Movement*, p. 180.
50. See Bekim Agai, "The Gülen Movement's Islamic Ethic of Education," in Yavuz and Esposito (eds.), *Turkish Islam and the Secular State: The Gülen Movement*, p. 59.
51. Cited in Helen Rose Ebaugh and Dogan Koc, "Funding Gülen-inspired Good Works: Demonstrating and Generating Commitment to the Movement," in Ihsan Yilmaz *et al.* (eds), *Muslim World in Transition: Contributions of the Gülen Movement* (London: Leeds Metropolitan Universtiy Press, 2007), p. 548.
52. Erol N. Gulay, "The Gülen Phenomenon: A Neo-Sufi Challenge to Turkey's Rival Elite?" *Critique: Critical Middle Eastern Studies,* Vol. 16, No. 1 (2007), p. 49.
53. Bill Park, "The Fethullah Gülen Movement as a Transnational Phenomenon," in Ihsan Yilmaz *et al.* (eds.), *Muslim World in Transition: Contributions of the Gülen Movement.* (London: Leeds Metropolitian University Press, 2007), p. 50.
54. See Balci, "Fethullah Gülen's Missionary Schools in Central Asia and Their Role in the Spreading of Turkism and Islam"; Elisabeth Özdalga, "Following in the Footsteps of Fethullah Gülen: Three Women Teachers Tell Their Stories," in Yavuz and Esposito (eds.), *Turkish Islam and the Secular State: The Gülen Movement*, pp. 85-114.
55. Park, "The Fethullah Gülen Movement as a Transnational Phenomenon," p. 51.
56. Bilici, "The Fethullah Gülen Movement and its Politics of Representation in Turkey," p. 12.
57. Ihsan Yilmaz, "Ijtihad and Tajdid by Conduct: The Gülen Movement," in Yavuz and Esposito (eds.), *Turkish Islam and the Secular State: The Gülen Movement*, p. 235.
58. This organization has chapters in Basingstoke, Brighton, Bristol, Exeter, Kent, Oxford, Southampton, Reading, and Swindon (www.fellowshipdialogue.net).
59. Yilmaz, "Ijtihad and Tajdid by Conduct: The Gülen Movements," p. 235; Hüseyin Gülerce, "Gülen's Message to European Union," in Today's Zaman (17.12.2004).
60. This approach is adopted among Alevis in Germany. See James Helicke, "Turks in Germany: Muslim Identity 'Between' States," in Yvonne Yazbeck Haddad and Jane I. Smith (eds.), *Muslim Minorities in the West: Visible and Invisible* (Oxford: Altamira Press, 2002).
61. This festival commemorates Abraham's willingness to sacrifice his son, Ishmael, for the love of God.
62. The Gülen movements rely on a primordial understanding of ethnic affiliation that unites modern Turks to their pre-modern attachment with Central Asian Turkmen. See Turam, "National Loyalties and International Undertakings" for further discussion.
63. The author has used pseudonyms in order to protect the identity of the participants.Though there are many benefits for those belonging to the Gülen movement, some *Fethullaci* (followers of Fethullah Gülen), claim to have experienced discrimination in Turkish universities and in the workplace due to their association with the Gülen movement.
64. Agai, "The Gülen Movement's Islamic Ethic of Education," p. 61.
65. Bilici, "The Fethullah Gülen Movement and its Politics of Representation in Turkey," p. 10.
66. Yavuz, *Islamic Political Identity in Turkey.*
67. Cited in Bilici, "The Fethullah Gülen Movement and its Politics of Representation in Turkey," p. 13.
68. www.tiecs.org/.
69. This term was first introduced by Arnold van Gennep in *The Rites of Passage* (London, Routledge and Kegan Paul, 1960 [original 1909]).
70. See Jeroen Doomernik, "State Politics and Islamic Institutions: Turks in the Netherlands and Germany," in Suha Taji-Farouki (ed.), *Muslim Communities in the Netherlands and Germany*

(Durham: Centre for Middle Eastern, 1995), pp. 7-19; Stephen Castles, Heather Booth and Tina Wallace (eds.), *Here for Good: Western Europe's New Ethnic Minorities* (London: Pluto Press, 1987); Castles and Miller, *The Age of Migration*.

71. See Castles *et al.*, *Here for Good*; Atalik and Beeley, "What Mass Migration has Meant for Turkey."

72. Gökçe Yurdakul, "State, Political Parties and Immigrant Elites: Turkish Immigrant Associations in Berlin," *Journal of Ethnic and Migration Studies*, Vol. 32, No. 3 (2006) pp. 435-53.

73. Ibid, p. 444.

74. Peggy Levitt, "Between God, Ethnicity, and Country," paper presented at workshop on *Transnational Migration: Comparative Perspectives*, June 30 to July 1, 2001, Princeton University, available at www.transcomm.ox.ac.uk, 2006, p. 17.

75. Yavuz, "Islam in the Public Sphere," p. 43.

76. *Religioscope*, "The Gulen Movement: a Modern Expression of Turkish Islam: Interview with Hakan Yavuz, www.religion.info, July 21, 2004.

77. Ibid.

78. Ibid.

79. Groups elect instead to take the name of cultural or dialogue centres such as the Dialogue Society of Scotland, the Dialogue Society (London), and Interfaith Dialogue Society (Brighton).

80. Lacey, "Exploring the Transnational Engagements of a Turkic Religio-cultural Community in Ireland."

81. Ibid; Lacey, "Reflecting on the Gülen Movement's Interfaith Dialogue Work through the Activities of NI-TECA."

82. Bilici, "The Fethullah Gülen Movement and its Politics of Representation in Turkey."

83. Yavuz, *Islamic Political Identity in Turkey*.

84. Bilir argues that the Gülen movement's emphasis on Turkish culture is likely to prove a hindrance in attempts to integrate Turks into German society; see Bilir, " 'Turkey-Islam.' "

85. The Baha'i faith was founded in nineteenth-century Persia (modern day Iran) by Bahá'u'lláh. Though it has its origins in Islam it is considered a separate religion. It lays stress on the spiritual universalism of mankind and believes in prophets from all the worlds' major religions. See Michael McMullen, *The Bahá'i: The Religious Construction of a Global Identity* (London: Rutgers University Press, 2000).

86. The Unification Church was founded by Sun Myung Moon in 1954 in Korea. Though Moon claims to be part of the Christian Church, his belief system is radically different from mainstream Christianity, with him claiming to be the Messiah. Among its many names, The Unification Church is also known as the Family Federation for World Peace and Unification (FFWPU). This name stresses the movement's avowed commitment to universal peace in the world. See David V. Barrett, *The New Believers: A Survey of Sects, Cults and Alternative Religions* (London: Cassel & Co., 2001).

87. SGI is a lay Buddhist organization, which emerged from the Japanese Buddhist sect Nichiren Shoshu. SGI shares many similarities with the Gülen movement, as it is a world-affirming, action-oriented movement that promotes education and dialogue. See Philip E. Hammond and David W. Machacek, *Soka Gakkai in America: Accomodation and Conversion* (Oxford: Oxford University Press, 1999).

88. Roland Robertson, *Globalization: Social Theory and Global Culture* (London: Sage Publications, 1998).

89. James A. Beckford, *Social Theory and Religion*. (Cambridge: Cambridge University Press, 2003).

90. The Dialogue Society was established in 1999 by second-generation Turks living in Britain.

91. Thomas Robbins, " 'Quo Vadis' the Scientific Study of New Religious Movements?"*Journal for the Scientific Study of Religion*, Vol. 39, No.4 (2000), pp. 515-23.

Afterword: Beyond a Methodologically Nationalist Perspective on Civil Society

THOMAS FAIST

Faculty of Sociology, Bielefeld University, Bielefeld, Germany

This collection of articles represents a welcome change from the prevalent focus on immigration, and particularly in Europe, on the social integration of Turkish migrants. This preoccupation on the integration of individual migrants into the sociopolitical order of immigrant societies is visible both in research, with a trend towards the "new assimilation" theory,[1] and in various public debates, both of which heavily focus on failures of social integration and thus on migration as a social problem. This special issue has taken another road. It self-consciously deals with the integration of collective agents, variously called migrant organizations, voluntary organizations, and community organizations throughout the issue. This perspective is much needed, not the least because it allows us to place immigration as part of the vital and effervescent debate in the social sciences on the present state and future prospects of civil society. In particular, these papers raise questions about transnational aspects of civil society.

One way to approach this question is: Why is there a renewed interest in migrant associations (of Turkish origin) right now? After all, there has been a spade of studies on associations founded by former "guestworkers" in Europe in the 1980s[2] or in the aftermath of postcolonial processes.[3] The focus of this earlier literature was on the conditions under which such associations formed and the tasks they fulfilled. The set of studies collected in this issue differ somewhat in that they mostly emphasize the links of such associations and organizations to formal channels of political participation in immigration states; to conditions of incorporation set by the nation-state regarding the acquisition and practice of citizenship; to the role of supranational "political opportunity structures;" and to public discourses around the practices of political or religious associations. In addition, a few contributions also deal with relations between migrants and countries with an elevated index of emigration. In contrast to the earlier wave of studies, it is the political function of civil society that looms large in all contributions. In order to understand the importance of the discussions on civil society, it is helpful to remember that civil society (often also "community") is regarded as a principle of social order next to "market" and "state." [4] Viewed in this way, civil society is important first, in the context of the global restructuring of capital and welfare states, as civil society associations are touted as, for example, as signs of economic development;[5] second, this kind of associations are relevant regarding issues of recognition of religious rights; and, third, civil society associations play an important role in terms of democratization. The authors of this issue focus on the second and third mentioned aspects.

Research on migrant organizations in the framework of civil society is particularly prone to fall into the trap of methodological nationalism. After all, external and internal borders of nation-states are among the most formidable boundaries that immigrants face. Nonetheless, it is another matter for researchers to assume that group boundaries along nation-state limits, or communities within states, form the quasi-natural dividing line of the social. This thinking would be an expression of methodological nationalism, which is an orientation that approaches the study of social, political, and cultural processes as if they were contained within the borders of individual nation-states. Nation-states are conflated with societies, and the members of those states are assumed to share a common history and set of values, norms, social customs, and institutions. Some writers label this orientation the "container" concept of society to highlight that most social theorists, including Émile Durkheim, Max Weber, and Talcott Parsons, have contained their concept of society within the territorial and institutional boundaries of the nation-state. [6] For migration studies, this orientation has been criticized not only regarding the view of the nation-state as a container but also regarding the exaggerated focus on migrants as members of ethnic or national groups, occluding the multi-stranded belongings and memberships of both migrants and those relatively immobile.[7] Essentialist characteristics of migrants as being mainly categorized along ethnic lines are replicated because of widespread assumptions that both newcomers and established persons and collectives would quasi-naturally organize along ethno-cultural lines.

The articles collected in this issue raise two important elements of methodological nationalism. These aspects concern, first, an overwhelming focus on the nation-state, with little consideration of local spaces or transnational spaces as social formations in their own right and, second, a heavy focus on the categories of ethnicity and religion.

First, from a state-centered perspective, it is plausible that the national opportunity structure would loom large in the explanation of political participation. Also, there is a wealth of evidence that some features of political participation may be explained by distinct national models of incorporation, citizenship, and state–society relations.[8] Overall, there are different "philosophies of integration," as Adrian Favell[9] outlined in the cases of France and the UK. Yet, and this is crucial from a methodological vantage point, positionality matters. For example, a viewpoint from civil society could favor other fields of research, such as locality. A lot of data of the contributions to this volume was collected on local levels—Toronto, Montreal, Vienna, Berlin, and Istanbul, to name just a few examples. Moreover, quite a few migrant associations may be concerned with locality. How can we extrapolate from the local to the national level? A methodological orientation, which takes seriously positionality of the collective agents studied, needs to carefully dissect the benefits and drawbacks from distinct starting points, such as the nation-state or local levels.

Second, the focus around collective agency is on the country of origin, either as an ethnic or national group, as in the articles by Pontus Odmalm, Saime Özçürümez, Laure Michon and Floris Vermeulen, and Jon Rogstad. Such groups may extend their ties transnationally, recreating cross-border ties along national lines from the immigration state(s) to the country of origin (see Şebnem Köşer Akçapar in this issue). Coupled with questions about political participation, one of the red threads running through the issue is what accounts for and hinders political participation of Turkish migrant associations. Yet the question comes up whether the "ethnic group" can be regarded as the quasi-natural unit of departure for analysis. In other words, one may ask: Why start with ethnically-grouped organizations? Today, the ethnic group continues to serve as the primary unit of analysis with which to study and describe migration settlement, transnational migration, and diaspora. Often termed "communities" or "diaspora," the ethnic group has become the bedrock of studies of immigrant incorporation. Yet such a view raises a host of questions: Why should a low degree of participation of Turkish migrants in Turkish associations, or a low impact of Turkish organizations on respective local or national politics be worrisome? Concomitantly, why should a single or stronger voice of such associations in the respective political arenas be desirable?

This brings up the question about other lines of engagement beyond and across ethnic lines. Especially since this issue is concerned with collective agency relating to Turkey, we may ask for agency outside associations along ethnic or national lines, such as in unions or non-ethnic voluntary associations. In addition, what about activities of and in immigrant social service organizations? This is an important issue because it concerns the boundaries of the political itself, which may not be restricted to formal channels of political participation in incorporated associations, political parties, and parliaments. What about less institutionalized politics, such as the "subpolitics"[10] of social service delivery in which migrant associations also lose forms of institutionalized social activities, such as networks of women active in mosques or churches? Focusing on the traditional forms and arenas of politics only would lead us to look for politics in the wrong places. In sum, there are sub-politics to be found in the everyday activities and choices of people and in the often informal and spontaneous political actions of social movements.

The articles on religious lines of organization offer a somewhat different viewpoint in that they open a window towards an understanding of incorporation, which focuses on the public sphere. These articles discuss competing visions of incorporation and relationships with states (Gökçe Yurdakul & Ahmet Yükleyen on two Islamic organizations in Germany), deal with one religious category—Alevis—in both Europe and Turkey interactively (Esra Özyürek), and analyze the strategies of a network of organizations, the Gülen movement in Ireland (Jonathan Lacey). The contributions suggest that more contextualization is needed above and below national opportunity structures in order to understand how identity and positions of agents are constantly made and remade. This allows a shift of focus from cultural difference to incentives offered for associations, such as those offered by the European Commission, European Parliament, nation-states, or local administrations. The interplay of different levels of politics and how ideas and interests criss-cross these levels transnationally is nicely illustrated by the fate of the travelling concept "minority," which is helpful in the EU arenas but, for historical reasons, not in Turkish domestic politics.

Overall, the contributions raise fundamental questions of civil society research. For example, in Rogstad's analysis of migrant associations in Norway two complementary visions of civil society are visible. The first refers to what he calls "voluntary associations." These offer training and breeding grounds for social skills, which stimulate and may sustain political engagement and participation. This argument, recently expounded by Putnam, [11] goes back to de Tocqueville's [12] path-breaking vision of political sociology in the first half of the nineteenth century. Other contributions, such as that of Michon & Vermeulen, ask whether this activation and maintenance aspect of associations is indeed the case. The second strand, less prominent in the contributions but still shining through in a number of articles, is the claim that associations may give a much-needed stimulus for general society. This argument was recently forcefully put forward by Jeffrey Alexander, who claims that civil society organizations, in his case above all social movement organizations such as the Civil Rights Movement of the 1960s, act as a sort of "repair shop" for society.[13]

In sum, this issue suggests ample opportunities for future research into genuinely transnational spaces across nation-states, localities, and supranational bodies— which are made up of civil society agents. As some of the contributions indicate, it is not only nation-states that provide opportunity structures and incentives for civil society actors such as migrant associations. Drawing on universalist ideas of human rights to justify religious incorporation and citizenship rights in struggles for political representation, actors ranging from local migrant associations to transnational religious-cultural movements bring in their particular agendas. It will be a tall but fascinating program to trace and account for how local agents use universal language in their own vernacular.

Notes

1. See Rogers Brubaker, "The Return of Assimilation? Changing Perspectives on Immigration and its Sequels in France, Germany, and the US,*Ethnic and Racial Studies* Vol. 24, No. 4 (2001), pp. 431-548.
2. For an early summary, see Barbara Schmitter Heisler, "Immigrant Settlement and the Structure of Emergent Immigrant Communities in Western Europe," *Annals of the American Academy of Political and Social Sciences*, Vol. 485 (1986), pp. 76-86.
3. See for example John Rex, Danièle Joly and Czarina Wilpert (eds.), *Immigrant Associations in Europe* (Aldershot: Gower, 1987).
4. Wolfgang Streeck and Philippe C. Schmitter, "Community, Market, State—and Associations? The Prospective Contribution of Interest Governance to Social Order," *European Sociological Review*, Vol. 1, No. 2 (1985), pp. 119-38.

5. Samir Dasgupta, and Nederveen Pieterse (eds.), *Politics of Globalization* (New Delhi: Sage, 2009); see also Thomas Faist, "Migrants as Transnational Development Agents: An Inquiry into the Newest Round of the Migration-Development Nexus," *Population, Space and Place*, Vol. 14, No. 1 (2008), pp. 21-42; Thomas Faist, "The Transnational Social Question: Social Rights and Citizenship in a Global Context," *International Sociology*, Vol. 24, No. 1 (2009), pp. 7-35.

6. For many, see Linda Basch, Nina Glick Schiller and Christina Szanton Blanc, *Nations Unbound: Transnational Projects, Postcolonial Predicaments and Deterritorialized Nation* (Langhorne: Gordon & Breach, 1994).

7. Andreas Wimmer and Nina Glick Schiller, "Methodological Nationalism, the Social Sciences, and the Study of Migration: An Essay in Historical Epistemology," *International Migration Review*, Vol. 37, No. 3 (2003), pp. 576-610.

8. For a recent review of the literature, see Gary P. Freeman, "National Models, Policy Types, and the Politics of Immigration in Liberal Democracies," *West European Politics*, Vol. 29, No. 2 (2006), pp. 227-47.

9. Adrian Favell, *Philosophies of Integration: Immigration and the Idea of Citizenship in France and Britain* (Basingstoke: Macmillan, 1998).

10. Ulrich Beck, *Die Erfindung des Politischen. Zu einer Theorie reflexiver Modernisierung* [The Invention of the Political: To a Theory of Reflexive Modernization] (Frankfurt: Suhrkamp, 1993).

11. Robert Putnam, "E Pluribus Unum: Diversity and Community in the Twenty-First Century," *Scandinavian Political Studies*, Vol. 30, No. 2 (2007), pp. 137-74.

12. Alexis de Tocqueville, *Democracy in America*, J.P. Mayer (ed.), translated by George Lawrence (New York: Harper & Row, 1988 [first published in French in 1835 and 1841]).

13. Jeffrey Alexander, *The Civil Sphere* (New York: Oxford University Press, 2006).

Index

Page numbers in *Italics* represent tables.
Page numbers in **Bold** represent figures.

For Product Safety Concerns and Information please contact our EU
representative GPSR@taylorandfrancis.com
Taylor & Francis Verlag GmbH, Kaufingerstraße 24, 80331 München, Germany

www.ingramcontent.com/pod-product-compliance
Lightning Source LLC
Chambersburg PA
CBHW050445280326
41932CB00013BA/2244